MW00581327

Windows® 10 & Office 2016

Windows® 10 & Office 2016

by Ciprian Rusen, Faithe Wempen, and Ryan Williams

A Wiley Brand

Windows® 10 & Office 2016 For Dummies®

Published by: **John Wiley & Sons, Inc.,** 111 River Street, Hoboken, NJ 07030-5774, www.wiley.com

Copyright © 2018 by John Wiley & Sons, Inc., Hoboken, New Jersey

Published simultaneously in Canada

For general information on our other products and services, please contact our Customer Care Department within the U.S. at 877-762-2974, outside the U.S. at 317-572-3993, or fax 317-572-4002. For technical support, please visit https://hub.wiley.com/community/support/dummies.

Wiley publishes in a variety of print and electronic formats and by print-on-demand. Some material included with standard print versions of this book may not be included in e-books or in print-on-demand. If this book refers to media such as a CD or DVD that is not included in the version you purchased, you may download this material at http://booksupport.wiley.com. For more information about Wiley products, visit www.wiley.com.

Library of Congress Control Number: 2017960438

ISBN: 978-1-119-48824-8; 978-1-119-47831-7 (ebk); 978-1-119-47830-0 (ebk)

Manufactured in the United States of America

10 9 8 7 6 5 4 3 2 1

Contents at a Glance

Table of Contents

Introduction

Windows 10 is the most modern operating system Microsoft offers, but your business requires more specialized tools than a notepad and a web browser. Though Office 2016 adds a powerful, cohesive suite of tools to your computer, you need a modern operating system to run it on. And we want to see you get the most value for your book-buying dollar. So, in the words of an Internet meme somewhere: "Why not both?"

This book tackles the functions of Windows 10 that you'll need in order to get up and running in the office as well as the highlights of the programs you'll use to actually get work done. This single volume covers all the major points you'll need to know in order to be more productive with these tools. And you don't need to keep juggling several books to get there. Efficiency is the key!

About This Book

You can start from page 1 in this book, especially if Windows 10 is new to you. In the business world, some companies can take the time to upgrade their technology. But Windows 10 represents the future, and Microsoft has made it easier than ever to upgrade.

But even if you've already logged in to Windows 10, this book offers some inside knowledge you can take advantage of. And Windows 10 has seen some major upgrades since it was first released. Take some time to make sure you're up-to-date.

This book also covers the bases of Office 2016, especially the power tools of Word, Excel, and PowerPoint. Again, whether you're new to these programs or an old hand who's loaded with confidence, Office 2016 is a constantly evolving package of functionality that you need to update yourself on.

Skip around for a refresher, or go to the beginning and run through the whole book. No matter what you need to do, this book is for you.

Part 1: Introduce Yourself to Windows 10

Learn the basics of Windows 10, from logging in to navigating the all-new Start menu. Even if you've used Windows before, this version is an all-new ball game. Get connected, find the information you're looking for, and get to work!

Part 2: Make Yourself at Home in Windows 10

Customize your Windows home and make yourself more comfortable. Put all the settings in place to make yourself more efficient. And yes, even change your background picture to that one photo of your family on vacation. You'll also personalize your account and learn privacy and safety tips to keep your valuable data secure.

Part 3: Introduce Yourself to Office 2016

Office 2016 lets you write, organize, process, and present your work to whatever audience you choose, even if it's just your boss. Get the fundamental functions under control and get yourself started.

Part 4: Communicating in Office 2016

Modern work demands instant communication. Learn how to send and organize your email and contact information, and then figure out how to construct professional presentations. This part includes everything you need to get your business known.

Part 5: The Parts of Ten

Windows 10 and Office 2016 contain more than enough functionality for books of their own, but we squeezed in everything we could. Some extras still demand some attention, though, and this part contains all the other info you need to know.

Icons Used in This Book

As you read this book, you'll see little icons in the margins that call out additional knowledge. These icons range in importance from a friendly tap on the shoulder to a somber warning, so keep that in mind as you go.

TIP

This handy icon gives you some extra information. Feel free to skip over it if you're in a hurry, though you might want to read it eventually.

REMEMBER

Store this info away, because you'll need it later.

WARNING

This icon is the somber warning we told you about in the introduction to this section. If you ignore this information, you could lose time, money, or data. We wouldn't want you to do that, so we tell you straight-up. You'll thank us later.

TECHNICAL STUFF

If we weren't geeks, we wouldn't write books like this one. And we sometimes get a little technical-minded. If you're fascinated by this kind of information, give it a read. We don't blame you for moving on and getting back to work, though.

Where to Go from Here

Go wherever you want, because it's your book! Start at the beginning or jump to the most important section for you right now. Make your work better and more efficient with the tools you need. Good luck!

In addition to what you're reading right now, *Windows 10 & Office 2016 For Dummies* comes with a free access-anywhere Cheat Sheet that's a great tool for getting started with Windows and Office. To get this Cheat Sheet, simply go to www.dummies.com and search for "Windows 10 & Office 2016 For Dummies Cheat Sheet" in the Search box.

1

Introduce Yourself to Windows 10

- » Using the new Start Menu to start your apps

- » Using the hidden WinX menu

- » Accessing the Desktop

- » Accessing Settings and Control Panel

- » Performing simple searches

- » Using notifications

- » Working with multiple apps and desktops at the same time

- » Closing apps and desktops

- » Signing out and locking your Windows 10 device

- » Shutting down and restarting Windows

Chapter **1**

Getting Started with Windows 10

Windows 10 is another revolution in the world of Microsoft operating systems. It's the first operating system to work on a huge number of devices, such as smartphones, tablets, traditional desktop PCs, consoles, and industrial devices. That also means it's designed to minimize hardware requirements. A Windows this slim and fast hasn't been built in a long time.

To make Windows 10 work on a variety of devices, with very different form factors, Microsoft developed a new user interface that's different from what you may have used with Windows 7 or Windows XP. Getting the first steps right when using Windows 10 goes a long way in having a pleasant user experience with this operating system. This chapter is your introduction to doing so.

Windows 10 uses concepts that may be new to you, such as the Lock Screen; a completely new Start Menu; the WinX menu; a new Settings panel that replaces the old Control Panel; the new Task View; and a new Action Center. Some items in this chapter are very simple to use, but you need to get them right in order to use Windows 10 productively. So roll up your sleeves and arm yourself with a bit of patience. It's time to go to work!

Use the Lock Screen

The first screen you see after Windows 10 loads on your computer or device is the Lock Screen. This concept was introduced in Windows 8 and continues in Windows 10. The Lock Screen is basically a full-screen wallpaper. By default, it shows you the time and the date and whether you're connected to a network (see Figure 1-1). You can customize it to also show the detailed status of an app as well as small icons representing your favorite apps so that you can see the status of those apps without leaving the Lock Screen. Along with all that, you can customize the Lock Screen's image.

FIGURE 1-1:
The Lock Screen
in Windows 10.

How you unlock the Lock Screen depends on the type of computer you're using:

>> **A Windows 10 desktop computer without touch:**

  - Press any key on the keyboard.

  - Click the mouse anywhere on the screen.

  - Drag upward from the bottom of the screen.

>> **A Windows 10 laptop with a touchpad:**

  - Press any key on the keyboard.

  - Click the mouse or the left-click trackpad button anywhere on the screen.

  - Hold down the left trackpad button and drag the cursor upward.

>> **Any Windows 10 device with a touchscreen (such as a tablet or a 2-in-1 device):**

  - Place your finger anywhere near the middle or bottom of the screen and flick upward.

TIP

Chapter 7 shows how to customize the Lock Screen.

Sign In to Windows 10

Once you get past the Lock Screen, you can sign in to Windows 10. You're asked to enter the password and click or tap the Sign In button for your user account (or the last account that was used on your device). The Sign In button is a right-pointing arrow (see Figure 1-2).

If other user accounts are on this computer, they're listed on the bottom-left side of the Sign In screen. To sign in with one of these other user accounts, click the account that you want, enter the password, and click or tap the Sign In button.

On the bottom-right of the Sign In screen, you see three accessible buttons:

>> Network Connections

>> Ease of Access options for starting such tools as the Narrator, Magnifier, and On-Screen keyboard

>> Session-ending options (such as Sleep, Shut Down, and Restart)

Other user accounts

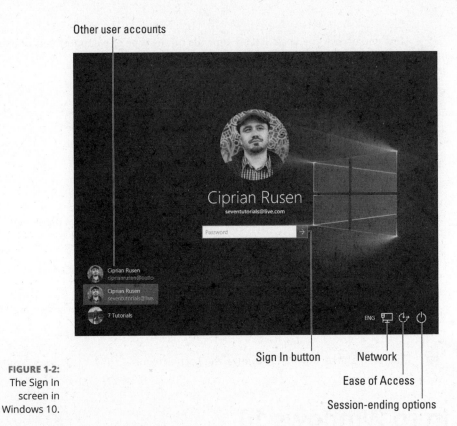

Sign In button   Network

Ease of Access

Session-ending options

FIGURE 1-2:
The Sign In
screen in
Windows 10.

Use the Start Menu

After you sign in to Windows 10, the user interface of the operating system loads:

>> On a classic PC, the desktop loads.

>> On a touch-enabled device that's set to work in Tablet mode, the Start Menu loads.

At the bottom of the screen you see the *taskbar*, a black bar with several buttons. If you click the button with the Windows logo (which is called the *Start button*), the Start Menu opens.

On classic PCs, the Start Menu covers only part of the screen and looks similar to the one shown in Figure 1-3.

FIGURE 1-3:
The Start
Menu on
Windows 10 PCs.

On the right side of the Start Menu, you see several tiles of different sizes. *Tiles* are like shortcuts, and clicking them opens the app that they represent. However, some tiles can also display up-to-date information for the apps they represent. These are interactive *live tiles.* You don't need to open the app to view the basic data a live tile offers. For example, after you configure the Weather app, it can show up-to-date weather information for a city, and the Photos app can show your pictures. This data appears on the Start Menu so that you have access to it without opening the app itself. The information is dynamic and changes as the information it represents does.

If you need to see more than a preview of the information, click the tile. The app opens in a window from which you can access all its features.

On the left side of the Start Menu, you see a column that contains your user account name, a list with your most-used apps, a Power button, and an All Apps button. Clicking an app's name opens that app.

If you're on a device that's working in Tablet mode, the Start Menu consumes the whole screen, so you don't see the desktop (see Figure 1-4).

The Start Menu displays a list with all your tiles, including the live tiles of apps that are pinned to the Start Menu. To expand the column on the left with your user account name, the list of your most used apps, the Power button, and the All Apps button, you tap what's called a *hamburger button* (or just *burger button),* located at the top-left corner of the screen. (The button is called a burger button because its three parallel lines look like a burger on a bun.) Tapping the burger button expands or minimizes this column, depending on its status.

FIGURE 1-4:
The Start Menu
on a Windows 10
device working in
Tablet mode.

REMEMBER

Wherever you see the burger button, clicking or tapping it opens a menu.

From here on, navigating the Start Menu works just like it does on desktop PCs. The only difference is that instead of clicking, you tap with your finger or stylus.

Use the All Apps List to Start Your Apps

All Apps is a list of all the apps that are installed on your Windows 10 device. Here's how to access the list and start any app you want:

1. **Sign in to Windows 10.**

   The desktop appears.

2. **Click the Windows logo.**

   The Start Menu appears.

3. **In the Start Menu, click the All Apps button.**

   A list with all your apps appears.

4. **Scroll down the list of apps until you find the one that you want to start (refer to Figure 1-4).**

5. **Click the app that you want to start.**

On touch-enabled devices that work in Tablet mode, after Step 2, tap the burger button and then follow the instructions from Step 3 onward. Also, don't forget to replace the click with a tap.

Use the WinX Menu

In Windows 10, a hidden menu, the *WinX* menu, produces shortcuts to such useful tools and apps as Computer Management, the Control Panel, the Command Prompt, and the Task Manager. The menu's name comes from the keyboard shortcut that you press to open the menu: Windows+X (see Figure 1-5).

FIGURE 1-5:
The WinX menu
in Windows 10.

You can also open the WinX menu with the mouse or by using touch:

>> With a mouse, right-click the Windows logo on the taskbar.

>> With a touch-sensitive screen, press and hold the Windows logo until the WinX menu appears.

To start any of the tools available in the WinX menu, simply click or tap them.

Access the Desktop

On a computer or device that isn't set to work in Tablet mode, you can access the desktop and its contents. If several apps are open and they completely cover the desktop, just press Windows+D on the keyboard. All apps are minimized, and you can see the desktop. Another solution is to minimize or close all apps, one by one.

Access Settings

In Windows 10, the old Control Panel is somewhat hidden, but it's there and you can use it. It's hidden because Microsoft developed an alternative "control panel" that works well on both classic desktop PCs with a mouse and keyboard and touch-enabled devices. This new control panel is named Settings, and it includes most of the settings that you adjust while using Windows 10 (see Figure 1-6).

FIGURE 1-6:
The Settings panel in Windows 10.

To access the Settings panel, follow these steps:

1. **Open the Start Menu.**

   If you're using a touch-enabled device in Tablet mode, tap the burger button now.

2. **Click Settings.**

   The Settings window appears.

3. **Click any of the sections to access the available settings.**

   On touch-enabled devices that work in Tablet mode, replace the click with a tap.

Access the Control Panel

The Control Panel still exists in Windows 10, and it works the same as in previous versions of Windows. The easiest way to access the Control Panel is to search for it, like this:

1. **Type** Control Panel **in the search box to the right of the Start button.**

2. **Tap Control Panel under the Best Match heading to see the screen in Figure 1-7.**

3. **When you're done, close the Control Panel.**

FIGURE 1-7:
The Control Panel
in Windows 10.

Perform Simple Searches

The previous section just introduced you to the search box. That's Cortana: an intelligent personal assistant that's built into Windows 10. With Cortana, you can do basic searches for apps and files on your computer, or you can interact by using voice and text and get all kinds of information.

Here's an example of finding an app and a file:

1. **Click inside the search box on the taskbar.**

2. **Type the name of the app that you want to use (for example,** Camera**).**

   A list of search results appears.

3. **In the list of search results, click the app that you want to use (see Figure 1-8).**

   The app starts.

4. **Click again inside the search bar on the taskbar.**

5. **Type the name of the file that you want to find.**

   A list of search results appears.

6. **In the list of search results, click the file that you want to find, and it opens.**

FIGURE 1-8:
Searching for
apps by using the
search bar on the
taskbar.

Use the Action Center

When you use Windows 10, you get all kinds of notifications. They can be notifications from apps, such as a new email message that was received, or notifications from Windows saying that it detected a removable disk that you just plugged into your computer. All these notifications are centralized in the Action Center, which you can access at any time (see Figure 1-9).

All your notifications are grouped according to the app that generated them:

» For more details about a notification, click it, and the app that generated it opens and shows you more details.

» After you open a notification, it disappears from the Action Center.

» To remove a notification without opening it, move the mouse cursor to its top-right corner and click the X button, shown in Figure 1-10.

» To remove all notifications without opening them, click Clear All at the top-right side of the Action Center.

At the bottom of the Action Center, you see such shortcuts as Tablet Mode, VPN, Connect, All Settings, Rotation Lock, and Location. The number of shortcuts displayed varies from device to device, depending on its capabilities. Click or tap on these shortcuts to start the tools that they represent and see what they do.

Work with Multiple Apps Simultaneously

Clicking a shortcut or a tile from the Start Menu starts the app that the shortcut represents.

On a desktop computer, these apps are opened one by one, and their icons appear on the taskbar. To switch to another app that's open, click its icon in the taskbar. Figure 1-11 shows an example of multiple opened apps and their icons on the taskbar.

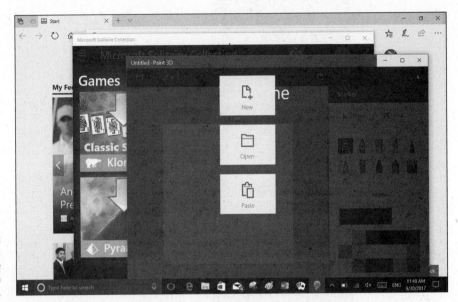

FIGURE 1-11:
Multiple apps, opened at the same time in Windows 10.

On a device that's running in Tablet mode, you switch between apps using the Task View. The following section shows how.

TIP

To switch between apps very quickly, you can also press Alt+Tab on the keyboard. This accesses a list with all opened apps. Keep the Alt key pressed and then press Tab to navigate between apps. When you reach the app you want to switch to, release both keys.

Switch Between Apps with the Task View

The Task View is like a more advanced Alt+Tab list that shows you the desktops that are open and the apps that are open in each desktop. (See the "Switch Between Multiple Desktops" section, later in this chapter, to find out how to use more than one desktop in Windows 10.) Here's how to use the Task View to switch between apps:

1. **On the taskbar, click the Task View button near the Search bar.**

    The Task View button looks like two rectangles stacked on each other (see Figure 1-12).

2. **In the list of apps that appears, click the app that you want to switch to.**

FIGURE 1-12:
How to use the
Task View in
Windows 10.

On a touch-enabled device, you can access the Task View by flicking from the left side of the screen to the right.

TIP

Close an App

You close apps in Windows 10 like you did in older versions of Windows. When you open an app on the desktop, you can close it by pressing Alt+F4 on the keyboard or by clicking the exit button (the X) located at the top-right corner of its window (see Figure 1-13).

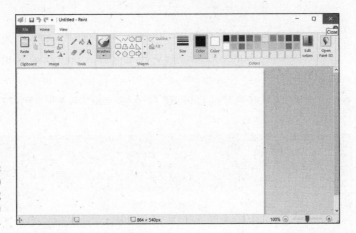

FIGURE 1-13:
The exit (or X)
button for closing
an app in
Windows 10.

If you're using Tablet mode on a touch-enabled device, apps consume the whole screen, and the exit button isn't shown. To close an app, use your finger to drag an app down from the top.

Create a New Desktop

Although Windows has long supported virtual desktops (with the help of third-party tools), Microsoft declined to make this feature available to users until Windows 10. Now you can easily create and manage multiple desktops, which you can use to separate related tasks into their own workspaces. This is useful in business environments where you can keep your personal apps and files in one desktop and your work-related apps and files in another.

To create a new desktop in Windows 10, follow these steps:

1. **Click the Task View button.**

   The Task View appears.

2. **Click New Desktop (see Figure 1-14).**

3. **A new desktop is created.**

4. **Click the desktop that you want to use.**

TIP

You can also use the keyboard shortcut Windows+Ctrl+D.

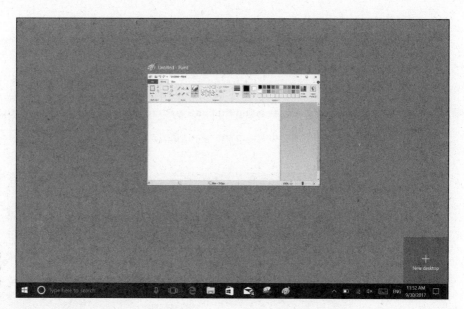

FIGURE 1-14:
The New Desktop
button in the
Task View.

Switch Between Multiple Desktops

Switching between desktops is as easy as switching between apps. Just use the Task View, like this:

1. Click the Task View button.

The Task View appears.

2. Click the desktop that you want to use.

You can also use these keyboard shortcuts: Windows+Ctrl+left arrow for the previous desktop and Windows+Ctrl+right arrow for the next desktop.

TIP

Send an App to Another Desktop

As you start populating each desktop with open apps, you may want to move an app from one desktop to another. Here's how to move an app:

1. Click the Task View button.

The Task View appears.

2. **Right-click the app that you want to move to another desktop.**

   The right-click menu appears.

3. **Click Move To.**

4. **Click the desktop that you want to move the app to (see Figure 1-15).**

5. **Click the desktop that you want to use.**

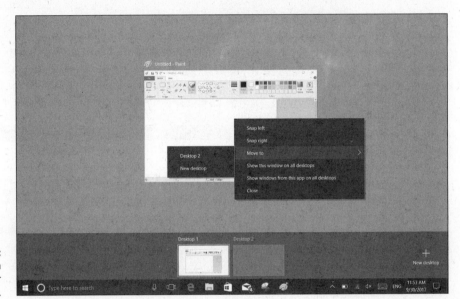

FIGURE 1-15:
How to move an app to another desktop.

Close a Desktop

You can close any desktop that you've opened, at any time. When you close a desktop, the apps that were open on it are moved to the remaining desktops. To close a desktop, follow these steps:

1. **Click the Task View button.**

   The Task View appears.

2. **Move the mouse to the top-right corner of the thumbnail of the desktop that you want to close.**

3. **Click the exit (X) button at its top-right corner (see Figure 1-16).**

4. **Click the desktop that you want to use.**

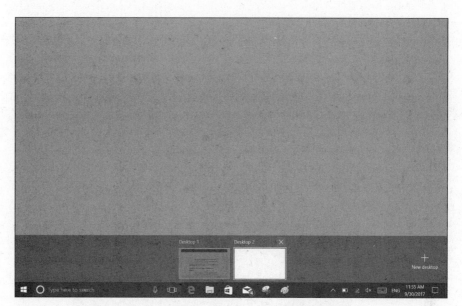

FIGURE 1-16:
How to close a
desktop in
Windows 10.

Sign Out or Lock Your Windows 10 Device

When you leave your desk, you need to secure your computer so that others can't access it. The easiest way to do so is by locking it. After you lock your computer, you must enter your user account password when you're ready to use your computer again. When you enter your password, the computer is just as you left it, with the same apps and files open. Lock your computer anytime you leave it unattended.

You can also sign out of your computer. When you sign out, you're prompted to save any open files, and you might be prompted to close open apps. With that done, Windows closes your computing session as if you were turning off the computer, but it doesn't turn off the computer. You're signed out of your user account, and you can let others use your computer, if they want to sign in with their user account. You can also log on again to start a new computing session.

To lock your Windows 10 computer or to sign out, follow these steps:

1. **Click the Windows logo (Start button.)**

The Start Menu appears.

2. **If you're in Tablet mode, tap the burger button.**

3. **Click your icon.**

A menu appears beneath your username.

4. Click Lock or Sign Out, depending on what you want to do (see Figure 1-17).

FIGURE 1-17:
How to lock or sign out from Windows 10.

You can quickly lock your computer by pressing Windows+L on the keyboard.

TIP

Shut Down or Restart Windows 10

If you need to shut down or restart your Windows 10 computer or device, close all your open files and apps and follow these steps:

1. **Click the Windows logo (Start button.)**

   The Start Menu appears.

2. **Click the Power button. (The icon is the Power symbol; see Figure 1-18.)**

   A menu appears with power-related options.

3. **Click Shut Down or Restart, depending on what you want.**

The Power button is available also on the Sign In screen, and this button offers you the same options as when you access it from the Start Menu.

TIP

FIGURE 1-18:
How to shut
down or restart
Windows 10.

Chapter **2**

Using the New Start Menu

One of the most important changes in Windows 8 was replacing the Start Menu with the Start screen. Most people didn't like this change and were quite vocal in saying so. As a result, Windows 10 brings the old Start Menu back, but in a modified form that mixes the best of Windows 7 and Windows 8. So, if you're a Windows 7 user, you'll feel right at home and have no trouble getting up to speed with the new Start Menu. If you use Windows 8 and love the Start screen, the good news is that you can easily set the Start Menu to utilize the whole screen and to behave like the former Start screen.

This chapter shows you how to use the new Start Menu, how to customize it, and how to improve the privacy of the data shown by the tiles you pin to it.

Access the All Apps List in the Start Menu

For a list of all the apps that you can access from the Start Menu, follow these steps:

1. **Click Start to open the Start Menu.**

The Start button is in the left corner on the taskbar. It has the Windows logo.

2. **Click All Apps. It's the icon that looks like a checklist, right next to the Calendar app shown in Figure 2-1.**

A list of apps appears.

FIGURE 2-1:
The Start Menu in
Windows 10.

3. **Navigate the list to find the app you want.**

4. **Select the app that you want to start.**

Expand the Start Menu in Windows 10

You can expand the new Start Menu so that it fills the entire screen and shows more shortcuts, tiles, live tiles, and data for these tiles. (Chapter 1 explains live tiles.)

To expand the Start Menu, follow these steps:

1. **Click Start to open the Start Menu.**

2. **Move the mouse cursor to the right margin of the Start Menu.**

You should see a double-arrow icon, pointing both left and right.

3. **Click the double-arrow icon and drag the Start Menu to the right side of the screen to expand it.**

   The Start Menu fills more of the screen and shows more data.

4. **Click anywhere outside the Start Menu to close it.**

REMEMBER

The Start Menu remembers your last setting. If you expand the Start Menu, it always opens in an expanded form until you manually restore it to its default size.

Restore the Start Menu in Windows 10

If you no longer want to use the Start Menu in expanded form, here's how to restore it to its default size:

1. **Click the Start button to open the Start Menu.**

2. **Move the mouse cursor to the right margin of the Start Menu.**

   You should see a double-arrow icon, pointing both left and right.

3. **To resize the Start Menu, click the double-arrow and drag the menu to the left side of the screen.**

   The Start Menu is resized.

4. **Click Start to close it.**

Again, use a mouse here, even for touchscreen devices.

REMEMBER

The Start Menu remembers your last setting. If you restore the Start Menu, it always opens with its default size until you expand it.

Pin Apps to the Start Menu

You can easily pin any app to the Start Menu. Follow these steps:

1. **Click Start to open the Start Menu.**

2. **Click All Apps.**

3. **Scroll down to find the app that you want to pin to the Start Menu, and then right-click the app.**

4. **In the list, click Pin to Start (see Figure 2-2).**

   The app is now pinned to the right side of the Start Menu.

5. **Click Start to close the Start Menu.**

Pin Executable Files to the Start Menu

Pinning files to the Start Menu is just as easy as pinning apps.

The only rule is that you can pin only executable files with the file extension .exe.

REMEMBER

To pin an executable file to the Start Menu, follow these steps:

1. **Click the File Explorer icon on the taskbar to start this application.**

2. **Navigate to the location of the executable file that you want to pin and right-click it.**

3. **In the list that appears, click Pin to Start (see Figure 2-3).**

4. **Close File Explorer and then click Start.**

   The file is pinned to the bottom of the Start Menu.

Move Tiles and Shortcuts Across the Start Menu

You can reorganize and change the position of apps, files, and websites that are pinned to the Start Menu. To move a tile or shortcut to another place on the Start Menu, follow these steps:

1. **Click Start to open the Start Menu.**

2. **Click and hold the left mouse button on the tile or shortcut that you want to move.**

   The item you select is highlighted, and the others are grayed out, which means they're disabled.

3. **Still pressing the left mouse button, move the selected item to the desired location (see Figure 2-4).**

   Other elements automatically change their positions to make room for your item.

4. **Release the left mouse button when the item is where you want it.**

TIP

You can use these steps to arrange all the items on the Start Menu just as you want them to be.

FIGURE 2-4:
Moving tiles and
shortcuts across
the Start Menu.

Resize Tiles and Shortcuts

You can change the size of all the items on the Start Menu. The choices are Small, Medium, Wide, and Large.

To change the size of a tile or shortcut on the Start Menu, follow these steps:

1. **Click Start to open the Start Menu.**

2. **Right-click the item that you want to resize.**

3. **In the list that appears, click Resize (see Figure 2-5).**

4. **In the list of available sizes, click the size you want for the item (see Figure 2-5).**

   The selected item is now resized.

**TECHNICAL
STUFF**

The maximum size that you can set for a tile or shortcut varies from app to app. For example, only a few apps have tiles that can be set as Large. Shortcuts to desktop apps can be set only to Small or Medium.

FIGURE 2-5:
Resizing tiles and
shortcuts on the
Start Menu.

Name Groups of Tiles and Shortcuts

One of the not-so-obvious features of the Start Menu is the capability to name groups of shortcuts and tiles, which enables you to organize them more efficiently. To name a group, follow these steps:

1. **Click Start.**

2. **Move the mouse to the top-right corner of the group of tiles and shortcuts that you want to name.**

    A symbol resembling the equal (=) sign appears at the top-right corner of the group.

3. **Click on the empty space at the left of the equal sign.**

    An empty text box appears.

4. **Type the name that you want for that group (see Figure 2-6).**

5. **After you name the group, click somewhere else in the empty space available on the Start Menu or the desktop.**

    The group now uses the name you chose.

TIP

If you no longer want to use a name for a group of shortcuts and tiles, follow the same procedure and delete the existing name you typed in Step 4.

FIGURE 2-6:
Naming a group
of shortcuts
and tiles.

Store and Display Recently Opened Programs

By default, Windows 10 stores and displays recently opened programs and items in the Start Menu and on the Taskbar. However, on computers that are managed by network administrators, this feature might be disabled. Here's what you need to do to enable this feature:

1. **Open Settings.**

2. **Click Personalization.**

   A list with personalization options and settings appears, split into several categories.

3. **Click Start.**

4. **Find the switch that says Show Recently Opened Items in Jump Lists on Start or the Taskbar.**

5. **Set this switch to On if you want it to display recently opened programs (see Figure 2-7).**

   Set the switch to Off if you don't want it to display recently opened programs.

6. **Close Settings.**

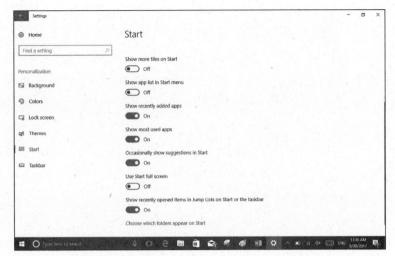

FIGURE 2-7:
Customizing the
programs shown
on the Start
Menu.

Unpin Items from the Start Menu

To remove a tile or shortcut from the Start Menu, follow these steps:

1. **Click Start.**

2. **Right-click the tile or shortcut that you want to unpin.**

3. **In the list that appears, click Unpin from Start (see Figure 2-8).**

4. **Click Start to close the Start Menu.**

FIGURE 2-8:
Unpinning an
item from the
Start Menu.

Chapter **3**

Connecting to Wi-Fi Networks and the Internet

To be productive, you need to connect to your company's network as well as to the Internet. If you have a laptop or a 2-in-1 device with Windows 10, you probably need to connect to the company's network through Wi-Fi. That's why in this chapter I first show you how to turn the Wi-Fi on and off in Windows 10 and how to connect to all kinds of wireless networks.

Business workers also travel a lot, and they need to connect to the Internet from all kinds of places, like airports, coffee shops, and business and public buildings. One way to connect to the Internet is to use a mobile USB modem that connects to your telecom's network. This chapter shows you how.

When you connect to any new network, Windows 10 asks whether you want to find PCs, devices, and content on that network. Depending on your answer, Windows 10 assigns a specific network profile that determines whether you can share with others on the network — and determines your level of security and firewall protection. This chapter shows what a network profile is, how to assign it correctly, and how to change it if you didn't get it right the first time.

Finally, many companies use proxy servers as intermediaries between their company PCs and devices and the Internet. Proxies bring many benefits, ranging from bandwidth savings to privacy and security improvements. This chapter shows you how to set up and disable a proxy server on your Windows 10 work computer or device.

Turn the Wi-Fi On and Off

Before connecting to a wireless network, you need to ensure that your Wi-Fi network card is turned on. Windows 10 offers a quick way to switch your Wi-Fi network card on or off. Here's how:

1. **On the desktop, either slide from the right side of the screen to the left (on a screen with touch) or click the Notifications icon in the notification area on the taskbar.**

   The Action Center appears on the screen, as shown in Figure 3-1.

2. **Click or tap the Wi-Fi icon to change the status of the wireless network.**

   If the Wi-Fi is turned on, you just turn it off, and vice versa.

FIGURE 3-1:
The Action Center.

Connect to a Wireless Network

If you need to connect to a wireless network, the procedure is simple. You just need to know the network name and its password. To connect to the wireless network, follow these steps:

1. **Click the Wireless Network icon on the taskbar.**

A list appears, showing all wireless networks in the area.

2. **Click the network you want to connect to (see Figure 3-2).**

FIGURE 3-2:
Connecting to a
wireless network.

3. **Leave the Connect Automatically box selected; then click Connect.**

You're asked to enter the password or the network security key.

4. **Type the password or the network security key in the appropriate field.**

5. **Specify whether you want to share the network connection details with your contacts, and then click Next.**

You're asked whether you want to allow your PC to be discoverable by other PCs and devices on this network. If you answer Yes, you can find PCs, devices, and content on the network you connected to.

6. **Click Yes or No, depending on what you prefer.**

You're now connected to the network, and you can start using it. In the future, Windows 10 automatically connects to this network every time the network is detected in your area. You don't have to complete this procedure again. You should enable this setting only for networks you trust, though. Your company network is fine, but think twice about a random airport or coffee shop network. And *never* connect to a network named "Why Would I Steal Anything from You? C'mon!"

WARNING

Specifying whether you want to find PCs, devices, and content on the network you connected to affects what you can do on the network and how secure your Windows computer or device is after you connect. To better understand how this setting works and its effects, see the "Set the Correct Network Profile" section, later in this chapter.

Connect to a Hidden Wireless Network

A *hidden* wireless network broadcasts its signal in a geographical area without making its name public. When you look for wireless networks in Windows 10, hidden networks aren't visible in the list with wireless networks. However, some companies use hidden wireless networks in some of their offices. In that case, you need to know the network's name, security type, and password before connecting to it. Follow these steps to connect to the hidden network:

1. Open the Control Panel.

2. Click Network and Internet.

A list with network and Internet-related settings appears.

3. Click Network and Sharing Center.

A window with the same name opens.

4. Click Set Up a New Connection or Network.

The Set Up a Connection or Network Wizard opens.

5. Select Manually Connect to a Wireless Network, and then click Next.

You're asked to enter the name (SSID) for the network and other details, such as the security type, encryption type, and security key (See Figure 3-3.).

6. Type the network name in the appropriate field.

7. In the Security Type field, choose the type of security used for the hidden wireless network.

8. In the Security Key field, type the network password.

9. **Indicate whether you want to start this connection automatically, and then click Next.**

Windows 10 notifies you that it has successfully added the wireless network.

10. **Click Close.**

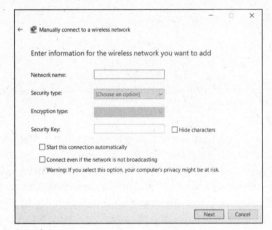

FIGURE 3-3:
Connecting to a hidden wireless network.

Connect to the Internet Using a Mobile USB Modem or SIM Card

If you have a laptop or a 2-in-1 device with Windows 10, you can connect to the Internet while on the go, by using a USB mobile modem from your telecom provider. To use it, you need to plug the modem into a USB port and wait for Windows 10 to detect and install it.

Once that's done, find the setup of a desktop app that's made available by the telecom provider on your modem. You need to install this app in order to connect to the mobile network of your telecom provider.

TECHNICAL STUFF

The app's name depends on your telecom provider. For example, in the United States, AT&T offers AT&T Communication Manager for its users who have mobile modems that can connect to their networks and the Internet.

After you install the app, you can use it to connect to your telecom's mobile network and the Internet.

Figure 3-4 shows an example of a desktop app that's offered by Vodafone, a major telecom provider in Europe.

FIGURE 3-4:
The desktop app
offered by
Vodafone for its
mobile USB
modems.

These desktop apps vary from provider to provider, and there's no single way of doing things.

Your Windows 10 device may have a slot for inserting a SIM card that you can then use to connect to the network of your telecom provider. If that's the case, plug in the SIM card and then go to the Windows Store. There, search for the app offered by your telecom and install it. You can use that app to connect to your telecom's mobile network and the Internet. For example, in the United States, Verizon offers the Verizon Connection Manager app, which you can use to manage your mobile broadband experiences (see Figure 3-5, which shows this app's Windows Store page).

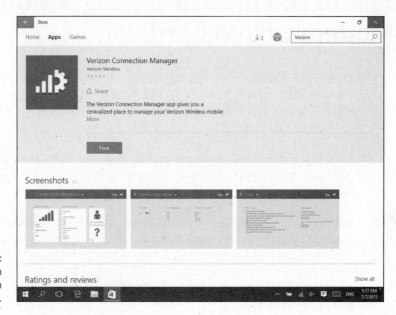

FIGURE 3-5:
The Verizon
Connection
Manager app.

Set the Correct Network Profile

When you connect for the first time to a new network — through a wireless network, a cable network, or a mobile USB modem — you're asked whether you want to allow your PC to be discoverable by other PCs and devices on that network. If you select Yes, your computer can find PCs, devices, and content on this network and automatically connect to devices like printers and TVs. When you select Yes, you set the network profile to Private.

TIP

Make your home or work network private if it's used by people and devices you trust. By default, network discovery is turned on, and you can see other computers and devices that are part of the network. This allows other computers from the network to access your computer.

If you select No, you disable all these preceding features, and you set the network profile to Public. This profile is appropriate when you're in public places such as airports, cafés, and libraries. Network discovery and sharing are turned off. Other computers from the network can't see your computer. This setting is also useful when your computer is directly connected to the Internet (such as via direct cable/modem connection or mobile Internet).

A third network location profile, called a *domain network*, is available for enterprise workplaces. Only a network administrator can set it or change it. This profile is applied only when you're connected to the network at your workplace.

Except for a domain network, you can easily change profiles for a network after you connect to it, as you can see in the next section.

Change the Network Profile

If you set an incorrect profile when you connect to a new network, you can always change the profile. If you agreed to allow Windows 10 to find PCs, devices, and content on your network, you have set the Private network profile, which makes your Windows 10 device discoverable on the network. If you didn't agree to let Windows 10 find PCs, devices, and content, you set the Public network profile, which doesn't allow network sharing.

To change the network profile in Windows 10, follow these steps:

1. **Open Settings.**

2. **Click Network & Internet.**

   The list of network- and Internet-related settings appears.

3. **Click Ethernet or Wi-Fi, depending on the type of network you're connected to.**

Information about the network you're connected to appears.

4. **Click the name of the network you're connected to.**

The list of settings available for your network connection is shown.

5. **Set the Make This PC Discoverable switch to Off or On, depending on whether you want to turn on sharing (see Figure 3-6).**

6. **Close Settings.**

FIGURE 3-6:
Changing the
network profile in
Windows 10.

REMEMBER

To enable network sharing, set the Make This PC Discoverable switch to On. To disable network sharing, set the switch to Off.

Manage Your Wi-Fi Settings

With the help of the new Wi-Fi feature named Wi-Fi Sense, Windows 10 can connect to Wi-Fi hotspots and networks that your contacts share with you. You can also share your networks and their details with your contacts. When Wi-Fi Sense is enabled, you agree that this feature can use your location in order to work and do what it was designed to do. Obviously, you can easily disable this feature, if you don't want to use it. You can also set whether you want to exchange Wi-Fi network access with your contacts and which group of contacts you want to make this exchange with.

Here's how to customize your Wi-Fi settings:

1. **Click the Wireless Network icon on the taskbar.**

   The list of available wireless networks appears.

2. **Click Network Settings.**

   Your wireless network settings are shown.

3. **Click Wi-Fi.**

4. **Set the Connect to Suggested Open Hotspots switch to Off if you want to disable this feature (see Figure 3-7).**

5. **If you want to keep these features turned on but customize which contacts you're sharing with, select the types of contacts you're interested in and deselect those you don't want to share with.**

FIGURE 3-7: Setting up Wi-Fi Sense.

Forget a Wireless Network You Connected To

You can easily "forget" a wireless network you connected to in the past. When you do so, Windows 10 deletes all the information it stored about the network, and it can't connect to it automatically. If you want to connect to it later, you must complete the whole procedure of connecting to that network, as though you're connecting to it for the first time.

TIP

Forgetting a network is useful when its settings have been changed, such as its security password.

Because Windows 10 stored details about a wireless network that are no longer valid, you may no longer be able to connect to it. Forgetting a wireless network forces Windows 10 to ask you for its latest connection details the next time you try to connect to it. Here's how to forget a wireless network in Windows 10:

1. **Click the Wireless Network icon on the taskbar.**

The list of available wireless networks appears.

2. **Click Network & Internet Settings.**

Your wireless network settings are shown.

3. **Click Wi-Fi.**

4. **Click Manage Known Networks.**

You can see all wireless networks that are known by Windows 10.

5. **Click the network that you want to forget; then click Forget (see Figure 3-8).**

FIGURE 3-8:
Forgetting a
wireless network.

TECHNICAL STUFF

If you chose to "forget" a network because you could no longer connect to it and you still can't connect after forgetting it, talk to your company's network administrator or IT support department. The problem may be that the network is now set up so that it's no longer compatible with the wireless network card on your Windows 10 device.

Set Up a Proxy Using an Automatic Configuration Script

A *proxy server*, which is an intermediary between your PC or device and the Internet, makes requests to websites, servers, and services on the Internet for you. Say that you use a web browser to visit www.wiley.com and your browser is set to use a proxy server. After you type www.wiley.com, the request is sent to the proxy server. The server then sends the request to the server where the website is hosted. The home page of the Wiley website is returned to the proxy server, which, in turn, returns the home page to you.

TECHNICAL STUFF

One reason companies use proxy servers is that doing so helps them save precious bandwidth. Proxy servers can compress traffic, cache files, and web pages from the Internet, and even strip ads from websites before they reach your computer. This allows companies to save bandwidth, especially when they have hundreds or thousands of employees accessing mostly the same popular websites (such as CNN News or *The New York Times*). Other benefits include improved security and privacy.

By default, Windows 10 is set to automatically detect proxy settings. However, this may not work when you're connected to your company's business network. One way to set up a proxy is to specify a script address that is given to you by the network administrator or by the company's IT department. When using a configuration script for a proxy server, note that its address is similar to a *URL* (the address of a website), such as http://my.proxy.server:8000/.

To set a proxy using an automatic configuration script, follow these steps:

1. **Open Settings.**

2. **Click Network & Internet.**

   The list of network- and Internet-related settings appears.

3. **Click Proxy.**

   The list of available proxy settings appears.

4. **In the Automatic Proxy Setup section, set the Use Setup Script switch to On (see Figure 3-9).**

5. **Enter the script address as it was given to you; then click Save.**

6. **Close Settings.**

TIP

To disable the proxy, follow the same steps and, at Step 4, set the Use Setup Script switch to Off.

FIGURE 3-9:
Setting up an automatic proxy configuration script.

Set Up a Proxy Manually

Another way to set a proxy is to manually enter its IP address and port number. The address of a proxy server is similar to that of any computer on the network, and it could be something like this: 192.168.1.211. The port can be any combination of up to four figures. It can be any combination of digits, including 80 or 8080, depending on how its administrator(s) set it. The IP address and port of your company's proxy server are given to you by the network administrator or by the company's IT department. Here's how to set a proxy manually in Windows 10:

1. **Open Settings.**

2. **Click Network & Internet.**

   The list of network- and Internet-related settings appears.

3. **Click Proxy.**

   The list of available proxy settings appears.

4. **In the Manual Proxy Setup section, set the Use a Proxy Server switch to On (see Figure 3-10).**

5. **In the Address field, type the IP address.**

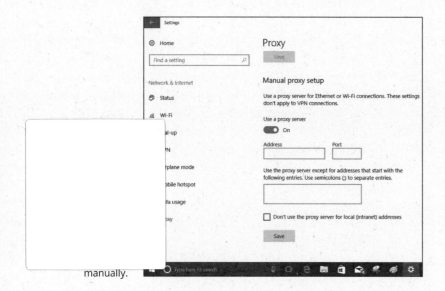

manually.

6. **In the Port field, type the port.**

7. **Click Save; then close the Settings window.**

TIP

To disable the proxy, follow the same steps; at Step 4, set the Use a Proxy Server switch to Off.

» **Downloading files and manage your downloads**

» **Working with multiple tabs**

» **Adding web pages as favorites and access them later**

» **Pinning a website to the Apps list in the Start Menu**

» **Changing the home page**

» **Setting Internet Explorer to start with tabs from the last session**

» **Adding a website to Compatibility View**

» **Browsing the web using InPrivate Browsing**

» **Deleting your browsing history**

Chapter **4**

Using Internet Explorer

Windows 10 is the first Microsoft operating system with two web browsers: Internet Explorer and Microsoft Edge. When Windows 10 was released, Microsoft Edge wasn't fully finalized. Edge has cer-tainly gotten better since then, but adoption is still minimal. If you also con-sider that many businesses don't have modern web apps and intranet websites that work with Microsoft Edge, it's obvious that Microsoft couldn't ditch Internet Explorer in Windows 10 — at least not in the version for enterprise customers. We don't expect many businesses to provide support for Microsoft Edge for quite some time, so we cover Internet Explorer 11 in this book. It's the browser that you're most likely to use at work to access your company's web-sites and web services.

In this chapter, we start by showing you the basics on using Internet Explorer: how to visit websites, how to download files, and how to manage downloads and work with multiple tabs simultaneously. Then we move on to more advanced tasks, such as adding web pages to your favorites and accessing them, adding websites to the list of apps in the Start Menu, and changing the Internet Explorer home page.

Finally, we provide some productivity tips, such as how to set Internet Explorer to start with tabs from the previous session, how to add sites with rendering issues to the Compatibility View list, how to browse the web privately, and how to delete your browsing history in Internet Explorer.

Browse the Web in Internet Explorer

The following example shows the basics of using Internet Explorer. To start Internet Explorer, type a website address, navigate to that website, and then use the Back and Forward buttons to move to the previous page and the next page, respectively.

1. **Click in the search bar on the taskbar.**

2. **Type the word** internet.

   A list of search results appears.

3. **Click the Internet Explorer search result.**

4. **Click in the address bar located at the upper-left of the Internet Explorer window.**

5. **Type** dummies.com; **then press Enter (see Figure 4-1).**

   The For Dummies website appears.

6. **Click the Shop for Books link on the For Dummies website.**

7. **After the For Dummies Store page loads, click the Back (left-pointing arrow) button, located at the top-left corner of the Internet Explorer window (see Figure 4-2).**

   You're now back at the For Dummies home page.

8. **Click the Forward button (right-pointing arrow), located at the top-left corner of the Internet Explorer window.**

   You're now back at the For Dummies Store page.

9. **Close Internet Explorer.**

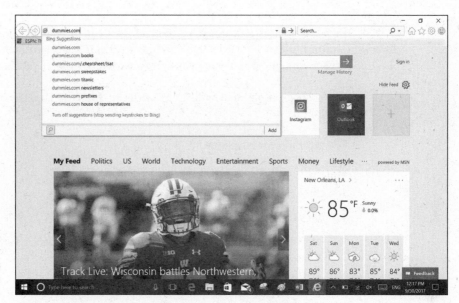

FIGURE 4-1:
How to enter
a website's
address in
the address bar.

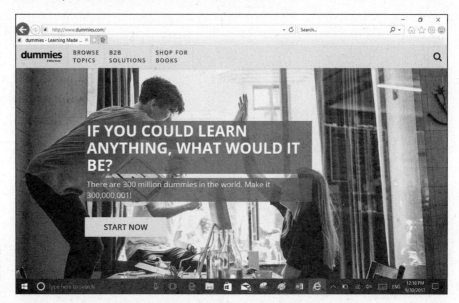

FIGURE 4-2:
Using the Back
and Forward
buttons.

Download Files in Internet Explorer

Downloading files in Internet Explorer involves just a few clicks. If you download an executable file, Internet Explorer asks whether you want to run it or save it. When you download other types of files, such as PDF documents or file archives, Internet Explorer asks whether you want to open or save them.

TIP

It's better to save a downloaded file and then run or open it. Directly opening or running a file without selecting Save means that it's saved to a temporary location on your computer, and when you close a temporary file, it's difficult to find.

Here's an example of downloading a file in Internet Explorer from the Skype website:

1. **Start Internet Explorer.**

2. **In the address bar, type skype.com; then press Enter.**

3. **Once the Skype website loads, click Download Skype.**

4. **Click Download.**

Internet Explorer shows a prompt asking whether you want to run or save the SkypeSetup.exe file.

5. **Click Save (see Figure 4-3).**

After the file is downloaded and saved on your computer, you receive a message to that effect.

FIGURE 4-3:
How to download
Skype in Internet
Explorer.

6. **In the window informing you that the download has completed, click Open Folder.**

A File Explorer window appears, showing you where the downloaded file is stored.

7. **Close File Explorer.**

8. **Close Internet Explorer.**

TIP

Downloads are saved, by default, in the Downloads folder of your user account.

View and Manage Your Downloads in Internet Explorer

In Internet Explorer, you can download multiple files at the same time, and you can manage them from the View Downloads window. Here, you see a list of the files that were downloaded recently. This window will also show any ongoing downloads. You can also pause active downloads or cancel them (see Figure 4-4).

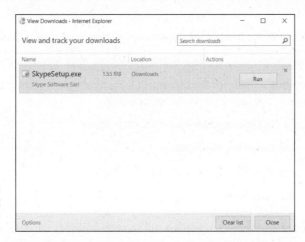

FIGURE 4-4:
Tracking
downloads in
Internet Explorer.

You can also remove a downloaded file from the list by selecting it and then clicking the small x at the top-right corner of its entry, as shown in Figure 4-5.

When you browse the web with Internet Explorer, here's how to access the View Downloads window and use it to manage downloads:

1. **Click the Tools button in Internet Explorer.**

   The Tools button is shaped like a gear wheel.

2. **In the Tools menu that appears, select View Downloads.**

   The View Downloads window shows the files that have been downloaded and files that currently are downloaded (if any).

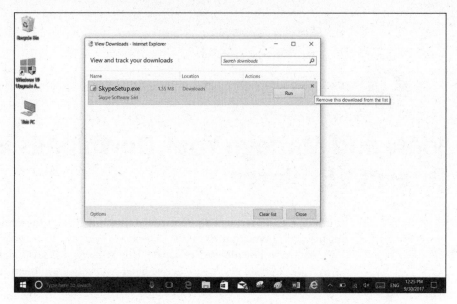

FIGURE 4-5:
How to remove a
download from
the list.

3. Click the Pause button for the download that you want to pause.

4. When you're ready to resume the download, click Resume.

5. To remove a file from the list, select it by clicking it and then click the small x at the top-right corner of its entry.

6. To open files that you downloaded, click Open.

7. Close the file that you opened.

8. Close the View Downloads window.

9. Close Internet Explorer.

TIP

The keyboard shortcut Ctrl+J opens the View Downloads window.

Work with Multiple Tabs in Internet Explorer

Tabbed browsing is an Internet Explorer feature that allows you to open multiple websites in a single browser window. You can open web pages in new tabs and switch between the pages by clicking their tabs. Here's how to do so:

1. Start Internet Explorer.

2. In the address bar, type dummies.com; then press Enter.

The For Dummies website appears.

3. **Click the New Tab button, located near the For Dummies tab (see Figure 4-6).**

FIGURE 4-6:
How to open a
new tab in
Internet Explorer.

4. **Click the small x at the right of the new tab to close it (see Figure 4-7).**

   Now only the *For Dummies* website tab remains.

5. **Close Internet Explorer.**

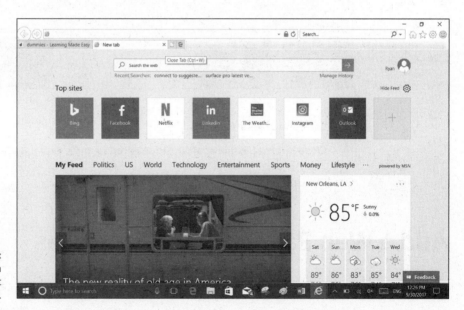

FIGURE 4-7:
How to close a
tab in Internet
Explorer.

TIP

The keyboard shortcut Ctrl+T opens a new tab in Internet Explorer.

Access Your Favorite Web Pages in Internet Explorer

You can mark a web page as a favorite and then access it very quickly, with just a few clicks, without having to type its address or remember it, which is quite useful, especially when you encounter a web page with content that you want to return to later. Favorites are organized as lists of shortcuts to web pages that can also be grouped in folders. (The following section shows how to add a favorite.) Here's how to access your favorites:

1. **Start Internet Explorer.**

2. **In the top-right corner of the Internet Explorer window, click the button that looks like a star. (It's referred to as the View Favorites, Feeds, and History button. See Figure 4-8)**

   A list with your favorites appears.

FIGURE 4-8:
Accessing your favorites in Internet Explorer.

3. **Click one of your favorites.**

4. **Close Internet Explorer after the selected favorite web page loads.**

The keyboard shortcut Alt+C opens the list of favorites.

TIP

Add a Web Page to Your Favorites

To add a web page to the list of Internet Explorer favorites, follow these steps:

1. **Start Internet Explorer.**

2. **In the address bar, type the address of the web page that you want to add as a favorite; then press Enter.**

3. After the web page loads, click the button that looks like a star, at the top-right of the Internet Explorer window. (It's referred to as the View Favorites, Feeds, and History button.)

4. Click Add to Favorites.

5. Click inside the Create In drop-down list, and choose the folder where you want to save your favorite; then click Add to Favorites (see Figure 4-9).

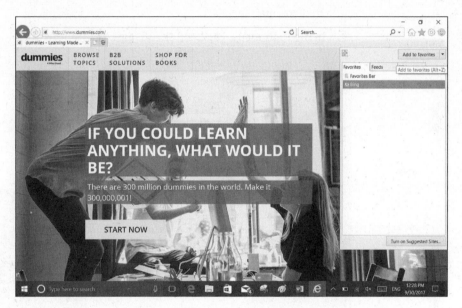

FIGURE 4-9:
How to add a web page as a favorite.

6. Access the list of favorites again to see the newly added entry in the folder that you selected.

7. Close Internet Explorer.

Pin a Website to the List of Apps in the Start Menu

In Windows 10, you can pin a website to the list of apps that's shown when you access the Start Menu. Once you pin a website, its shortcut appears in the All Apps list, as though it were an app. If you use a website often (such as a corporate intranet page or a vendor's website), having it in the list of apps will save time.

To pin a website to the list of apps shown in the Start Menu, follow these steps:

1. **Start Internet Explorer.**

2. **In the address bar, type the address of the web page that you want to pin; then press Enter.**

   The web page is loaded in Internet Explorer.

3. **Click the Tools button (shaped like a gear wheel).**

   The Tools menu appears.

4. **In the Tools menu, click Add Site to Apps (see Figure 4-10).**

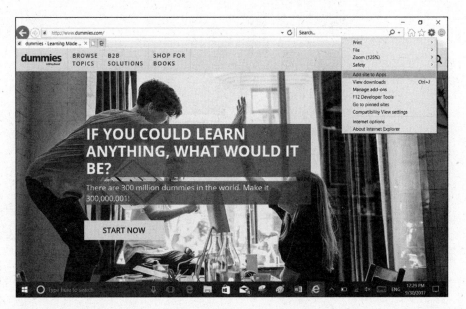

FIGURE 4-10:
How to add a site to All Apps.

5. **Click Add to confirm.**

   The website loads again in a new Internet Explorer window, which has the website's logo as an icon, in the top-left corner of the window.

6. **Close Internet Explorer.**

If you open the Start Menu and go to All Apps, you see the newly pinned website in the list of available apps.

Change the Home Page in Internet Explorer

The *home page* in Internet Explorer is the page that loads automatically every time you start this browser. You can easily change the home page and make it anything you want. It can be any web page on the Internet or a web page from your company's internal network. It can be the default page provided by Internet Explorer when you install Windows 10, the current page that's loaded in the active tab, or a new, empty tab.

To change the Internet Explorer home page, follow these steps:

1. **Start Internet Explorer.**

2. **In the address bar, type the address of the web page that you want to set as the home page, and press Enter.**

The web page is loaded in Internet Explorer.

3. **Click the Tools button (shaped like a gear wheel).**

The Tools menu appears.

4. **Click Internet Options.**

The Internet Options window appears.

5. **In the General tab, find the Home Page section.**

6. **Click the Use Current button (see Figure 4-11).**

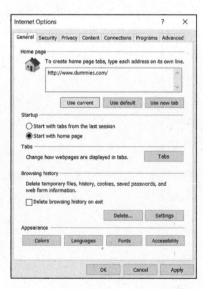

FIGURE 4-11:
How to change the home page in Internet Explorer.

7. Click OK (see Figure 4-11).

8. Close Internet Explorer.

Set Internet Explorer to Start with the Tabs from the Last Session

You can set Internet Explorer so that it automatically loads the tabs that were open the last time you closed it. This is handy if you regularly work on several websites or web pages. Here's how to do so:

1. Start Internet Explorer.

2. Click the Tools button (shaped like a gear wheel).

The Tools menu appears.

3. Click Internet Options.

The Internet Options window appears.

4. In the General tab, find the Startup section, not quite halfway down.

5. Select Start with Tabs from the Last Session; then click OK (see Figure 4-12).

6. Close Internet Explorer.

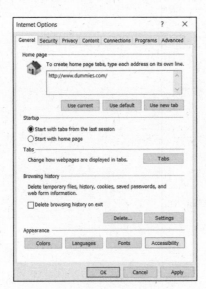

FIGURE 4-12:
How to set Internet Explorer to start with tabs from the last session.

When you set Internet Explorer to start with tabs from the last session, it ignores the home page that you set.

Add a Website to Compatibility View

Sometimes websites don't look like you expect them to. Images might not appear correctly, menus might be out of place, and text may be jumbled. Such problems can be caused by incompatibility between Internet Explorer and the website you're on. This situation may be especially the case with intranet websites that companies created many years ago. However, incompatibility can also happen with public websites on the Internet.

If a website doesn't look right in Internet Explorer, you may be able to fix the problem by adding the site to the Compatibility View list. Once you turn on Compatibility View, Internet Explorer automatically shows that site in Compatibility View every time you visit the site. You can turn off the Compatibility View for that site by removing it from your compatibility list.

Here's how to add websites to the Compatibility View list:

1. **Start Internet Explorer.**

2. **In the address bar, type the address of the website you're having trouble with and press Enter.**

    The website is loaded in Internet Explorer.

3. **Click the Tools button (shaped like a gear wheel).**

    The Tools menu appears.

4. **Click Compatibility View Settings.**

    The Compatibility View Settings window appears (see Figure 4-13).

5. **Click Add and then click Close.**

    The site loads again, using Internet Explorer's Compatibility View.

If you add a site to the Compatibility View list and the page looks worse, the problem may not be compatibility. In this case, remove the site from the list.

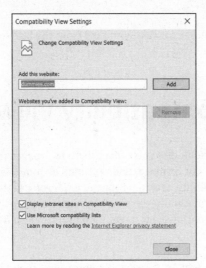

FIGURE 4-13:
How to add a
website to the
Compatibility
View list.

Browse the Web Using InPrivate Browsing

InPrivate Browsing in Internet Explorer enables you to surf the web without leaving a trail in your browser. This helps prevent others using your computer from seeing what sites you visited and what you looked at on the web.

When you start InPrivate Browsing, Internet Explorer opens a new browser window. The protection that is provided is in effect only during the time that you use that window. You can open as many tabs as you want in that window, and they're all protected. However, if you open another browser window, that window isn't protected by InPrivate Browsing. You can see an InPrivate Browsing window in Figure 4-14.

While you're surfing the web using InPrivate Browsing, Internet Explorer stores some information, like cookies and temporary Internet files, so that the web pages you visit work correctly. However, at the end of your InPrivate Browsing session, this information is discarded.

Here's how to start InPrivate Browsing in Internet Explorer:

1. **Start Internet Explorer.**

   The window that opens isn't protected by InPrivate Browsing.

2. **Click the Tools button (shaped like a gear wheel).**

   The Tools menu appears.

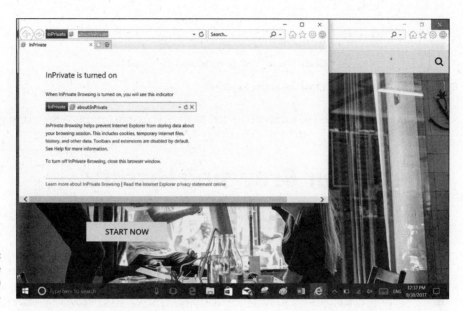

FIGURE 4-14:
InPrivate
Browsing in
Internet Explorer.

3. **Click Safety (see Figure 4-15).**

The Safety menu appears.

4. **Click InPrivate Browsing (see Figure 4-15).**

An InPrivate Browsing window opens.

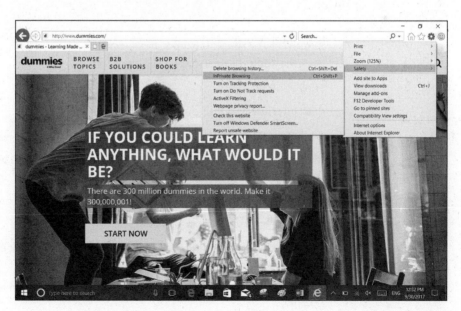

FIGURE 4-15:
How to start
InPrivate
Browsing in
Internet Explorer.

5. Navigate the web as usual in this window.

6. Close the InPrivate window when you finish.

7. Close Internet Explorer.

TIP

The keyboard shortcut Ctrl+Shift+P starts an InPrivate Browsing session.

Delete Your Browsing History in Internet Explorer

As you use Internet Explorer, the browser stores temporary files, your browsing history, cookies from the websites that you're visiting, saved passwords, and web form information. All web browsers do this so that they can load web pages faster and quickly provide you with the data you need. However, over time the browser may start to slow down. One way to speed it up is to delete the entire stored browsing history.

TIP

Deleting your browsing history is useful when you don't want others to see which websites you visited.

To clear the entire browsing history stored by Internet Explorer, follow these steps:

1. Start Internet Explorer.

2. Click the Tools button (shaped like a gear wheel).

   The Tools menu appears.

3. Click Internet Options.

   The Internet Options window appears.

4. In the General tab, find the Browsing History section (at the bottom of the Internet Options window shown in Figure 4-16).

5. Click the Delete button.

   The Delete Browsing History window opens.

6. Select all the types of data that you want removed and click Delete (refer to Figure 4-16).

   After Internet Explorer deletes the selected browsing history, a message confirms it.

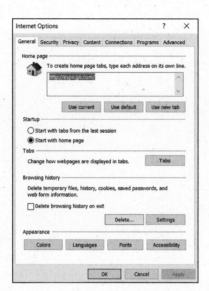

FIGURE 4-16:
How to delete
your browsing
history in Internet
Explorer.

7. **Click OK in the Internet Options window.**

8. **Close Internet Explorer.**

If you always want to delete your browser history whenever you close Internet Explorer, select the Delete Browser History on Exit check box. This step eliminates a lot of convenience for finding sites you browsed in the past, but you'll never forget to empty your history this way.

Chapter **5**

Managing Files and Folders

When you work on a Windows computer or device, you spend a lot of time browsing and managing files and folders. You may want to look at your pictures, create documents, watch movies, and organize your files. Or you may just wonder where that one document you created got to before your meeting in five minutes.

File Explorer is Windows' most important tool for doing all the above, and, once you're familiar with it, you find that you can do a lot with File Explorer, which is what this chapter tells you about.

Key Terms

Before getting down to the business of working with File Explorer in Windows 10, I'd like to go over a few basic terms. Once you understand them, the rest of the chapter is much clearer:

>> **Files:** A file is any unique, stand-alone piece of data. It can be a document, a presentation, a picture, or a video.

  To help keep track of your files, you save them in folders.

>> **Folders:** Folders on your computer are the digital equivalent of the file folders used to hold papers, and just like those file folders, the folders on your computer hold data that's grouped together in a logical way.

  Windows has several folders ready for you to use: Desktop, Documents, Downloads, Music, Pictures, and Videos.

>> **Subfolders:** These are folders within other folders.

  A folder can contain any number of subfolders and files. You create subfolders to organize your data, which you then place in folders.

>> **Libraries:** These are virtual collections of folders on your computer.

  Libraries aren't actual folders, although they may appear to be. Instead, libraries hold references or shortcuts to files or folders that are stored elsewhere. Windows 10 has several default libraries for you to use: Camera Roll, Documents, Music, Pictures, Saved Pictures, and Videos. You can also create your own libraries.

Open File Explorer

You can start File Explorer in many ways in Windows 10, but here's a list of the most common ones:

>> On the Taskbar, click the icon that looks like a folder.

>> Click the Start button to access the Start Menu. When it appears, click the File Explorer shortcut (see Figure 5-1).

>> Press Windows+E on your keyboard.

>> Right-click the Start button; then click the File Explorer shortcut.

>> Click in the search bar on the taskbar, type **file explorer**, and press Enter on the keyboard or click the File Explorer search result.

FIGURE 5-1:
The File Explorer
shortcut in the
Start Menu.

Navigate File Explorer

When you start File Explorer, the Quick Access view is shown, which contains a list of the folders you browse most frequently and the files that you recently opened. This list changes as you use different folders, and you can customize it by pinning folders and libraries that you'd like to access as quickly as possible. Figure 5-2 shows the Quick Access section in File Explorer. (Chapter 6 shows how to pin items to Quick Access.)

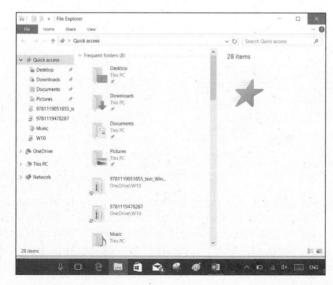

FIGURE 5-2:
The Quick Access
section in File
Explorer.

On the left side of the File Explorer window, you find the *Navigation pane*, which is a column with several shortcuts. When you open File Explorer, you see these shortcuts in the Navigation pane:

>> **Quick Access:** Shortcuts to the folders you frequently access and the files you opened recently.

>> **OneDrive:** Files and folders that are stored on your OneDrive.

>> **This PC:**

- Your user folders (Desktop, Documents, Downloads, Music, Pictures, and Videos)

- Devices and drives that are available on your computer (see Figure 5-3)

- Network locations

>> **Network:** Other computers and devices that are connected to the network. If they have shared files and folders, you can access those as well.

>> **HomeGroup:** Members of your HomeGroup, if you have one. If they have shared files and folders, you can access those, too.

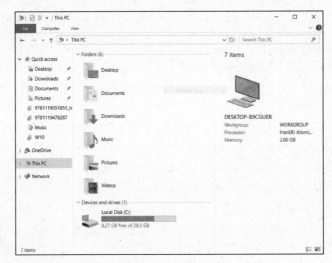

FIGURE 5-3:
This PC in File Explorer.

When you click any shortcut in the Navigation pane, its contents are shown on the right side of the File Explorer window. To open a file or folder shown on the right, double-click it. As soon as you start navigating your Windows computer or device, the Back, Forward, Recent Locations, and Up buttons are activated, as is the Address Bar (see Figure 5-4).

FIGURE 5-4:
Back, Forward,
Recent Locations,
Up, and
Address Bar.

Here's how to use these buttons and the Address Bar to browse your computer:

1. **Open File Explorer.**

2. **Click OneDrive.**

   The OneDrive folder and its contents are shown.

3. **Click the Back button.**

   You're taken right back to the Quick Access screen.

4. **Click the Forward button to go to your OneDrive folder again.**

5. **Click the Recent Locations button.**

6. **In the menu that appears, click Quick Access.**

   You return to the Quick Access screen.

7. **Click This PC.**

8. **Double-click Documents.**

   As you open a new folder, its shortcut is added in the Address Bar. If you click on any of the elements in the Address Bar, you're taken to them.

9. **In the Address Bar, click This PC.**

   File Explorer quickly jumps from the current folder to This PC.

10. **Click the Back button to go back to the previous folder.**

11. **Close File Explorer.**

Navigate the File Explorer Ribbon

File Explorer uses a graphical user interface feature, called the *Ribbon*, that runs across the top of the File Explorer window. Several tabs comprise the Ribbon, such as File, Home, Share, and View. Depending on what you're browsing on your computer, additional tabs, such as Manage, may be displayed. Figure 5-5 shows the Ribbon in File Explorer.

FIGURE 5-5:
The Ribbon in File
Explorer.

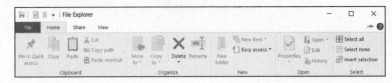

By default, the Ribbon is minimized, and you can see only the names of each tab. When you click a tab like Home, you see several buttons and options that are organized in logical sections.

Here's how to navigate the Ribbon in File Explorer:

1. **Open File Explorer.**

2. **Click This PC.**

3. **Click Documents.**

   The Documents folder and its contents are shown.

4. **Click the Home tab.**

   This tab includes tools for common operations such as Copy, Cut, and Paste, creating new folders and files, moving data, and deleting files and folders.

5. **Click the Share tab.**

   This tab includes tools for sharing files and folders with others through the network, the HomeGroup, by email, or by burning your data to a disc.

6. **Click the View tab.**

   This is where you can change how files are displayed in File Explorer, and you can also enable or disable different user interface elements.

7. **In the Navigation pane, click This PC.**

   The ribbon is minimized again.

8. **Double-click the C drive, which is usually named Local Disk (C).**

   The Manage tab appears on the Ribbon.

9. **Click the Manage tab (see Figure 5-6).**

   Here you find contextual options for managing the C drive.

10. **Click File on the Ribbon.**

    A menu appears with options for opening a new File Explorer window, starting the Command Prompt and PowerShell, changing folder and search options, getting help, and accessing your most frequent places.

11. **In the File menu, click Close to exit File Explorer.**

FIGURE 5-6:
The Manage tab
on the File
Explorer Ribbon.

Maximize or Minimize the Ribbon in File Explorer

By default, the Ribbon is minimized in File Explorer. If you find it useful and you often need to use it, you may want to maximize it all the time. Here's how to maximize and minimize the Ribbon in File Explorer:

1. **Open File Explorer.**

2. **Double-click the Home tab on the Ribbon.**

The File Explorer window changes to make room for the maximized Ribbon (see Figure 5-7).

3. **Close File Explorer.**

4. **To minimize the Ribbon, open File Explorer again.**

From now on, the Ribbon is maximized every time you open File Explorer.

5. **Click the Share tab to open it.**

The Share tab is shown on the Ribbon.

6. **Double-click the Share tab.**

The Ribbon is minimized.

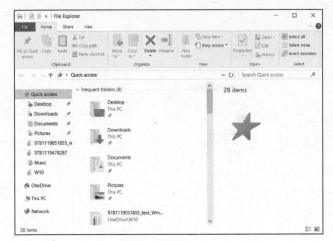

FIGURE 5-7:
The Ribbon,
maximized in File
Explorer.

7. **Close File Explorer.**

8. **Open File Explorer again.**

Now the Ribbon is minimized when you open File Explorer.

File Explorer remembers whether the Ribbon was minimized or maximized the last time you closed it and will open it that way the next time you open File Explorer.

Identify Common File Formats in File Explorer

You can open and view hundreds of file types on your Windows computer or device. The most common types of files are documents, music, pictures, videos, and executable files. You may also work with specialized files from third-party apps, such as PDF files, but usually the types of files you encounter are the common ones.

What File Explorer shows you depends on what you're doing on your computer. You see either several columns with information or a preview of each file. For example, when you open the Downloads folder, you see these columns: Name, Date Modified, Type, and Size (see Figure 5-8).

For folders, the type is always File Folder. But if you're looking at previews of files, you really can't tell what kind of file you're looking at, so it's best to use the Details view, where you can get more useful information. (Turn to Chapter 6 to find out how to change the view in File Explorer.)

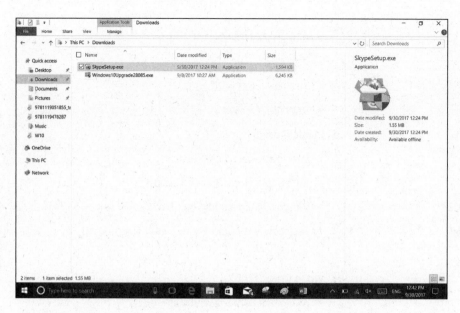

FIGURE 5-8:
The columns
shown for the
Downloads
folder.

Here's how to identify the type of each file shown in File Explorer:

1. **Open File Explorer.**

2. **Click Downloads.**

The Downloads folder and its contents are shown.

3. **Look at the first five to eight files and check their type in the Type column.**

Here are the most common types of files that you may encounter on your Windows 10 computer:

» Microsoft Office files:

- Microsoft Word (.doc and .docx)

- Microsoft PowerPoint (.ppt and .pptx)

- Microsoft Excel (.xls and .xlsx)

- Microsoft Publisher (.pub and .pubx)

- Microsoft OneNote (.one)

» Picture files:

- JPEG files (.jpg and .jpeg)

- GIF files (.gif)

- Bitmap files (`.bmp`)

- PNG files (`.png`)

- TIFF files (`.tif` and `.tiff`)

- RAW files (`.raw`)

» **Music files:**

- Windows audio files (`.wav`)

- MP3 audio files (`.mp3` and `.m3u`)

- Windows Media audio files (`.asx`, `.wm`, `.wma`, and `.wmx`)

- Free Lossless Audio Codec files (`.flac`)

- AAC files (`.aac`)

» **Video files:**

- Audio Video Interleaved files (`.avi`)

- Motion JPEG files (`.avi` and `.mov`)

- Windows Media files (`.wm`, `.wmv`, and `.asf`)

- Matroska multimedia files (`.mkv`)

- Apple QuickTime files (`.mov` and `.qt`)

- MPEG Movie files (`.mp4`, `.mov`, `.m4v`, `.mpeg`, `.mpg`, `.mpe`, `.m1v`, `.mp2`, `.mpv2`, `.mod`, `.vob`, and `.m1v`)

» **Other types of popular files:**

- *Application files* (`.exe`): Executable files that can run with a double-click

- *Text documents* (`.txt`): Simple text documents without any kind of formatting

- *Compressed* (`.zip`): Archives of other files and folders

- *Portable Document Format files* (`.pdf`): A very popular type of file generally used for sharing non-editable documents that need to look the same on all devices, no matter which operating system you use

- *OpenOffice and LibreOffice documents* (`.odt`, `.ott`, `.oth`, and `.odm`): Documents created using free open-source productivity applications, such as OpenOffice and LibreOffice

TIP

By default, file extensions aren't shown in the lists you see while using File Explorer. Depending on the folder that you're viewing and its content, File Explorer may show a column named Type, where you can see the type of each file. (See Chapter 6 for more on changing how File Explorer displays data.)

Open a File in File Explorer

To open a file in File Explorer, browse the locations on your PC, find the file, and double-click it. An app, set by default for a file's type, automatically opens the file. To use another app to open a file type, start File Explorer and follow these steps:

1. Browse to the location of the file that you want to open and select it.

2. Click the Home tab on the Ribbon.

The Home tab is displayed.

3. In the Open section, click the down-pointing arrow beside the Open button.

The Open menu is displayed.

4. In the Open menu, click the app that you want to use to open the file (see Figure 5-9).

Now the app you selected opens your file.

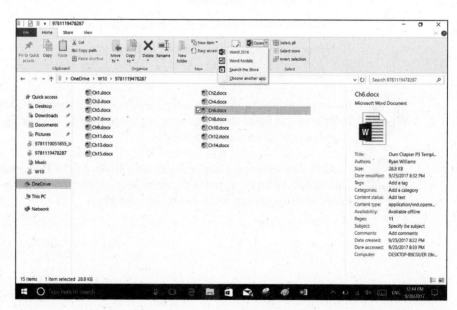

FIGURE 5-9:
The Open menu in File Explorer.

Move a File or Folder in File Explorer

You can move one or more files or folders to another location in several ways. One way is to use the Cut and Paste commands. To do so, open File Explorer and follow these steps:

1. **Browse to the file's or folder's location and select it by clicking on it.**

2. **Click the Home tab on the Ribbon.**

   The Home tab is displayed.

3. **In the Clipboard section, click the Cut button (see Figure 5-10).**

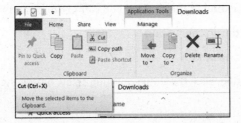

FIGURE 5-10:
The Cut button in
File Explorer.

4. **Browse to the folder where you want to move that file.**

5. **Click the Home tab on the Ribbon.**

   The Home tab is displayed.

6. **Click the Paste button in the Clipboard section.**

   The selected file is now in the new folder.

7. **Close File Explorer.**

TIP

Instead of using the mouse, you can also use the keyboard. Follow the preceding procedure and press Ctrl+X on your keyboard instead of clicking the Cut button, and press Ctrl+V instead of clicking Paste.

Another way to move a file or folder also starts on the Home tab of the Ribbon. Click the Move To menu in the Organize section, and then click on the name of the folder where you want to move the selected item.

TIP

Rename a File or Folder in File Explorer

You can easily rename files and folders (unless they're system files that the operating system installs in folders, such as Windows and Program Files).

WARNING

Don't fiddle with the files in folders such as Windows and Program Files because you could create problems that you might not be able to fix. And don't change the file extensions of any file unless you absolutely know what you're doing. That change could cause programs to not open the file correctly.

When it comes to your own files (such as documents, pictures, videos, and music), there's no stopping you from renaming files as you prefer. To rename a file or folder, open File Explorer and follow these steps:

1. Browse to the file or folder that you want to rename.

2. Click the file or folder to select it.

3. Click the Home tab on the Ribbon.

The Home tab is displayed.

4. In the Organize section, click the Rename button (see Figure 5-11).

You can now edit the name of the selected item.

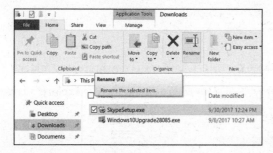

FIGURE 5-11:
The Rename button in File Explorer.

5. Type the new name.

6. Press Enter or click somewhere else in the File Explorer window.

The selected file or folder now has the name that you typed.

7. Close File Explorer.

TIP

The keyboard shortcut for the Rename command is F2.

Create a Folder in File Explorer

You can create as many folders as you want, either directly on a drive on your computer or within other folders. Using multiple folders enables you to better organize your files, so create as many as you need. To create a folder, open File Explorer and follow these steps:

1. **Go to the location where you want to create the folder.**

It can be a drive on your computer or another folder.

2. **Click the Home tab on the Ribbon.**

The Home tab is displayed.

3. **In the New section, click the New Folder button (see Figure 5-12).**

A new folder is created with the name New Folder.

FIGURE 5-12:
The New Folder button in File Explorer.

4. **Type the name that you want for the newly created folder.**

5. **Press Enter or click somewhere else in the File Explorer window.**

The newly created folder now has the name that you typed.

6. **Close File Explorer.**

TIP

The keyboard shortcut for the New Folder command is Ctrl+Shift+N.

Create a File in File Explorer

You can create files in File Explorer. Actually, you can create them almost anywhere, except in system folders such as Windows and Program Files. When creating a new file, you first choose its type and then give it a name. To do so, open File Explorer and follow these steps:

1. **Go to the location where you want to create the file.**

2. **Click the Home tab on the Ribbon.**

   The Home tab is displayed.

3. **In the New section, click the New Item button (see Figure 5-13).**

   A menu appears with several types of files.

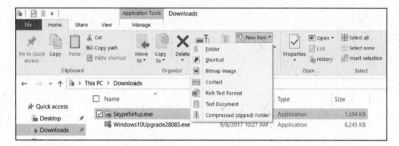

FIGURE 5-13:
The New Item
button in File
Explorer.

4. **Click the type that you want, and the file is created.**

5. **Type the name that you want for that file.**

6. **Press Enter or click somewhere else in the File Explorer window.**

7. **Close File Explorer.**

The file that you created is an empty one. To add content to it, you must open it in an application that can edit that type of file and add the content that you want.

Save Your Files

Many apps work with all kinds of files and allow you to create files on your computer that you can use later. For example, you can use the Microsoft Word app to create documents and share them with your coworkers, or you can use Paint to create simple drawings and share them with your child. To save a file, you locate the Save button and click it. Some apps also offer a Save As button or menu so that you can choose between multiple file formats before saving a file. Figure 5-14 shows the Save As menu in Paint (the drawing app that's bundled with Windows 10). Paint enables you to select from among several image formats to save a drawing.

When you save a file, you're asked to select the folder where you want to save it, provide a name for the file, and select the type. To keep things organized, take advantage of the user folders and libraries that are available in Windows: Desktop, Downloads, Documents, Pictures, Music, and Videos.

Save your documents in the Documents folder, your pictures in the Pictures
folder, your downloads in the Downloads folder, and so on. This way, you can easily find them when you need them.

TIP

Another advantage to using these user folders to store your files is that Windows 10
automatically indexes them, so you can easily search for and find everything that's
stored in them. Searching for files stored in other locations takes much longer.

Here's an example of how to save files in Windows 10 desktop apps:

1. **Click inside the search bar on the taskbar and type** wordpad.

    A list of search results appears.

2. **Click the WordPad search result to create a new document.**

    The Document – WordPad window appears.

3. **Type** Hello!

4. **Click File.**

    The File menu appears (see Figure 5-15).

5. **In the File menu, click Save.**

    The Save As window appears.

6. **Select the** Documents **folder in the column on the left.**

7. **Type a name for the file; for example,** My Document.

8. **Click the Save As Type drop-down list.**

FIGURE 5-15:
The File menu.

9. Select the file type that you want to use.

10. Click Save.

11. Close WordPad.

If you go to the Documents folder in File Explorer, you now see the file you just created.

Create a Shortcut to a File or Folder in File Explorer

You may want to create a shortcut to a file or folder and place it on the desktop for quick access or in some other location that you go to frequently. To create a short-cut, open File Explorer and follow these steps:

1. Locate the file for which you want to create a shortcut.

2. Right-click that file and, in the menu that appears, select one of these options (see Figure 5-16):

   - *Click Create Shortcut.*

     This creates a shortcut in the folder where the file is found. You can then move the shortcut to another folder.

   - *Click Send To; then click Desktop (Create Shortcut).*

     This creates a shortcut to the file on the desktop.

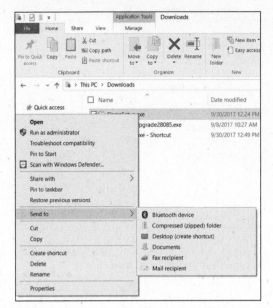

FIGURE 5-16:
The right-click
menu in File
Explorer.

TIP

Shortcuts are references to the files and folders that they point to. When you delete a shortcut, the item it points to remains on your computer. On the other hand, if you delete or move the file or folder it points to, the shortcut doesn't work.

Select Multiple Files or Folders in File Explorer

When you're working with files and folders in File Explorer, sometimes you may want to select more than one item. For example, you may want to select a group of files and delete them or select multiple folders and move them to another folder.

Here's the quickest way to select items in File Explorer (also see Figure 5-17):

1. **Click the first file or folder that you want to select.**

2. **Press and hold the Ctrl key on your keyboard.**

3. **With the Ctrl key still pressed, click each file and folder that you want to select.**

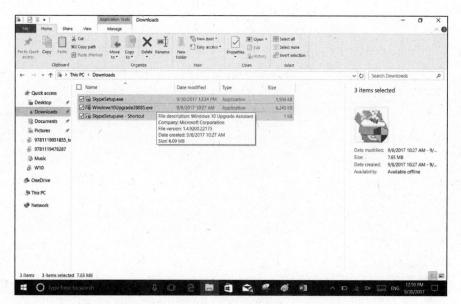

FIGURE 5-17:
Selecting files and
folders in File
Explorer.

4. **Release the Ctrl key after you select the items.**

Each of the selected items is highlighted with a blue bar in File Explorer. Now you can apply commands like Cut, Copy, or Delete to all selected items.

Another way to select files or folders in File Explorer is to use the Ribbon. Click the Home tab for access to the Selection section, as shown in Figure 5-18.

Several options in the Selection section of the Home tab let you select and deselect groups of files:

>> **Invert Selection:** Selects the currently unselected files and folders, and deselects the currently selected files and folders.

Every time you click Invert Selection, the selected and deselected files and folders switch.

>> **Select All**: Selects every file and folder.

>> **Select None**: Deselects every file and folder.

TIP

The keyboard shortcut for the Select All command is Ctrl+A.

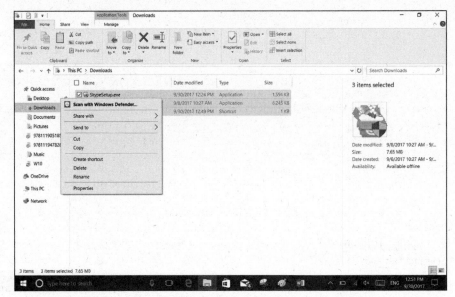

Delete a File or Folder in File Explorer

When you no longer need to use a file or folder, you can remove it from your computer to free up storage space. To do so, open File Explorer and follow these steps:

1. Locate the file or folder that you want to delete.

2. Select that file or folder by clicking on it.

3. Click the Home tab on the Ribbon.

The Home tab is displayed.

4. In the Organize section, click the Delete button (see Figure 5-19).

The selected item is moved to the Recycle Bin.

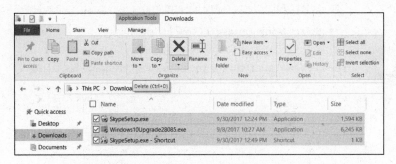

TIP

You can use two keyboard shortcuts for the Delete command: Delete and Ctrl+D. Also, you can use Shift+Delete on your keyboard and delete files and folders without moving them to the Recycle Bin. When you do that, you can't restore them, because they are no longer stored in the Recycle Bin.

Restore Deleted Files and Folders

The files and folders that you delete without using the Shift+Delete keyboard shortcut are moved to the Recycle Bin. This is a folder that temporarily stores references to the items that you delete from your Windows 10 computer or device. The items in the Recycle Bin aren't fully deleted, even though they no longer show up in their original location. The data from the files and folders that you delete remain on your computer's hard drive until the Recycle Bin is emptied and other files write data on top of them in the same location on your hard disk.

Here's how to recover deleted files and folders from the Recycle Bin:

1. **Go to the desktop.**

2. **Double-click the Recycle Bin shortcut.**

   You now see a list of deleted files and folders that you can recover.

3. **Select the item that you want to restore by clicking on it.**

4. **Click the Manage tab on the Ribbon (see Figure 5-20).**

   The Manage tab is displayed.

5. **In the Restore section, click the Restore the Selected Items button.**

6. **Close the Recycle Bin window.**

7. **Go to the original location of the selected item.**

   The item now appears there.

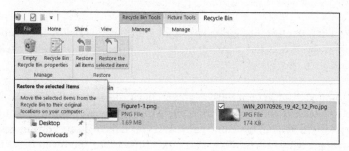

FIGURE 5-20:
Restoring items in the Recycle Bin.

WARNING

Items that are deleted using Shift+Delete aren't displayed in the Recycle Bin and can't be recovered using the preceding method. You have to use specialized third-party data recovery desktop apps (such as Recuva) to restore the items.

View the Properties of a File or Folder

When you use the default configuration of File Explorer, a lot of information about the properties of each file and folder is hidden from view. For example, the file extension is hidden by default, and you can't view when the file or folder was created or last accessed. If you want a complete overview of the properties of any file or folder, open File Explorer and follow these steps:

1. **Select the file or folder whose properties you want to see.**

2. **Click the Home tab on the Ribbon.**

   The Home tab is displayed.

3. **In the Open section, click the Properties button (see Figure 5-21).**

   The Properties window for the selected item appears. The available tabs (such as General Details) show information about that item.

4. **Close the Properties window when you're done.**

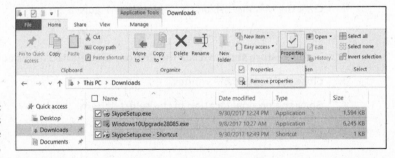

FIGURE 5-21:
The Properties button in File Explorer.

TIP

You can use the Alt+Enter keyboard shortcut instead of the Properties button to open the Properties window for an item. You can also right-click a file or folder and click Properties.

TIP

If you see a file icon with a green check mark on it in your OneDrive folder or elsewhere, that file more than likely has a copy stored in the cloud. Any edits you make will sync to the cloud copy, and you'll have a safe copy in case anything goes wrong with your computer. We talk a little more about OneDrive in Chapter 22.

Archive Files and Folders in a ZIP File

An *archive* is a file containing one or more files along with their data. You use archives to collect multiple files into a single file for easier portability and storage, or simply to compress files to use less storage space. Archives are also useful when you want to send multiple files to someone by email. Rather than attach several large files, archive them into one file. That file takes less space than sending all the files separately, and it's easier to attach and send by email.

The most popular format for archiving files is `.zip`, and Windows 10 can automatically work with this type of archive without having to install third-party apps. To archive several files and folders into a `.zip` file, open File Explorer and follow these steps:

1. **Select the files and folders that you want to archive.**

2. **Click the Share tab on the Ribbon.**

   The Share tab is displayed.

3. **In the Send section, click the Zip button (see Figure 5-22).**

   An archive is automatically created in the same folder as the files and folders that you selected. You can edit the name of the archive.

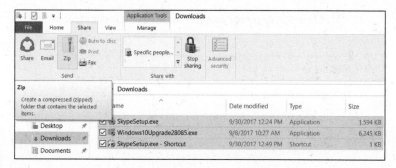

FIGURE 5-22: The Zip button in File Explorer.

4. **Type the name that you want for the archive file.**

5. **Press Enter or click somewhere else in the File Explorer window.**

   You can now use the newly created `.zip` archive and send it by email or store it where you want on your computer.

TIP

If you want to save space on your hard disk, it's a good idea to delete the files and folders that you placed in an archive, because you can always extract them from the archive, using the steps described in the next section of this chapter.

View and Extract the Contents of a ZIP File

When you receive an archive in the `.zip` format, you can view its contents and extract it in File Explorer. Here's how:

1. Open File Explorer.

2. Go to the location of the archive file.

3. Double-click the file to view its contents.

4. Click the Extract tab on the Ribbon.

The Extract tab is displayed.

5. Click the Extract All button (see Figure 5-23).

A wizard appears, asking you to select where to extract the files.

6. Click Browse.

7. Select where you want to extract the files.

8. Click Select Folder.

9. Click Extract.

The files are extracted. File Explorer opens the folder that you specified, where you can view all the files and folders that were in the archive.

10. Close File Explorer and the archive you just extracted.

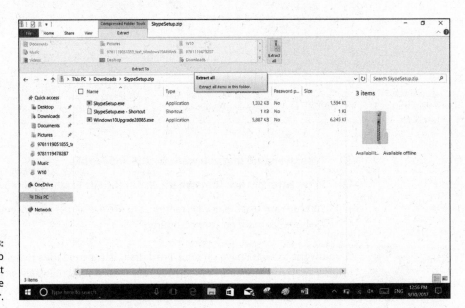

FIGURE 5-23: The Extract tab and the Extract All button in File Explorer.

The Extract tab on the File Explorer Ribbon also gives you options for extracting individual files to standard user folders like Documents, Pictures, and Downloads.

Find Files in File Explorer

The name of the search bar, which is located in the top-right corner of the File Explorer window, always starts with *Search*, followed by your current location in File Explorer. This search bar functions differently from the search bar found on the taskbar. First, you can use File Explorer's search bar only to search for files and folders. Also, the search is performed only in your current location. For example, if you're in Quick Access and you type the name of a file, Windows 10 searches for it only in the locations found in Quick Access. Similarly, if you go to the Pictures folder and you type the name of a file, Windows 10 searches for it only in the Pictures folder.

Here's an example of a search:

1. **Click the This PC shortcut in File Explorer.**

2. **Double-click the C drive, usually named Local Disk (C).**

3. **In the search bar at the top-right corner of the File Explorer window, type** notepad.

4. **Press Enter.**

   A progress bar appears at the top of the File Explorer window until the search finishes. The results returned are all from the C drive of your computer (see Figure 5-24).

5. **Click the** Documents **folder in the Quick Access section.**

6. **In the search bar, type a different filename, one that's found in your documents.**

7. **Press Enter.**

   The results returned are from the Documents folder, not from other locations on your computer. Also, because you're searching in a location that's indexed by Windows 10, you receive the results much faster than you did in the previous search.

8. **Close File Explorer.**

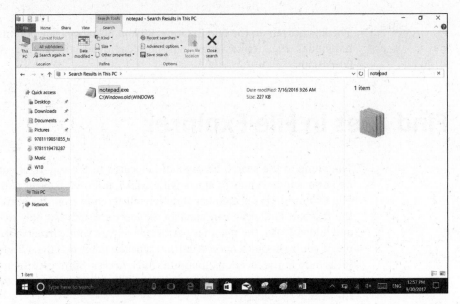

FIGURE 5-24:
Search results
returned by File
Explorer.

View or Hide Filename Extensions

By default, File Explorer hides the extensions of each file that it displays, which makes it hard to figure out the type of each file. We prefer to see the extensions of each file so that we're not easily fooled by viruses and malware disguising themselves as something else. To view or hide filename extensions, open File Explorer and follow these steps:

1. **Go to a folder with lots of files, such as** Documents.

2. **Click the View tab on the Ribbon.**

   The View tab is displayed.

3. **In the Show/Hide section, select File Name Extensions (see Figure 5-25).**

   You can now see the file extension for each file.

TIP

To hide file extensions, click the View tab and uncheck File Name Extensions.

FIGURE 5-25:
Reveal filename
extensions in File
Explorer.

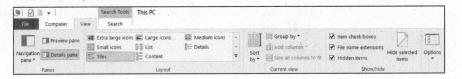

View or Hide Hidden Files or Folders

The Windows 10 operating system, as well as some apps, install folders and files that are hidden from File Explorer. They exist and can be used, but they aren't shown to you. Also, you can mark some files as hidden so that others can't see them. Luckily, File Explorer enables you to set whether to view or hide hidden items. Just follow these steps:

1. **In File Explorer, click This PC.**

2. **Double-click the C drive, usually named Local Disk (C).**

A list of folders appears.

3. **Click the View tab on the Ribbon.**

The View tab is displayed.

4. **In the Show/Hide section, select Hidden Items (refer to Figure 5-25).**

More folders appear on the C drive. You should now see a new folder named ProgramData, which wasn't shown earlier. The number of hidden folders that you see depends on your device.

TIP

To conceal the hidden items, click the View tab and uncheck Hidden Items.

Chapter **6**

Customizing File Explorer

When using Windows 10, you can customize in detail how File Explorer works, just like other Windows features. You may want to customize File Explorer in order to improve the way it works and be more productive when using it day by day. For example, you can add your own folders to Quick Access, enable libraries and make them easily accessible, or use check boxes to select files and folders.

This chapter is filled with many useful steps, such as how to change File Explorer's start location, how to enable or disable the different navigational elements, how to use the different Views that are available for an enhanced view of what's inside your folders, and how to use grouping and filtering options.

Change the File Explorer Start Location

When you start File Explorer, by default, it opens Quick Access. You can change the start location to This PC by opening File Explorer and following these steps:

1. **Click the File tab on the Ribbon.**

The File menu appears.

2. **Click Options.**

The Folder Options window appears.

3. **In the General tab, click the Open File Explorer To drop-down list.**

A list with two options is shown: Quick Access and This PC.

4. **Select This PC (see Figure 6-1).**

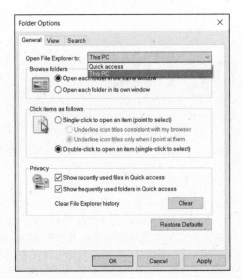

FIGURE 6-1:
The Folder
Options window.

5. **Click OK.**

6. **Close File Explorer.**

The next time you open File Explorer, it displays This PC rather than Quick Access.

Pin Folders to Quick Access

As we mention in the previous section, when you start File Explorer, it displays Quick Access, where you see a list of the folders you browse most frequently and the files that you recently accessed. This list changes over time as you use different folders. You can always pin to Quick Access the folders and libraries that you want to access as quickly as possible. Here's how to do so:

1. **Open File Explorer.**

2. **Navigate to the folder that you want to pin to Quick Access.**

3. **Select that folder by clicking on it.**

4. **Right-click the folder.**

5. **Select Pin to Quick Access from the, menu that appears (see Figure 6-2).**

   The selected folder is now listed in Quick Access.

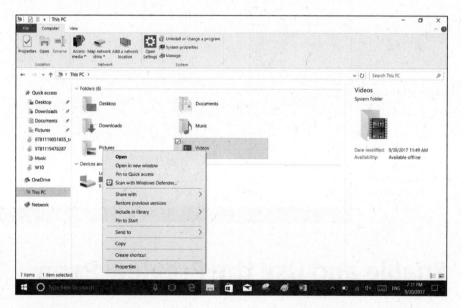

FIGURE 6-2:
The Pin to Quick
Access button in
File Explorer.

TIP

You can also pin a folder by right-clicking it and selecting Pin to Quick Access in the right-click menu.

Unpin Folders from Quick Access

To unpin a folder from the Quick Access section, open File Explorer and follow these steps:

1. **Click the Quick Access section.**

2. **Right-click the folder that you want to unpin.**

   The right-click menu appears.

3. **In the right-click menu, click Unpin from Quick Access (see Figure 6-3).**

   The selected folder is no longer listed in Quick Access.

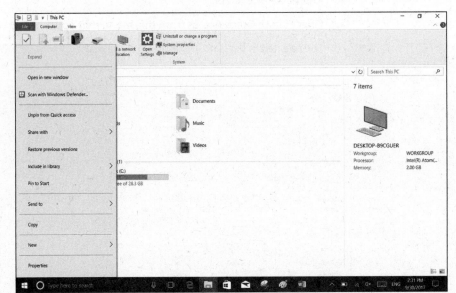

FIGURE 6-3: The Unpin from Quick Access option in the pop-up menu.

Enable and Use the Preview Pane

In File Explorer, you can enable a Preview pane that is shown on the right side of the window. As its name implies, you can use it to preview the contents of certain types of files. For example, if you select an image file in File Explorer, you can see a preview of it; if you select a text file, you can preview its contents. Figure 6-4 shows the Preview pane in File Explorer.

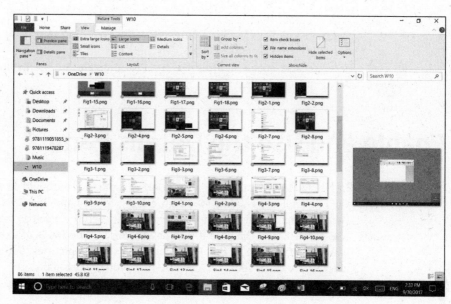

FIGURE 6-4:
The Preview pane
in File Explorer.

**TECHNICAL
STUFF**

You can see previews of only certain file types: text, images, and videos.

To enable the Preview pane, open File Explorer and follow these steps:

1. **In the File Explorer window, click the View tab.**

The View tab is shown.

2. **In the Panes section, click the Preview Pane button (see Figure 6-5).**

The Preview pane is added to the right side of the File Explorer window.

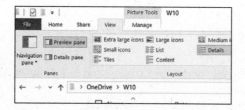

FIGURE 6-5:
Enabling the
Preview pane in
File Explorer.

3. **Select several files one by one.**

You can preview their contents in the Preview pane, if they are text, images,
or videos.

To disable the Preview pane, just follow the preceding steps.

You can also enable and disable the Preview pane in File Explorer by pressing Alt+P on your keyboard.

TIP

Enable and Use the Details Pane

In File Explorer, you can enable a Details pane that is shown on the right side of the File Explorer window (see Figure 6-6). As its name implies, you can use the Details pane to find more information about each file, such as its size, the date it was created, and the date it was last modified. The fields of data shown in this pane vary from file to file. For some files, such as pictures, you see lots of data; whereas for other files, such as PDF files, you see less data.

FIGURE 6-6:
The Details pane in File Explorer.

To enable the Details pane, open File Explorer and follow these steps:

1. **In the File Explorer window, click the View tab.**

   The View tab is shown.

2. **In the Panes section, click the Details Pane button (see Figure 6-7).**

   The Details pane is added to the right side of the File Explorer window.

3. **To see a file's details, click it to select it.**

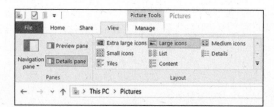

FIGURE 6-7:
Enabling the
Details pane in
File Explorer.

To disable the Details pane, just follow the preceding steps.

TIP

You can also enable and disable the Details pane in File Explorer by pressing Alt+Shift+P on your keyboard.

Disable or Enable the Navigation Pane

In File Explorer, the Navigation pane is shown, by default, on the left side of the window. As its name implies, you can use it to quickly jump to different locations on your computer.

When the Navigation pane is disabled and you start File Explorer, either Quick Access or This PC is loaded, depending on the start location for File Explorer.

WARNING

We don't recommend disabling the Navigation pane, because doing so makes navigation more difficult.

If you decide to disable the Navigation pane, follow these steps:

1. **Open File Explorer.**

2. **Click the View tab.**

   The View tab is shown.

3. **In the Panes section, click the Navigation Pane button.**

   The Navigation Pane menu appears.

4. **In the menu, click Navigation Pane (see Figure 6-8).**

   The Navigation pane no longer appears at the left side of the File Explorer window.

TIP

To enable the Navigation pane, follow the preceding steps.

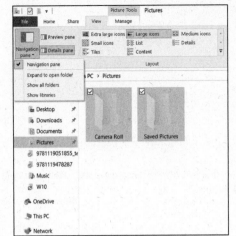

FIGURE 6-8:
Disabling the
Navigation pane
in File Explorer.

Enable the Libraries Section in the Navigation Pane

By default, the Navigation pane doesn't show the Libraries in Windows 10, as it did in Windows 7. Fortunately, the libraries aren't gone; they're just hidden. To enable and use the libraries in Windows 10, open File Explorer and follow these steps:

1. **In the File Explorer window, click the View tab.**

The View tab is shown.

2. **In the Panes section, click the Navigation Pane button.**

The Navigation Pane menu appears.

3. **In the menu, click Show Libraries (see Figure 6-9).**

The Libraries are now added to File Explorer.

4. **Click the Libraries shortcut in the Navigation pane to view your libraries.**

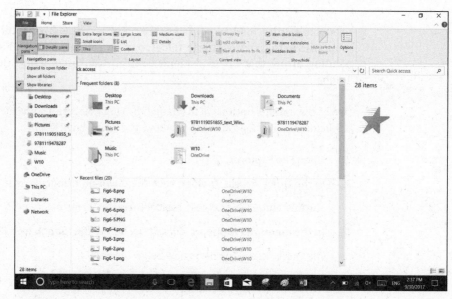

FIGURE 6-9:
Enabling the
Libraries section
in File Explorer.

Change the Position of the Quick Access Toolbar

The Quick Access Toolbar is located at the top-left corner of the File Explorer window. You can see it highlighted in Figure 6-10.

FIGURE 6-10:
The Quick Access
Toolbar.

By default, this toolbar contains only three buttons: one for accessing the properties of the selected file or folder, one for creating a new folder, and a down-pointing arrow that opens a menu you can use to configure the Quick Access Toolbar.

One of the menu's options is to change the Quick Access Toolbar's position so that it's below the Ribbon rather than above it. Here's how:

1. **Open File Explorer.**

2. **In the Quick Access Toolbar, click the down-pointing arrow.**

The Customize Quick Access Toolbar menu appears.

3. **In the menu that appears, click Show Below the Ribbon (see Figure 6-11).**

The Quick Access Toolbar is now below the Ribbon.

FIGURE 6-11:
The menu for the Quick Access Toolbar.

TIP

To place the Quick Access Toolbar back at the top of the Ribbon, follow the preceding steps and, at Step 3, click Show Above the Ribbon.

Add Buttons to the Quick Access Toolbar

You can make the Quick Access Toolbar more useful by adding more buttons to it; for example, the Undo, Redo, Delete, and Rename buttons. In File Explorer, follow these steps for each new button that you want to add:

1. **In the Quick Access Toolbar, click the down-pointing arrow.**

   The Customize Quick Access Toolbar menu appears.

2. **In the menu that appears, click the function you want to add to the Quick Access Toolbar (such as Undo, Redo, or Delete; refer to Figure 6-11).**

Use Views to Better Examine Your Folders' Contents

When you first browse a folder, File Explorer automatically applies a view that's optimized for the contents of that folder. However, the Ribbon has a multitude of view options in the Layout section of the View tab (as shown in Figure 6-12):

» **Details:** For each file and folder, the Details view shows several columns with information, such as Name, Date Modified, Type, and Size.

   Each file has its own small icon that represents the file type.

» **Content:** Each file and folder appears on a separate row, where you see detailed information about it, such as the date the file was last modified, its size, its author, and its length (for audio and video files).

   For picture and video files, you see a small preview of the content rather than a file icon.

» **List:** Displays a simple list of folders and files, each with an identifying icon.

» **Tiles:** Displays a medium-size icon representing each file and folder, along with information about their types and sizes.

» **Extra Large Icons:** Displays extra-large icons that are representative of the contents of each file.

   For pictures and video, you see a preview of each file.

» **Large Icons:** Displays large icons that are representative of the contents of each file.

   For pictures and video you see a preview of each file.

FIGURE 6-12:
The Layout section of the View tab on the File Explorer ribbon.

>> **Medium Icons:** Displays medium icons that are representative of the contents of each file.

For pictures and video you see a preview of each file.

>> **Small Icons:** Displays small icons that are representative of the contents of each file.

You can easily switch between these views by clicking on them.

TIP

File Explorer remembers the last view that you used for a folder and applies it the next time you open it.

Sort Files and Folders

File Explorer offers the Sort tool for sorting the files and folders that you're viewing based on criteria such as their name, type, size, authors, and more. To sort the files within a folder, open File Explorer and follow these steps:

1. **Navigate to the folder that you want to sort.**

2. **Click the View tab on the Ribbon.**

    The View tab is shown.

3. **In the Current View section, click the Sort By button (see Figure 6-13).**

    The Sort By menu appears.

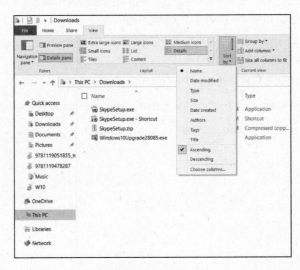

FIGURE 6-13:
The Sort By menu in File Explorer.

4. **Click the sorting criteria that you want to use to apply it.**

The files and folders for your current location are now sorted using the criteria you selected.

Group Files and Folders

With File Explorer, you can group the files and folders that you're viewing based on criteria such as their name, type, size, authors, and more. To group the files within a folder, open File Explorer and follow these steps:

1. **Navigate to the folder whose contents you want to group.**

2. **Click the View tab on the Ribbon.**

The View tab is shown.

3. **In the Current View section, click the Group By button (see Figure 6-14).**

The Group By menu appears.

4. **Click the grouping criteria that you want to use to apply it.**

The files and folders for your current location are now grouped using the criteria you selected.

FIGURE 6-14:
The Group By button and menu in File Explorer.

Customize File Explorer with Folder Options

You can reconfigure certain ways that File Explorer works. All the configuration settings are in a window named Folder Options. This window has three tabs filled with settings. Here's how to access the Folder Options window, browse its settings, change them, and apply your desired configuration:

1. Open File Explorer.

2. Click File.

The File menu appears.

3. Click Change Folder and Search Options.

The Folder Options window appears at the General tab. Here are settings for browsing folders in File Explorer, opening an item in File Explorer, and whether to show recently used files and folders in Quick Access.

4. In the General tab, change the settings that you're interested in.

5. Click the View tab (see Figure 6-15).

Here you find settings for viewing files and folders in File Explorer.

TIP

The list of settings is long. Browse through the list and read what they do. Each name is self-explanatory.

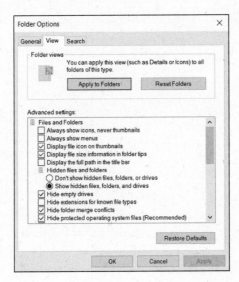

FIGURE 6-15:
The View tab in
Folder Options.

6. **Change any advanced settings that you want.**

7. **Click the Search tab (see Figure 6-16).**

   Here you find settings for using search in Windows 10 and in File Explorer.

8. **Change how search works.**

9. **To apply your settings, click OK.**

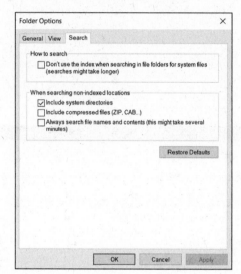

FIGURE 6-16:
The Search tab in
Folder Options.

Use Check Boxes to Select Files and Folders

You can set File Explorer to display check boxes near the name of each file and folder. You can then use these check boxes to select files and folders. These check boxes look similar to those in Figure 6-17.

To enable check boxes in File Explorer, follow these steps:

1. **Open File Explorer.**

2. **Click the View tab on the Ribbon.**

   The View tab is shown.

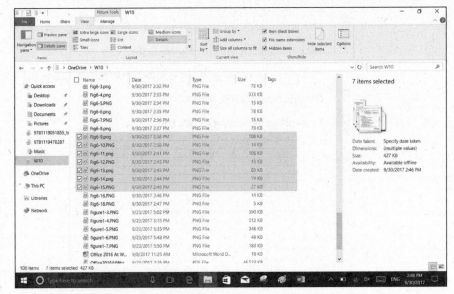

FIGURE 6-17:
Using check
boxes to select
items in File
Explorer.

3. **In the Show/Hide section, click Item Check Boxes (see Figure 6-18).**

   Check boxes are now shown every time you move the cursor on top of a file or folder. Click the check box to select that item.

4. **Close File Explorer.**

FIGURE 6-18:
How to enable
Item Check Boxes
in File Explorer.

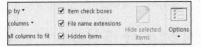

To disable the check boxes, follow the preceding steps.

TIP

Clear File Explorer's History of Recently Used Files and Folders

By default, File Explorer remembers all the files and folders that you've accessed and displays them in different places, like in Quick Access. If you want to clear your history of accessed files and folders, open File Explorer and follow these steps:

1. **Click File.**

   The File menu appears.

2. **Click Change Folder and Search Options.**

   The Folder Options window appears.

3. **In the General tab, look for the Privacy section.**

4. **Click the Clear button (see Figure 6-19).**

5. **Click OK.**

6. **Close File Explorer.**

FIGURE 6-19: The Clear button in the Folder Options window.

2

Make Yourself at Home in Windows 10

» **Changing the Windows theme**

» **Changing the resolution and the mouse pointer**

» **Customizing the Start Menu and the Lock Screen**

» **Customizing the taskbar**

» **Changing the sound volume**

» **Setting the date, time, time zone, and country**

» **Adding a new keyboard input language**

» **Downloading a language pack**

» **Tuning which settings get synchronized**

Chapter 7

Customizing Windows 10

This chapter focuses on customizing how Windows 10 looks and works, especially on how to customize the appearance of the operating system. We show you how to customize the desktop background, the colors Windows 10 uses, the theme, the icons that are displayed, the screen resolution, and the mouse pointer size and color. You also find out how to customize the Lock Screen, what it looks like, and the information it displays. You discover how to customize the taskbar and how to change the sound volume.

This chapter also covers how to change the date and time, the time zone, and the country on Windows 10, which should be especially interesting to those of you who travel to other countries or work with different languages. You also find out how to add a new keyboard input language and how to download a language pack in Windows 10.

Finally, we show you how to set which Windows 10 settings are synchronized across your devices, which is handy if you use a Microsoft account on your work computers.

Change the Desktop Background

Windows 10 allows you to change the desktop background to another picture that's bundled with the operating system or with a picture of your own. To change the desktop background, follow these steps:

1. **Open Settings.**

2. **Click Personalization.**

   All available personalization settings are shown.

3. **In the Background section, choose a picture from those included in Windows 10 by clicking on it (see Figure 7-1).**

4. **Click the down-pointing arrow in the Choose a Fit drop-down list.**

   A list is shown with such choices as Fill, Fit, Stretch, Tile, Center, and Span.

5. **From the drop-down list, choose how you want the picture to fit your desktop.**

6. **Close the Settings window.**

TIP

If you want to use your own picture, at Step 3 click Browse, navigate to the picture that you want to use, and click Choose Picture; continue with Steps 4, 5, and 6.

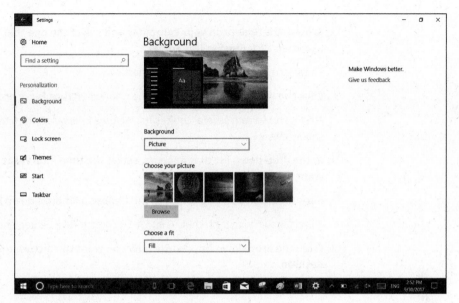

FIGURE 7-1:
How to change
the background
picture in
Windows 10.

Set a Slideshow of Pictures as the Desktop Background

You can use your Pictures folder (or any other folder with pictures) to create a "slideshow" background on your desktop. When you do that, at regular intervals, Windows 10 automatically shows a rotating series of the pictures in your Pictures folder.

To create a slide show with your own pictures as the desktop background, follow these steps:

1. **Open Settings.**

2. **Click Personalization.**

   All available personalization settings are shown.

3. **Click the down-pointing arrow in the Background drop-down list.**

   A list is shown with such choices as Picture, Solid color, and Slideshow.

4. **In the drop-down list that appears, select Slideshow.**

   By default, the Pictures folder is used as the source for the slideshow (as shown in Figure 7-2).

5. **To choose another folder, click Browse.**

   The Select Folder window appears.

6. Browse the folders on your computer and select the one that you want to use; then click Choose This Folder.

The selected folder is used for the slideshow.

7. Click the down-pointing arrow in the Change Picture Every drop-down list.

A list is shown with several choices for the time interval at which the pictures should change.

8. In the drop-down list that appears, select the time interval at which you want the pictures to change.

9. Click the down-pointing arrow in the Choose a Fit drop-down list.

A list is shown with such choices as Fill, Fit, Stretch, Tile, Center, and Span.

10. From the drop-down list, choose how you want the picture to fit your desktop.

11. Close the Settings window.

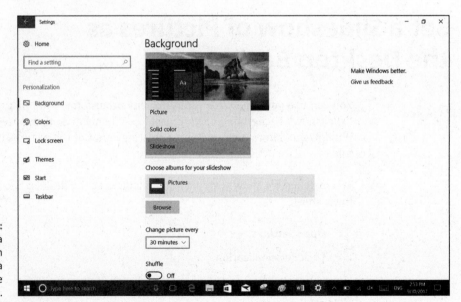

FIGURE 7-2:
How to set a
folder with
pictures as a
slideshow on the
desktop.

Set the Colors Used by Windows 10

Windows 10 allows you to change the main color that's used throughout the operating system. By default, this color is chosen from the desktop background. Windows 10 simply picks the desktop's accent color and uses it automatically.

You can override this setting and choose your own accent color. Black is the default color for the Start Menu, the taskbar, and the Action Center. You can change this setting and have these elements use the accent color that you set. You can also make the Start Menu, the taskbar, and the Action Center transparent so that you can see through them.

Here's how to change the color-related settings in Windows 10:

1. **Open Settings.**

2. **Click Personalization.**

   All available personalization settings are shown.

3. **Click Colors.**

   The color-related settings are shown.

4. **To pick a custom accent color, set the switch Automatically Pick an Accent Color from My Background to Off; then choose an accent color from the list of options (see Figure 7-3).**

5. **Set the Show Color on Start, Taskbar, and Action Center switch to On or Off, depending on what you want.**

6. **Set the Make Start, Taskbar, and Action Center Transparent switch to On or Off, depending on what you want.**

7. **Close the Settings window.**

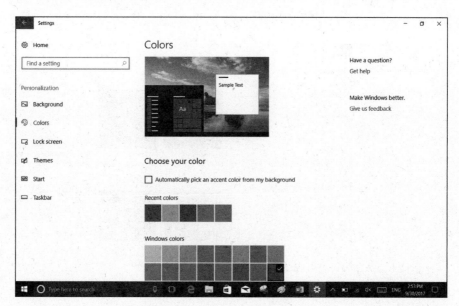

FIGURE 7-3:
How to set the colors used by Windows 10.

Change the Windows Theme

A Windows *theme* includes the wallpaper used on the desktop as well as settings such as the standard desktop icons (for example, Computer, Network, and Recycle Bin), the visual styles applied to Windows and apps, the mouse cursors, the screen–saver that runs when the computer isn't in use, and the sound scheme applied to the operating system. If you get bored with any of the items that are included in the theme, you can change the theme and freshen things up a bit.

To change the Windows theme, follow these steps:

1. **Open Settings.**

2. **Click Personalization.**

   All available personalization settings are shown.

3. **Click Themes.**

   The themes-related settings are shown.

4. **Click Theme Settings.**

   The Personalization window opens.

5. **In the Personalization window, click the new theme that you want to apply (see Figure 7-4).**

6. **Close the Personalization window.**

7. **Close Settings.**

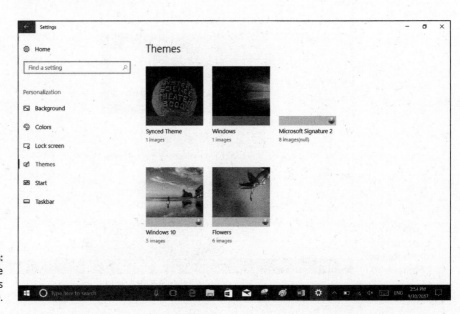

FIGURE 7-4:
How to change the Windows theme.

TIP

If you want access to more diverse Windows themes, try the gallery provided by Microsoft at `http://windows.microsoft.com/en-us/windows/themes`.

Change the Icons Displayed on the Desktop

You can change the icons shown on the desktop. For example, you can enable or disable any of the following icons: Computer, Control Panel, Network, Recycle Bin, and Users' Files. You can also create your own shortcuts on the desktop, just like in previous versions of Windows.

To enable or disable a standard icon on the desktop, follow these steps:

1. **Open Settings.**

2. **Click Personalization.**

   All available personalization settings are shown.

3. **Click Themes.**

   The themes-related settings are shown.

4. **Click Desktop Icon Settings.**

   A window by the same name opens (see Figure 7-5).

5. **Check the desktop icons that you want to enable.**

FIGURE 7-5:
How to change the icons displayed on the desktop.

6. Deselect the desktop icons that you want to disable.

7. Click OK.

8. Close Settings.

Change the Resolution of the Screen

Since the beginning of computers, *resolution* has been described by the number of pixels arranged horizontally and vertically on a monitor — for example 640 x 480 = 307,200 pixels. The choices were determined by the capability of the video card, and they differed from manufacturer to manufacturer. The resolutions built into Windows were quite limited, so if you didn't have the driver for your video card, you were stuck with the lower-resolution screen that Windows provided. As monitor quality improved, Windows began offering a few more built-in options, but the burden was still mostly on the graphics card manufacturers, especially if you wanted a high-resolution display.

The more recent versions of Windows, such as Windows 10, can detect the default screen resolution for your monitor and graphics card and adjust accordingly. This doesn't mean that what Windows chooses is always the best option, but now it works better than it did. As you expect, you can change the resolution manually. When you do that, you get a preview of what it looks like; you can decide whether you want to keep the new screen resolution.

Here's how to change the resolution of your screen in Windows 10:

1. Open Settings.

2. Click System.

   The list of available system settings appears.

3. Click Display.

4. Click the down-pointing arrow in the Resolution drop-down list.

   A list appears with multiple resolutions you can choose from. Your options vary according to your display's size and specifications.

5. In the list of available options, select the resolution that you want to use by clicking on it (see Figure 7-6).

6. Click Apply.

   The new resolution is applied. You're asked whether you want to keep these displayed settings.

7. Click Keep Changes.

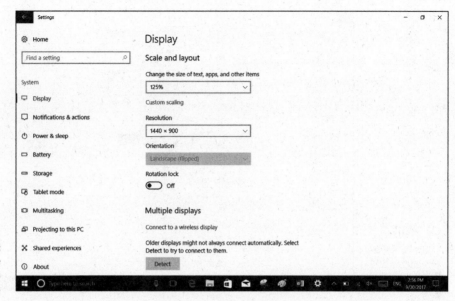

FIGURE 7-6:
How to change
the resolution in
Windows 10.

Change the Mouse Pointer Size and Color

If you want to, you can make the mouse pointer bigger and also change its color
from white to black. Here's how:

1. **Open Settings.**

2. **Click Ease of Access.**

   The list of available ease-of-access settings appears.

3. **Click Mouse.**

   The available mouse-related settings appear (see Figure 7-7).

4. **In the Pointer Size section, click the size that you want to use.**

5. **In the Pointer Color section, click the color that you want to use.**

6. **Close Settings.**

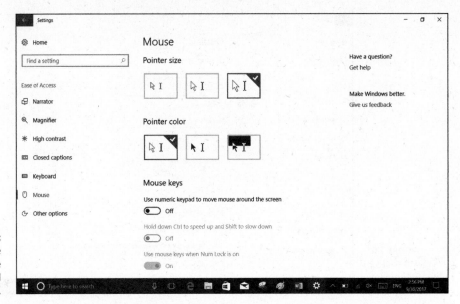

FIGURE 7-7:
How to change
the mouse
pointer size and
color.

Customize the Behavior of the Start Menu

The Start Menu is more customizable in Windows 10 than it was in Windows 7 and Windows XP. In Settings, there's a big section of settings that allow you to decide whether to

>> Show your most used apps.

>> Show your recently added apps.

>> Use the full-screen Start Menu.

>> Show recently opened items in Jump Lists on Start or on the taskbar.

Figure 7-8 shows the entire list of settings, which is mostly a list of simple switches that you can turn on or off. There's also a link that opens a new window where you can choose which folders appear on the Start Menu.

To access the settings that allow you to customize how the Start Menu works, follow these steps:

1. **Open Settings.**

2. **Click Personalization.**

   All the available personalization settings are shown.

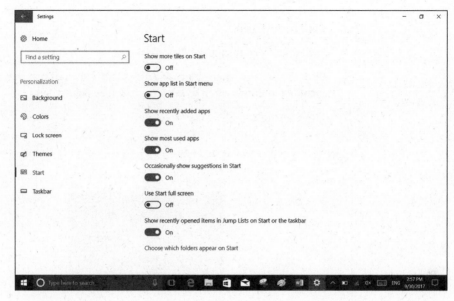

FIGURE 7-8:
The Start Menu
customization
options.

3. **Click Start.**

   The previous Start Menu customization options are shown.

4. **Set the Start Menu as you want it to behave, using the available switches.**

5. **When done, close Settings.**

If you want to set which folders appear on the Start Menu, start the preceding steps. At Step 4, click Choose Which Folders Appear On Start, and then set the folders that you want to appear to On and those that you don't want to appear to Off.

TIP

Change the Picture Shown on the Lock Screen

If you're bored with the picture used for the Lock Screen in Windows 10, you can change it. Follow these steps:

1. **Open Settings.**

2. **Click Personalization.**

   All available personalization settings are shown.

3. **Click Lock screen.**

   The Lock Screen-related settings are shown.

4. **Click the picture, then select another picture from those that are included in Windows 10 by clicking on it (see Figure 7-9).**

5. **Close Settings.**

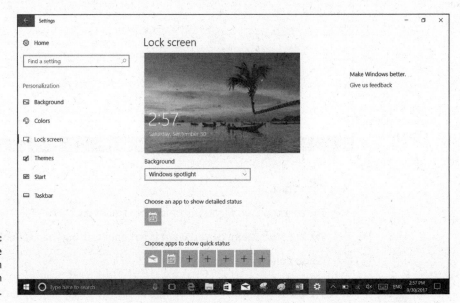

FIGURE 7-9:
How to change
the Lock Screen
picture in
Windows 10.

TIP

If you want to use your own picture, at Step 4 click Browse, navigate to the picture that you want to use, click on the picture, and then Choose Picture.

Change the Apps That Show Their Status on the Lock Screen

You can set one app that shows its detailed status on the Lock Screen and seven other apps that show a quick status. To change which apps show their status on the Lock Screen, follow these steps:

1. **Open Settings.**

2. **Click Personalization.**

   All available personalization settings are shown.

3. **Click Lock Screen.**

    The Lock Screen-related settings are shown.

4. **Click the App icon shown in the Choose an App to Show Detailed Status section.**

    A list of apps appears.

5. **Click to select a new app from the list (see Figure 7-10).**

6. **In the Choose Apps to Show Quick Status section, click the icon of an app that you want to change.**

    A list of apps appears.

7. **In the app list, click the replacement app.**

8. **Close the Settings window.**

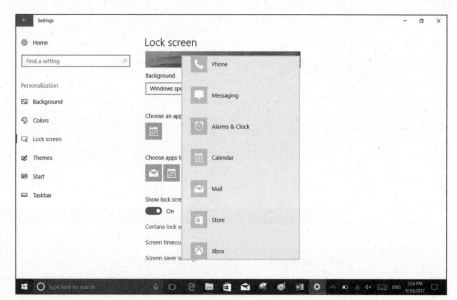

FIGURE 7-10: How to change the app showing the detailed status on the Lock Screen.

Customize the Taskbar

Just as in older versions of Windows, in Windows 10 you can customize the taskbar in the following ways:

» Lock the taskbar so that other users can't change it.

» Set the taskbar to auto-hide.

>> Set the taskbar to use small buttons.

>> Change the taskbar's location on the screen from the bottom to the top, or to the left or right of the screen.

>> Set how taskbar buttons appear: always combined with the labels hidden, combined only when the taskbar is full, or never combined.

>> Set whether to use the Peek feature to preview the desktop when you move your mouse to the Show Desktop button at the end of the taskbar.

Figure 7-11 shows all these settings.

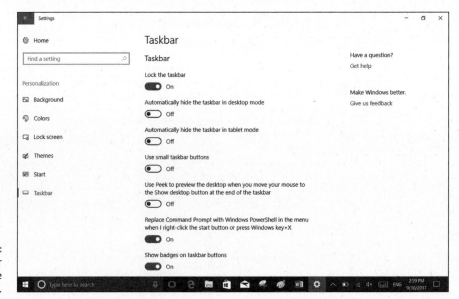

To customize the taskbar, follow these steps:

1. **Right-click the taskbar.**

   The right-click menu appears.

2. **Click Properties.**

3. **In the Taskbar tab, set how you want the taskbar to behave by selecting the available settings.**

4. **Click OK.**

Set Which Icons Appear on the Taskbar

You can customize the settings to show more or fewer icons on the right side of the taskbar. Here's how:

1. **Open Settings.**

2. **Click Personalization.**

3. **Click Taskbar.**

4. **Click Select Which Icons Appear in the notification area.**

   A long list of icons is shown. Each has a switch to turn it on or off.

5. **In the list of icons that appears, set the icons you want displayed to On and the icons you don't want displayed to Off (see Figure 7-12).**

   The icons that you set to On are immediately shown in the taskbar.

6. **Click the left-pointing arrow (the Back arrow) to go back.**

   The settings for notifications and quick actions are shown.

7. **Click Turn System Icons On or Off, in the Quick Actions section.**

   A list of system icons is shown.

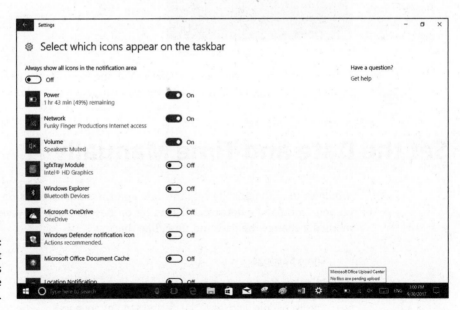

FIGURE 7-12: How to select which icons appear in the taskbar.

8. **In the list of icons that appears, set the icons you want displayed to On and the icons you don't want displayed to Off.**

   The icons that you set to On are shown in the taskbar immediately.

9. **Close the Settings window.**

Change the Sound Volume

If you want to change the volume of the speakers to be louder or softer, follow these steps:

1. **Click the Volume icon at the right side of the taskbar.**

   A volume slider appears above the taskbar.

2. **With the mouse, set the slider to the desired sound level (see Figure 7-13).**

3. **Click anywhere outside the slider to hide it.**

FIGURE 7-13:
How to change
the sound volume
in Windows 10.

If you want to mute the sound, click the Volume icon, shown near the slider. The sound level changes to 0. Alternatively, you can move the volume slider to 0.

TIP

Set the Date and Time Manually

Windows 10 automatically sets the date and time with servers on the Internet or on your company's network, depending on how it's set. However, you can also manually change the date and time, like this:

1. **Open Settings.**

2. **Click Time & Language.**

   The list of time- and language-related settings appears.

3. **In the Date & Time section, set the Set Time Automatically switch to Off and click Change.**

   The Change Date and Time window appears.

4. **Set the date and time you want to use; then click Change (see Figure 7-14).**

5. **Close the Settings window.**

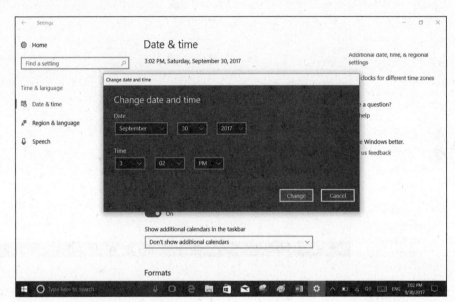

FIGURE 7-14:
How to change
the date and time
in Windows 10.

Set the Time Zone

If you travel a lot, you can change the time zone when you arrive in a new country or in an area with a different time zone than your usual one. To change the time zone, follow these steps:

1. **Open Settings.**

2. **Click Time & Language.**

   The list of time- and language-related settings appears.

3. **In the Date & Time section, click the down-pointing arrow in the Time Zone drop-down list (shown in Figure 7-15).**

   A list appears with all the time zones.

4. **Click the time zone that you want to use.**

The time zone is now changed.

5. **Close the Settings window.**

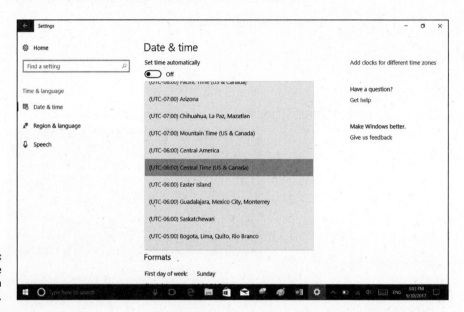

FIGURE 7-15:
How to set the
time zone in
Windows 10.

REMEMBER

When you get back home, change the time zone again so that Windows and its apps use and display the correct time.

Set the Country You're In

Some Windows apps might use your country or region to display local content that's personalized for you. For these apps to display the correct content, you need to set the country you're in. Follow these steps:

1. **Open Settings.**

2. **Click Time & Language.**

The list of time- and language-related settings appears.

3. **Click Region & Language.**

The settings for configuring the country, region, and languages are shown (see Figure 7-16).

4. **Find the Country or Region section and click the down-pointing arrow in the box labeled Window and Apps Might Use Your Country or Region to Give You Local Content.**

A list of all countries in the world appears.

5. **Click the country that you're in.**

6. **Close the Settings window.**

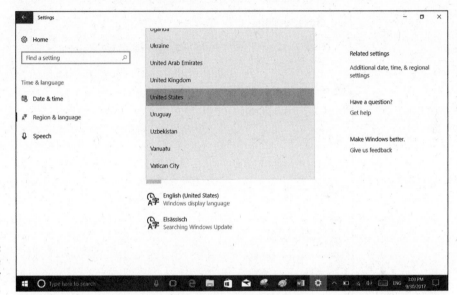

FIGURE 7-16:
How to change
the country
you're in.

Add a Keyboard Input Language

If you frequently work with multiple languages, you may want to add a keyboard input language or two. To add a keyboard input language, follow these steps:

1. **Open Settings.**

2. **Click Time & Language.**

The list of time- and language-related settings appears.

3. **Click Region & Language.**

The settings for configuring the country, region, and languages are shown.

4. **In the Languages section, click the plus-sign (+) button beside Add a Language.**

The Add A Language window appears, showing all available languages.

5. **Scroll the list of languages (shown in Figure 7-17) until you find the one that you're looking for.**

6. **Click the language that you want to add.**

   A list with multiple dialects of that language appears.

7. **Click the dialect that you want to add.**

   You're informed that a new feature is added to Windows. The language is downloaded in the background; you can resume using Windows.

8. **Close Settings.**

   Now you can use the added keyboard input language.

FIGURE 7-17: How to add a keyboard input language.

Download a Language Pack

Using Windows Update, you can install a language pack for languages other than your own. After you download a language pack and activate it, the Windows 10 operating system is translated into that language. Depending on the language, either the entire operating system is translated or only part of it. When no translation is available, Windows 10 uses English to display the elements that haven't been translated by Microsoft.

To install a language pack, you first need to install the keyboard input language using the procedure in the preceding section of this chapter. Once the keyboard input language is installed, you can use only the new language to type. To translate the entire operating system, follow these steps to install the language pack:

1. **Open Settings.**

2. **Click Time & Language.**

   The list of time- and language-related settings appears.

3. **Click Region & Language.**

   The settings for configuring the country, region, and languages are shown.

4. **Click the language for the language pack you want to install (see Figure 7-18).**

5. **Click Options.**

   A new window appears with several language options.

6. **Find the Download button in the Language Options section.**

7. **Click the Download button to begin the installation.**

   Be patient — the download takes a while.

   When the install is complete, you receive a message to that effect.

8. **Close the Settings window.**

FIGURE 7-18:
How to download a language pack in Windows 10.

TECHNICAL STUFF

At Step 4, the languages that have a language pack available to download and install are marked by a line of text that says *Language pack available*. If a language pack isn't mentioned as being available for a particular language, you can't download a language pack for it. You can use that language only as a keyboard input language, not as a display language.

Set Which Settings Are Synchronized

If you're using a Microsoft account, you can customize Windows 10 to automatically synchronize settings for you across all your Windows 10 devices. By default, Windows 10 synchronizes the following elements: the Windows theme, the web browser settings for Internet Explorer and Microsoft Edge, your passwords, your language preferences, and your ease-of-access settings, among others.

You can adjust settings to sync with your other Windows 10 devices. Follow these steps:

1. **Open Settings.**

2. **Click Accounts.**

The settings for configuring user accounts are shown (see Figure 7-19).

3. **Click Sync Settings.**

The available synchronization settings are shown.

4. **Set the Sync Settings switch to On.**

5. **Set the switches to On for the settings that you want to sync.**

6. **Set the other switches to Off.**

7. **Close the Settings window.**

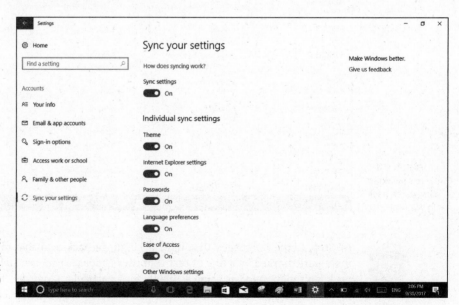

FIGURE 7-19: How to customize settings that Windows 10 synchronizes.

Chapter **8**

Capturing Pictures and Screenshots

In the course of your work, you likely need to use all kinds of images. For example, you may need to take a quick screenshot and add it to a presentation or document. Hey, you may even want to take the occasional selfie and send it to a friend or coworker.

Windows 10 offers you the tools you need for taking pictures and screenshots. This chapter covers them in detail. As you can see in the following instructions, these tools are user-friendly and fun to use.

Start the Camera App

If you have a webcam on your Windows 10 computer or device, you can use the Camera app to take pictures. But, before you do that, here's how to start the Camera app in Windows 10:

1. Click Start to open the Start Menu.

2. Click All Apps.

A list of all your apps appears.

3. Scroll down the list to apps that start with the letter *C*, and click the Camera app shortcut (see Figure 8-1).

4. If you're asked whether the Camera app can use your webcam and microphone, click Allow.

FIGURE 8-1:
The shortcut for
the Camera app.

Take a Picture

When you start the Camera app, it's already set to take pictures. To take a picture, just follow these steps:

1. Start the Camera app.

2. Arrange the camera so that you capture the subject you're interested in.

3. When you frame the subject the way you want, click the button that looks like a camera (see Figure 8-2).

4. If you want to take another picture, click that button again.

TIP

After you take your first picture, a Picture icon appears in the top-left corner of the Camera app window. You can use it to look at the pictures you take with the Camera app. Your pictures are stored as JPEG files in the `Camera Roll` folder, located in the `Pictures` library/folder.

FIGURE 8-2:
The button for
taking pictures in
the Camera app.

View Pictures

If you're using the Camera app and want to quickly view the pictures you've just taken, follow these steps:

1. **In All Apps, click the Photos app icon.**

    The Photos app window appears and shows the last picture taken.

2. **To navigate backward in the stored photos, move the mouse cursor to the left corner of the app window and click the Back arrow (see Figure 8-3).**

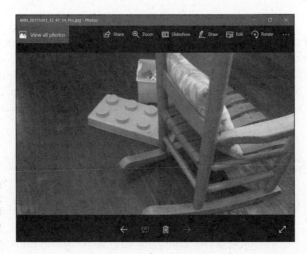

FIGURE 8-3:
The Back
and Forward
arrows in the
Photos app.

3. **Click the Back arrow until you've looked at all the pictures you're interested in.**

4. **To navigate forward, move the mouse to the right corner of the Photos app window and click the Forward arrow.**

Here are two other ways to view the pictures you take with the Camera app:

>> Using File Explorer, go to the Pictures library and find the Camera Roll folder, which, as we mention earlier, is where photos are automatically stored.

>> Open the Photos app and browse your collection of pictures, which includes those taken with the Camera app.

Capture Instant Screenshots

Capturing an entire screen in Windows 10 and saving it as a file is a one-step process. How you do it depends on whether your Windows 10 device has a keyboard:

>> **With a keyboard,** press the Windows and Print Screen (PrtScn) keys simultaneously.

>> **Without a keyboard,** press the Windows logo on your device and the Volume Down key at the same time.

>> **On a Windows 10 tablet,** the Windows logo usually is on the screen, and the Volume Down key is on the side of the case.

TECHNICAL
STUFF

The traditional way to take a screenshot in Windows is to press PrtScn (Print Screen) on your keyboard, paste the screenshot into an image-editing program such as Paint, and save the image as a file on your computer. Though this method works in all versions of Windows (including Windows 10), it isn't the fastest way to take a screenshot in Windows 10. The preceding options are faster.

Capture Custom Screenshots
with the Snipping Tool

If you have a desktop or laptop computer with Windows 10, the best tool for taking screenshots is the Snipping Tool. With the Snipping Tool, you can take full-screen screenshots, screenshots of a specific window, and rectangular or free-form screenshots. Once you've taken a screenshot, you can edit it and use tools such as pens, highlighters, and erasers. Here's how to use the Snipping Tool to take a screenshot of a specific app window:

1. **Open the app for which you want to take a screenshot.**

2. **In the search box on the taskbar, type the words** snipping tool.

   A list with search results appears.

3. **Click the Snipping Tool search result.**

   The Snipping Tool desktop app opens.

4. **In the Snipping Tool window, click the down-pointing arrow, located near the New button.**

5. **On the menu that appears, click Window Snip.**

   Figure 8-4 shows the screenshot-taking tools available in the Snipping Tool window.

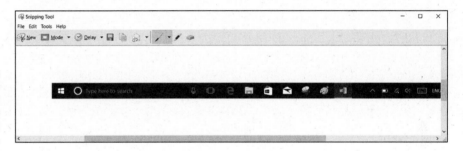

FIGURE 8-4:
The screenshot-taking tools available in the Snipping Tool window.

6. **Click the app window that you want to capture.**

   The screenshot is loaded into the Snipping Tool.

7. **Click the Save button in the Snipping Tool window.**

8. **Type a name for this screenshot.**

9. **Select where to save the screenshot.**

10. **Click Save.**

11. **Close the Snipping Tool.**

Chapter **9**

Working on the Road

I f you travel as part of your job, you probably need access to your company's network in order to do your work. That's where virtual private networks (VPNs) come in. VPNs establish secure connections to a company's private network. So we start this chapter by showing you how to work with VPN connections in Windows 10.

On the other hand, perhaps you work from home on your personal devices and need to access your files at work. This is where the Work Folders feature, first introduced in Windows 8, comes in. With the help of Work Folders, you can access your work on personal devices that are connected to the Internet. You don't have to take your work computer or laptop with you. You just need to set up Work Folders on your work computer and your personal devices; your work always is available, no matter which device you use. If this feature is available on your company's network, be sure to check out this chapter's discussion on how to use it from just about anywhere.

You may need to connect remotely to your work computer, either from home or from another location in your company's network. If so, this chapter shows how Remote Access works in Windows 10.

Traveling also means that you need as much battery power as possible. For example, if you're taking a long flight and need to do some work, you'll appreciate the new Battery Saver feature that's included in Windows 10. With this feature, you can squeeze in more time for work and also find out what's using up most of your battery. Also, this chapter explains how to further improve the use of your battery by manually adjusting Windows settings.

Create a VPN Connection

VPNs allow users to connect to private networks from the Internet in a secure manner. Many companies provide VPN services for their employees so that they can connect to the enterprises' networks as needed. If your workplace has this service, depending on how it's set up and implemented, you may be able to connect to the VPN service either straight from Windows 10, using the features offered by the operating system, or via a special VPN client app that's provided by your company.

TECHNICAL STUFF

If your workplace uses a special VPN client app, the network administrator or the IT department must provide you with the specific instructions for that app.

However, if you connect straight to the VPN service from Windows 10, you need information about your company's VPN. Depending on your company's setup, you may need to know the following details to connect with VPN:

» The VPN server name or address

» The VPN type (such as PPTP, L2TP/IPsec, SSTP, or IKEv2)

» The sign-in details (usually your username and password)

If your company uses Windows to create a VPN connection to the workplace network, here's what you need to do to connect to its VPN service:

1. **Click the Notifications icon on the right side of the taskbar.**

The Action Center appears.

2. **Click VPN.**

The Settings window appears.

3. **Click Add a VPN Connection (see Figure 9-1).**

A window with the same name opens.

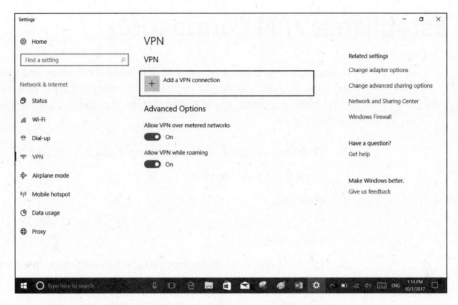

FIGURE 9-1:
Adding a VPN
connection.

4. **Type the name that you want to use for the connection and the other required details (such as server name or address, VPN type, username, and password; see Figure 9-2).**

5. **When you finish, click Save.**

   The VPN connection is now added to your list of VPN connections.

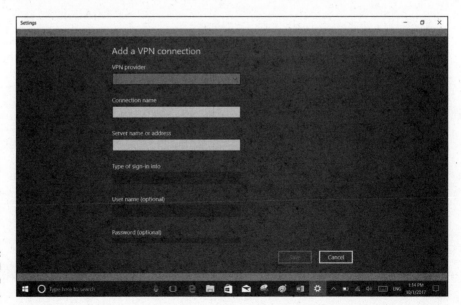

FIGURE 9-2:
Entering the VPN
connection
details.

Establish a VPN Connection

If you're connected to a network that's away from work and you have access to the Internet, you can try to connect to your company's private network using VPN. After you create the VPN connection in Windows 10, here's how to use the connection:

1. **Click the Notifications icon on the right side of the taskbar.**

   The Action Center appears.

2. **Click VPN.**

   The Settings window appears, where you can manage and create VPN connections.

3. **Click the VPN connection that you want to use; then click Connect (see Figure 9-3).**

   Windows 10 starts the VPN connection using the credentials you entered.

   Once the connection is established, you receive a confirmation from Windows 10.

4. **Close the Settings window.**

   Now you can use your VPN connection when needed.

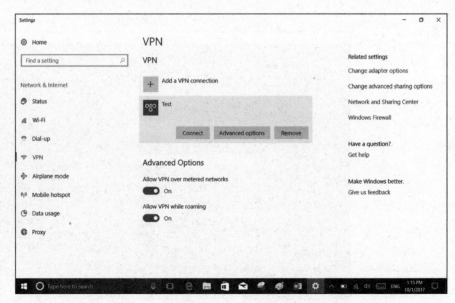

FIGURE 9-3:
Connecting
via VPN.

Not all public networks that have access to the Internet allow you to connect using VPN to your company's network. Some networks are configured so that they specifically block VPN connections of any kind. If that's the case for the network that you're connected to, your only solution is to change the network and try another one.

Disconnect from a VPN Connection

When you finish using your VPN connection, here's how to disconnect from it:

1. **Click the Notifications icon on the right side of the taskbar.**

   The Action Center appears.

2. **Click VPN.**

   The Settings window appears.

3. **Click the VPN connection that you want to disconnect from; then click Disconnect (see Figure 9-4).**

4. **Close the Settings window.**

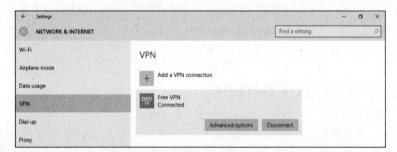

FIGURE 9-4:
Disconnecting
from VPN.

Remove a VPN Connection

If you no longer need to use a VPN connection that you created, you can remove it easily from Windows. Just follow these steps:

1. **Click the Notifications icon on the right side of the taskbar.**

   The Action Center appears.

2. **Click VPN.**

   The Settings window appears.

3. Click the VPN connection that you want to delete; then click Remove (see Figure 9-5).

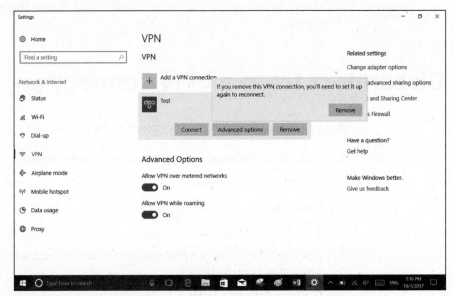

FIGURE 9-5:
Removing a VPN
connection.

4. Click Remove again to confirm your choice (see Figure 9-5).

5. Close the Settings window.

Set Up Work Folders

Work Folders is a feature that enables you to access your work files from your personal computer or device. With Work Folders, you can keep copies of your work files on your personal devices and have them automatically synchronized to your company's data center.

Here's an example of how an information worker (we'll call her Alice) might use Work Folders to separate her work data from her personal data while having the ability to work from any device:

Alice saves a document in the Work Folders directory on her computer at work. The document is synced to a file server controlled by her company's IT department. When Alice returns home that evening, she picks up her Microsoft Surface Pro device, where the document is already synced because she previously set up Work Folders on that device. She takes her Microsoft Surface Pro on a trip, and she has no Internet access while traveling. She works on the document offline, and when she returns home and an Internet connection is available, the document automatically is synced back with the file server from her company. The next day, she returns to her office and opens the document. All the changes that she made the previous evening are in her `Work Folders` directory on her work computer.

To set up Work Folders on your Windows 10 computer or device, follow these steps:

1. **Click the search bar on the taskbar.**

2. **Type** work folders.

A list of search results appears.

3. **Click Work Folders.**

The Work Folders window appears.

4. **Click Set Up Work Folders (see Figure 9-6).**

You're asked to enter your work email address.

FIGURE 9-6:
How to set up
Work Folders.

5. **Type your work email address; then click Next.**

You're asked to enter the username and password that you use on your company's network.

6. **Type the requested details and click OK.**

You're asked to enter a Work Folders URL.

7. **Type the URL address of your company's Work Folders server (see Figure 9-7).**

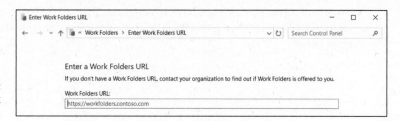

FIGURE 9-7:
Entering the Work
Folders URL.

8. **Click Next.**

You see information about the Work Folders feature and where your files will be saved on your computer.

9. **Click Next.**

The Accept Security Policies page appears.

10. **Select I Accept These Policies on My PC.**

11. **Click Set Up Work Folders (see Figure 9-8).**

Windows 10 spends some time configuring this feature and then sends a message informing you that Work Folders has started syncing with your PC.

FIGURE 9-8: Accepting the security policies for Work Folders.

12. **Click Close.**

You don't have to wait until syncing finishes. It runs automatically in the background.

TECHNICAL STUFF

Before setting up Work Folders on your devices and computers, you need to ask your company's IT department for the appropriate connection details. For example, you need to know the URL of the Work Folders server and the email address and password to use for this feature. If you're setting up Work Folders on your work computer, you may not have to complete Steps 6–8. These steps are generally activated only when you set up Work Folders on your computers and devices from home.

Use Work Folders

To use the Work Folders service, all you need is an active Internet connection and File Explorer up and running. In File Explorer you find a new folder called Work Folders. Click it and you see all files that are synced by Work Folders. Every file that you add to this folder is automatically synced to your work computer, and vice versa. Figure 9-9 shows the Work Folders folder in File Explorer.

FIGURE 9-9:
The Work Folders folder in File Explorer.

On the File Explorer status bar, you see the sync status and when Work Folders was last synchronized.

TIP

To manually sync a file in Work Folders, right-click it in File Explorer and, from the menu that pops up, select Sync Now.

Stop Using Work Folders

To stop using Work Folders on any of your Windows 10 computers and devices, follow these steps:

1. **Click the search bar on the taskbar.**

2. **Type** work folders.

   A list of search results appears.

3. **Click Work Folders.**

   The Work Folders window appears.

4. **In the column on the left, click Stop Using Work Folders.**

   You're asked to confirm that you want to stop using this feature.

5. **Click Yes (see Figure 9-10).**

6. **Close the Work Folders window.**

FIGURE 9-10:
How to stop using
Work Folders.

TIP

In the Work Folders window (opened in Step 3), you can see how much space is available on the Work Folders server, and you can also manage the credentials that you're using to log in to the Work Folders server.

Connect Remotely to Another Computer on the Network

The Remote Desktop Connection app allows you to connect to other computers or devices that are connected to your local network or that are on the Internet and have a public IP address. For example, you can use the Remote Desktop Connection app to connect to a colleague's computer from your desk or to your work computer when you're using another computer or device.

Here's how to use Remote Desktop Connection to connect remotely to another device:

1. **Click the search bar on the taskbar.**

2. **Type** remote desktop.

   A list of search results appears.

3. **Click Remote Desktop Connection.**

4. **In the Remote Desktop Connection window, type the IP address or the name of the Windows device that you want to connect to; then click Connect (see Figure 9-11).**

    Windows initiates the remote connection; then you're asked to enter your credentials.

FIGURE 9-11:
The Remote Desktop Connection app.

5. **Enter the username and password that you want to use on the computer you're connecting to; then click OK.**

6. **If you're informed that the remote computer couldn't be authenticated due to problems with its security certificate, click Yes to connect anyway (see Figure 9-12).**

    You're now connected to the remote computer and can use it as though it were your local computer.

FIGURE 9-12:
Problems with the security certificate.

7. **When you finish using the Remote Desktop Connection, close the app by clicking the x button on top of the window and then clicking OK.**

    The remote session is disconnected.

TIP

If Remote Desktop Connection says that it can't connect to the remote computer, check whether the remote computer is turned off, whether it isn't available on the network, or whether remote connections are disabled on it. The next section describes how to enable remote connections.

Allow Remote Access to Your Windows 10 Computer

By default, Windows 10 doesn't allow remote access to your computer or device. If you need this kind of access, you must manually enable it. Here's how:

1. **Click the search bar on the taskbar.**

2. **Type** remote desktop.

A list of search results appears.

3. **Click Allow Remote Access to Your Computer.**

The System Properties window appears.

4. **In the Remote tab, go to the Remote Desktop section and select the Allow Remote Connections to This Computer box (see Figure 9-13).**

5. **Click OK.**

FIGURE 9-13: How to allow remote connections to your computer.

Use Airplane Mode

Airplane mode turns off all radio chips on your device. In Windows 10, when Airplane mode is turned on, wireless network cards, Bluetooth chips, and mobile data connections are turned off. You should turn on Airplane mode when you board a plane. After take-off, you can turn on the Wi-Fi or the Bluetooth, if you need to use one of them. However, you must turn them off again when the plane prepares for landing.

This feature also helps you save power. Because some of your device's components are turned off, they aren't used and don't consume any power. Therefore, you get slightly better battery life. This benefit alone makes Airplane mode useful, even when you're nowhere near a plane but want to save as much power as possible.

Here's how to enable Airplane mode in Windows 10:

1. **Go to the notification area on the taskbar and click the Wireless icon.**

   The Action Center appears.

2. **Click Airplane Mode (see Figure 9-14).**

   The Wireless icon on the taskbar turns into an Airplane icon.

FIGURE 9-14: Turning on Airplane mode.

TIP

To disable Airplane mode, click the Airplane icon and then click the Airplane Mode button.

Save Battery Power on the Go

Windows 10 introduced the Battery Saver feature. As its name implies, this tool allows you to improve battery life on mobile devices (such as laptops, Ultrabooks, tablets, and 2-in-1 devices). In Windows 10, Battery Saver

» Turns Battery Saver on automatically if the battery falls below a certain level.

» Controls which apps can run in the background while your battery is low.

» Controls which push notifications are allowed when the battery is low and monitors what is using most of your battery.

Battery Saver automatically activates itself when your battery falls below 20 percent, but you can also enable the feature manually at any time. Here's how:

1. **Go to the notification area on the taskbar and click the Battery icon.**

A pop-up appears with information about your battery.

2. **Click the Battery Saver button (see Figure 9-15).**

The battery icon changes to reflect that the Battery Saver feature is turned on.

3. **Click anywhere outside the pop-up with information about your battery to resume normal computing activities.**

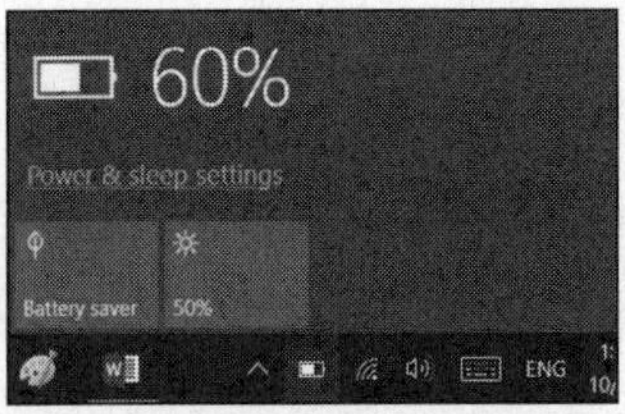

FIGURE 9-15:
Manually turning on the Battery Saver.

TIP

To turn off the Battery Saver, repeat the preceding steps.

See What's Using Your Battery Power

You can take steps to identify the services and features that eat up the most battery power. To check your battery use in Windows 10, follow these steps:

1. **Open Settings.**

2. **Click System.**

A list with system settings appears.

3. **Click Battery Saver.**

Here you see the percentage of battery life remaining and the estimated time remaining (see Figure 9-16).

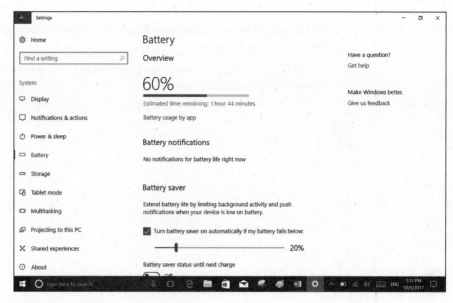

FIGURE 9-16:
Checking
battery use.

4. **Click Battery Usage By App.**

   A list appears, showing what is consuming most of your battery.

5. **When you finish, close the Settings window.**

Improve Your Power and Sleep Settings

When you're on the road and want to work productively, battery time can be vital. Though the new Battery Saver feature can help you save some battery time, you can extend that time by manually editing the Power & Sleep settings that are available in Windows 10; for example, when Windows 10 turns off your computer's and/or device's screens, when it goes into Sleep mode, and whether Wi-Fi remains connected while your device is asleep.

To extend the battery time by adjusting the Power & Sleep settings, follow these steps:

1. **Open Settings.**

2. **Click System.**

   A list with system settings appears.

3. **Click Power & Sleep.**

   The list of available power and sleep settings appears.

4. **In the Screen section, change when you want the screen to be turned off while on battery power.**

5. **In the Sleep section, change when your PC goes to sleep when it's running on battery power (see Figure 9-17).**

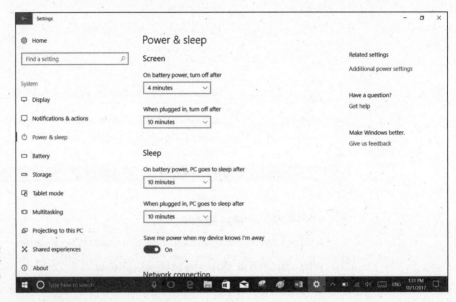

FIGURE 9-17: Improving your Power & Sleep settings.

6. **In the Wi-Fi section, change how the Wi-Fi behaves when on battery power.**

7. **Close the Settings window.**

Chapter **10**

Personalizing User Accounts

U ser accounts make it possible for multiple people to share a computer, with each person having a private Documents folder, apps, email inbox, and Windows settings. When you have your own account, you can do all the customization you want to your Windows environment without affecting other user accounts. Other users will have their own visual customization, their own app settings, and so forth. Windows 10 provides several types of user accounts, each with its own characteristics. This chapter starts by detailing them and what's different from user account to user account.

This chapter also shows how to personalize your own user account and do things such as set up a PIN or a picture password for quick sign-ins, switch between sign-in options, and change your account picture. Finally, you see how to set the sign-in policy in Windows 10.

Understanding the User Accounts
You Can Use

In Windows 10, several user accounts are available, each with its own characteristics.

In well-managed business environments, there is a network domain for the entire company or for a part of it. On this domain, each individual user has her own user account, called a *domain user account*. When you use a domain user account, your actions are limited by the access rights and privileges associated with the account. These rights and privileges are managed centrally by the IT department or by the network administrator and can't be changed by individual users.

With a domain user account, employees can log on to every computer in the company's network and quickly get access to their apps, files, and settings. A domain user account has two name formats that can be used to authenticate in Windows and in Windows apps:

>> **Email address or User Principal Name (UPN)**: Specifies an Internet-style name, such as UserName@Microsoft.com and ciprianrusen@wiley.com

The parts of the UPN are

- The user account name (before the @ character)
- The separator (the @ character)
- The domain name (after the @ character)

>> **Down-level logon name:** Specifies a domain and a user account in that domain, such as DOMAIN\UserName and CONTOSO\John.Smith

The parts of a down-level logon name are

- The domain name (before the \ character)
- The separator (the \ character)
- The user account name (after the \ character)

On your personal Windows devices as well as in smaller companies without a carefully managed IT environment, you don't use domain user accounts. Instead, you can use a Microsoft account or a local account.

A *Microsoft account* is an ID composed of an email address and a password, which you can use to log on to most Microsoft websites, services, and properties such as

Outlook.com, Xbox Live, and all Microsoft services (including OneDrive and Skype). You also use it in Windows 10 for synchronizing your computer settings, for using the Windows Store to purchase apps, and for other activities.

TIP

If you're already using Outlook.com, OneDrive, or Xbox Live, you already have a Microsoft account. You can use the same email address and password in Windows 10.

If you don't have a Microsoft account, you can easily create one in Windows 10 or on the Microsoft websites. Using a Microsoft account in Windows 10 is useful, particularly if you want to access all the features it has to offer without problems or limitations. In addition, a Microsoft account gives you access to almost all Microsoft products, services, properties, and websites. And you can use the same Microsoft account across many devices and have your settings, apps, and files synced automatically.

Local user accounts can be used only on your local computer. If you have multiple devices, you must create a separate local account for each device. A local account is the same as any account you've ever used to log in to a Windows 7 or Windows XP operating system. A local account grants you access to the system's resources in your own user space. You can install desktop apps, change settings, and work as usual. Although with local accounts you won't miss out on any familiar features in older versions of Windows, you can't access too many new features that Windows 10 has to offer, because local accounts can't use services like OneDrive or Skype, unless you manually enter a Microsoft account.

TECHNICAL
STUFF

In Windows 10, you can sign in with domain user accounts, Microsoft accounts, and local user accounts. However, your work computer might not allow every type of user account. That's because the company may impose certain rules about which types of user accounts can be used on the company's computers. In a company with carefully managed networks, usually you can use only your domain user account; you can't create or use a local account or a Microsoft account.

Understanding User Account Types and Permissions

User accounts in Windows 10 can be administrator accounts or standard user accounts. Accounts with administrator permissions are specified by the word *Administrator* in the Accounts section of the Settings window (see Figure 10-1).

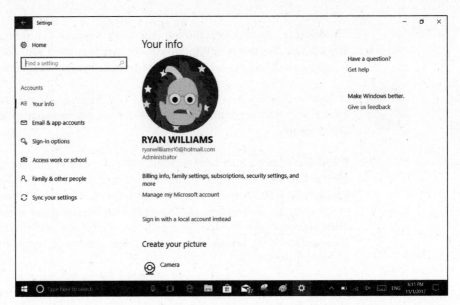

FIGURE 10-1:
A user account
that's set as an
administrator.

Administrators have full access to all user accounts. They can create and delete user accounts and change the name, password, and account types for other accounts. The administrator can also install software and hardware and configure every aspect of the operating system. As a rule, every computer must have at least one administrator.

A user account that isn't an administrator account is considered a standard user account and has limited permissions. Generally, a user with standard privileges has access to apps that have already been installed on the computer but can't install other software without the administrator password. Standard users can change their own passwords but can't change the account name or type without the administrator password.

In business environments, most users have standard user accounts with limited permissions that are set by the IT department or the network administrator. Individual users can't create and manage other user accounts. The rest of this chapter explains how to personalize your standard user account in Windows 10.

Set Up a PIN for Your User Account

To simplify how you log on to your computer, Windows 10 allows you to create a 4-digit PIN associated with your user account. After you create a PIN, you can use it to log on quickly to your user account. Here's how to set up a pin for your account:

1. **Open Settings.**

2. **Click Accounts.**

   The settings for user accounts are shown.

3. **Click Sign-In Options.**

   Your sign-in settings are shown.

4. **Click the Add button in the PIN section.**

   You're asked to verify your account.

5. **Enter your user account password.**

6. **Click Sign In.**

   The Set Up a PIN window opens.

7. **Type the PIN that you want to set in the New PIN and Confirm PIN boxes (see Figure 10-2).**

FIGURE 10-2:
How to set up
the PIN in
Windows 10.

8. **Click OK.**

9. **Close Settings.**

TIP

If you forget your PIN, you have to reset it. To reset the PIN, follow the preceding steps and, at Step 4, click I Forgot My PIN; then follow the wizard's instructions for resetting the PIN.

Set Up a Picture Password for Your User Account

The concept of picture passwords was first introduced in Windows 8. A picture password has two complementary parts: a picture and gestures that you draw on it. These gestures can be taps, clicks, circles, or lines. If your user account has a complicated password, using a picture password can make it easier to log on to your Windows 10 devices. Even though this feature is particularly recommended for use on touch-enabled devices such as tablets, you can also employ it on a desktop computer by using a mouse.

To create a picture password for your user account, follow these steps:

1. **Open Settings.**

2. **Click Accounts.**

   The settings for user accounts are shown.

3. **Click Sign-In Options.**

   Your sign-in settings are shown.

4. **In the Picture Password section, click the Add button.**

   You're asked to first verify your account info and type your password.

5. **Type your password as requested; then click OK.**

   The wizard for setting the picture password appears.

6. **Click Choose Picture (see Figure 10-3).**

   A browsing window opens.

FIGURE 10-3:
Welcome to picture password.

7. Navigate to where you stored the picture you want to use for the password and select it.

8. Click Open.

The selected picture is now open.

9. Drag the picture to the position that you want.

You can use your mouse (if you have one) or your finger (if you use touch).

10. Click Use This Picture.

You're asked to set up three gestures as your picture password.

11. Draw three gestures on your picture.

You can use any combination of circles, straight lines, and taps.

12. Confirm the three gestures by drawing them again (see Figure 10-4).

You receive a message that you successfully created your picture password.

FIGURE 10-4: Confirming your gestures for the picture password.

13. Click Finish.

14. Close Settings.

Switch Between Sign-In Options

After you set up more than one way to sign in to Windows 10, you need to know how to switch between them when signing in to Windows. When you're at the sign-in screen in Windows 10 and you want to use a way to sign in other than with your password, here's what to do:

1. **Select your user account from the list of available accounts.**

Your user account picture appears.

2. **Click the Sign-In Options link.**

A list of icons appears. Each icon represents a sign-in option. From top to bottom, they are picture password, password, and PIN.

3. **Click the icon for the sign-in option that you want to use (see Figure 10-5).**

4. **Sign in to Windows 10 using the option that you selected.**

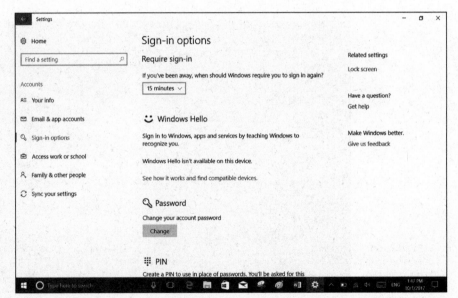

FIGURE 10-5:
Selecting the sign-in option that you want to use.

Change Your User Account Picture

In Windows 10, you can set a picture for your user account, and you can change it at any time. The picture you use is shown when you sign in to Windows 10, on the Start Menu, in apps that use this picture, and so on.

To change the picture that you're using for your account, follow these steps:

1. **Open Settings.**

2. **Click Accounts.**

   The settings for user accounts are shown.

3. **In your account, click the Browse for One link.**

   A browsing window opens.

4. **Navigate to where you stored the picture that you want to use and select it (see Figure 10-6).**

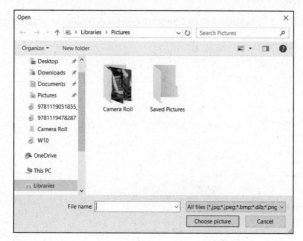

FIGURE 10-6:
Changing your
user account
picture.

5. **Click Choose Picture.**

   The new picture is shown alongside the previous one, if one was set.

6. **Close Settings.**

You can also click the Camera button to open the camera on your computer (if you have one) to take a quick selfie.

Set the Sign-In Policy

You can set Windows 10 to require you to sign in again if you stop using it for a certain period. You can also set it to never ask you to sign in.

TIP

Setting Windows 10 to always require you to sign in after you're away from your computer is a useful security precaution, especially in business environments where it's important that unauthorized people don't get access to your work.

Here's how to set the sign-in policy in Windows 10:

1. **Open Settings.**

2. **Click Accounts.**

   The settings for user accounts are shown.

3. **Click Sign-In Options.**

   Your sign-in settings are shown.

4. **Click the drop-down list in the Require Sign-In section (see Figure 10-7).**

   A list with options appears.

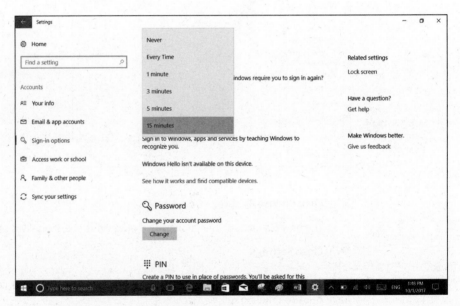

FIGURE 10-7:
Setting the sign-in option.

5. **Select the desired sign-in option.**

6. **Close Settings.**

TIP

Depending on the hardware provided by your company, you may be able to use Windows Hello or features that lock your computer when you walk away. Ask your IT department for availability.

Chapter **11**

Improving Your Privacy and Security

Security and privacy are especially important in business environments. Many employees work with confidential data that, if stolen, could be harmful to businesses. That's why most company networks have strict security rules and install several security tools. In this chapter, we present the key security features that Windows 10 offers. Your company may use some (or all) of them, so feel free to check out only the features pertinent to your needs, or check out all of them if you're just curious by nature.

Protecting your personal privacy is also important in today's computing world. By default, Windows 10 and your apps can access plenty of data about you; for example, your account name, picture, location, contacts, and calendar. This chapter shows you how to set all these privacy options so that Windows 10 and your apps can access only the data you allow.

Check Whether Windows Update Is Turned On

Depending on the size of the company you work for and your role in it, either you or an IT department is tasked with keeping Windows 10 up to date. If your company is a big one with a well-managed environment, the IT department probably manages updates. In this environment, you have no say about how your computer and devices are updated — and you don't have to worry about it, either. On the other hand, if you work for a small company, it may not have an IT department or even an IT person, so you may have to deal with Windows updates yourself. If that's the case, be glad that Windows Update is automatically turned on and Windows 10 updates itself automatically. We just recommend that you check whether Windows Update is turned on. Here's how to do so:

1. **Click Start.**

   The Start Menu appears.

2. **Click Settings.**

   The Settings window appears.

3. **Click Update & Security.**

4. **In the Update & Security list of settings, click Windows Update (see Figure 11-1).**

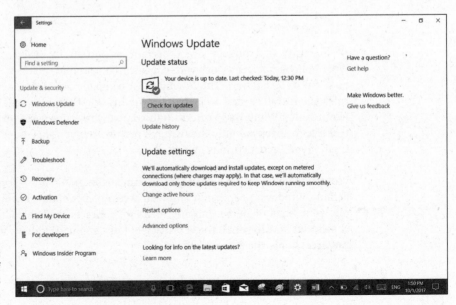

FIGURE 11-1:
The status of the Windows Update service.

If Windows Update is already turned on, you see this message: Available Updates Will Be Downloaded and Installed Automatically.

If Windows Update is turned off and you have the permission needed to change the setting, don't worry. We tell you how to turn on Windows Update in the following section.

Turn On Windows Update

Say that you start up your work computer and find that Windows Update is turned off. Assuming that your company doesn't have an official IT person and that you're allowed to change the Windows Update settings, here are the steps you can take to enable it:

1. **Open Settings.**

2. **Click Update & Security.**

   Your Windows update and Windows security settings are loaded.

3. **Click Windows Update to access this tool and its settings (see Figure 11-2).**

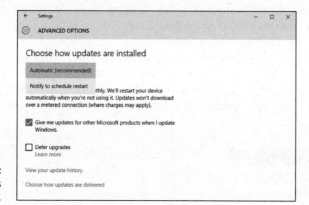

FIGURE 11-2: Run Windows Update.

Use the User Account Control (UAC)

The User Account Control (UAC) is a security feature that helps prevent unauthorized changes to your Windows 10 computer or device. These unauthorized changes can be initiated by users, apps, viruses, or other types of malware. UAC ensures that these changes are made only with the administrator's approval. If these changes aren't approved by the administrator, they will never be executed, and the system will remain unchanged.

Desktop apps in Windows 10 don't run with administrator permissions and consequently can't make automatic changes to an operating system. When a desktop app wants to make system changes (such as modifications that affect other user accounts, modifications of system files and folders, or installation of new software), Windows 10 issues what's called a UAC confirmation dialog box, where users can confirm whether they want those changes to be made. If the user clicks No, the changes won't be made. If the user clicks Yes, the app receives administrator permissions and makes the system changes it's programmed to make (see Figure 11-3).

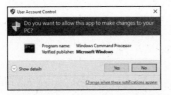

FIGURE 11-3:
The User Account Control (UAC) prompt.

These permissions will be granted until the app stops running or the user closes it.

When using Windows Store apps, UAC is never triggered because, by design, these apps can't modify system settings or files.

If you're on a locked computer and your user account doesn't have administrator permissions, the UAC prompt asks you to enter the password for an administrator account, as shown in Figure 11-4. If you don't type the correct administrator password, you can't run desktop apps that require administrator permissions.

FIGURE 11-4:
The UAC prompt on a locked-down account.

WARNING

When you encounter UAC prompts, it's important to pay attention to them. Look at the information displayed and determine which app wants administrator permissions. If it isn't an app that you started and want to run, click No.

Protect Yourself from Malware

Windows Defender originally provided protection only against spyware threats. With each new version of Windows, this product has been improved, and it now provides protection against more types of malware, including both viruses and spyware. Windows Defender doesn't compare in number of features and efficiency with most commercial security solutions, but it's one of the best free security solutions you can find for Windows. If your company hasn't installed another security product on the computers and devices used by its employees, Windows Defender is turned on by default, and it automatically protects your computer or device from malware. Windows Defender automatically scans all the files and folders through which you browse. If a threat is identified, it's immediately cleaned or quarantined, and you're informed of this action (see Figure 11-5).

FIGURE 11-5:
A Windows
Defender prompt.

Depending on the threat, you may not need to do anything, or you may need to restart your computer or device in order for Windows Defender to disinfect your computer.

WARNING

Pay attention to the prompts that Windows Defender displays. They're never false alarms, and these prompts should put you on guard that you're dealing with a possible malware infection.

REMEMBER

Scan your device again after Windows Defender has dealt with threats. This scan gives Windows Defender the chance to make a complete scan and identify all infected files.

Scan for Viruses

As we mention earlier in this chapter, Windows Defender automatically monitors your computer for malware threats. However, if a malware sample (such as a virus) is detected, you should run a manual full scan of your computer or of the drive where the threat was detected. Here's how to perform a manual scan with Windows Defender:

1. **Click inside the search box on the taskbar.**

2. **Type** defender.

A list of search results appears.

3. **Click Windows Defender.**

The Windows Defender window appears.

4. **In the Home tab, find the Scan Options section.**

5. **Select the type of scan that you want to perform (Quick, Full, or Custom).**

6. **Click Scan now (see Figure 11-6).**

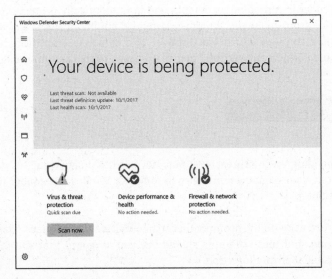

Windows Defender Security Center — □ ×

≡

⌂ ♡ ♥ (•)) ▭ ✕

Your device is being protected.

Last threat scan: Not available
Last threat definition update: 10/1/2017
Last health scan: 10/1/2017

🛡 Virus & threat protection
Quick scan due

💓 Device performance & health
No action needed.

((•)) Firewall & network protection
No action needed.

Scan now

⚙

FIGURE 11-6:
The Windows Defender desktop app.

7. **Wait for the scan to finish.**

8. **If threats were detected, click Clean PC and follow the instructions for removing threats.**

If no threats were detected, close Windows Defender.

TECHNICAL STUFF

At Step 5, if you've selected Custom, you're asked to select the location that you want to scan after Step 6. Browse your computer, select the folders or the drives that you want to scan, and click OK.

Increase the Security of Your Passwords

Regardless of how good your company's security products are, your computer or device is still vulnerable to security problems if you don't use good judgment about password security. If you use the same password everywhere, a malicious user might break into a forum or social website you're using and steal your password. That user can then use your password and the email address you used when you registered with the forum or social website to access more personal data and information from your Inbox, your accounts on social networks, and so on.

In corporate environments, you may be forced to change your password every month, but that doesn't mean that you aren't using guessable passwords. Large companies tend to be regular targets for hackers. Industrial espionage is also a common problem in large companies, and good password habits are critical for keeping your data safe.

To expose yourself as little as possible, follow these guidelines:

>> Don't use passwords with fewer than six characters. They're especially easy to break.

Your passwords should be at least eight characters long and shouldn't be recognizable words.

>> Include letters, numbers, and special characters such as +, #, and $ in your password.

>> Don't reuse the same password.

>> Use password-management solutions such as LastPass, KeePass, or RoboForm, which help you securely store and use your passwords.

These solutions help you identify your duplicate passwords, change them to new random passwords, generate secure passwords automatically, and store them safely so that you can use them whenever needed, and never lose them again.

3

Introduce Yourself to Office 2016

Master Word basics.

Work with Excel worksheets.

Use Excel formulas and functions effectively.

Create impressive Excel charts.

Chapter **12**

Getting to Know Office

Microsoft Office is a suite of applications. A *suite* is a group of applications designed to work together and that have similar user interfaces in order to cut down on the learning curve for each one. Office 2016 includes a word processor (Word), a spreadsheet program (Excel), a presentation graphics program (PowerPoint), and an email program (Outlook). Depending on the version of Office, it may also include other programs. Sweet, eh? Er . . . *suite.*

Because all the Office apps have similar interfaces, many of the skills you pick up while working with one program also translate to the others. In this lesson, we introduce you to the Office interface and show you some things the programs have in common. For the examples in this lesson, we mostly use Word and Excel because they are the most popular of the applications. Keep in mind, though, that the skills you learn here apply to the other applications, too.

Throughout this book, the examples all show Windows 10 as the operating system. Wherever Windows 7 or 8 are substantially different, we let you know what to expect.

Starting and Exiting an Office Application

There are several ways to start Office applications. For example, you can select it from the Start menu's All Apps list. You can also use the Search feature: With the Start menu open, begin typing the application's name and then click its name when it appears. Depending on how your PC is set up, you might also have short-cuts to one or more of the Office apps on your desktop or taskbar, or pinned to the top level of the Start menu.

TIP

You can also double-click a data file that's associated with one of the Office applications to start that application.

The following steps explain how to start an Office application in Windows 10; if you're using earlier versions of Windows, check out the Tips throughout this book that point out differences:

1. **On the taskbar, click the Start button.**

   If the application you want to run appears at the top of the Start menu, click it and you're done with these steps.

2. **Click All Apps (as shown in Figure 12-1).**

3. **Scroll down to the section for the first letter of the application name.**

   For example, to run Word, scroll down to the W section (as shown in Figure 12-2).

FIGURE 12-1:
Click Start
and then click
All Apps.

FIGURE 12-2:
Scroll to the W section and click the desired application.

4. **Click the desired application.**

5. **Press the Esc key to bypass the Start screen that appears.**

TIP

In Word, Excel, and PowerPoint, a Start screen appears when you run the application from which you can select a template for a new document or open an existing document.

6. **Click the Close (X) button in the application window's upper-right corner to close the application (as shown in Figure 12-3).**

TIP

If you have any unsaved changes, you're prompted to save them here. See "Saving Your Work," later in this chapter, for more information about saving.

Now try opening and closing again, this time using a different method for both.

7. **Click in the Search box on the taskbar (as shown in Figure 12-4).**

FIGURE 12-3:
The Close button shuts down an application.

FIGURE 12-4:
Click in the Search box.

8. **As shown in Figure 12-5, begin typing the name of the application to open (for example, type** Excel**).**

9. In the search results that appear, find the name of the application you're typing and then click that name.

The application opens.

10. Press Alt+F4 to close the application.

FIGURE 12-5:
Search for the application's name and then click it in the search results.

Now that you know how to start and exit Office applications, let's take a look at the interface of a typical Office application.

Working with the Ribbon

All Office applications have a common system of navigation called the *Ribbon*, which is a tabbed bar across the top of the application window. Each tab is like a page of buttons. You click different tabs to access different sets of buttons and features. To explore the Ribbon, follow these steps:

1. Open an Office application, as discussed in the previous section, and, if needed, press Esc to bypass the Start screen.

2. On the Ribbon, click the desired tab (as shown in Figure 12-6).

3. Click the desired command.

FIGURE 12-6:
Click a tab, and then click the desired command.

Here are some key facts to know about Ribbon commands:

(A) Not all commands are available all the time. For example, you can't paste content until you first cut or copy it. Commands that appear gray (dimmed) are currently unavailable.

(B) Buttons are organized into groups, as shown in Figure 12-7. The group names appear at the bottom.

(C) Some groups have dialog box launchers; these open a dialog box or task pane relating to the commands in that group. The one in the Font group, for example, opens the Font dialog box.

(D) Some buttons, such as Bold or Italic, are on/off toggles. Each time you click the button, it switches its state from one to the other.

(E) Some groups contain drop-down lists from which to choose settings such as fonts or sizes.

(F) Some buttons work as a group from which only one button can be selected at a time. One example is the four buttons in the Paragraph group that control horizontal alignment of paragraph text.

(G) Some buttons have a small arrow on them. In some cases, if you click the button face (not the arrow), the current setting is applied. If you click the arrow, on the other hand, a menu opens for changing the current setting. In other cases, clicking the arrow or the button face has the same effect: opening a menu.

(H) Some groups, such as the Styles group, contain galleries from which you can choose settings by graphical example.

(I) You can hide the Ribbon to save space by clicking the Collapse the Ribbon arrow or pressing Ctrl+F1. When you do so, the tab names remain onscreen; click a tab name to reopen the Ribbon. Then click the Pin the Ribbon icon (the tiny pushpin) at the far right end of the Ribbon to re-pin it open.

(J) Depending on the width of the application window, some groups may appear collapsed (as shown in Figure 12-8). When a group is collapsed, it appears as a single button with the group's name. When you click the button, a palette appears, containing all the group's individual commands.

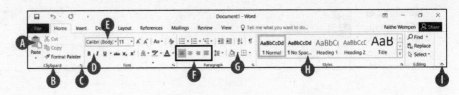

FIGURE 12-7:
Ribbon controls.

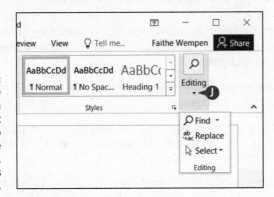

FIGURE 12-8:
When the
application
window is not
wide enough to
display all the
Ribbon content,
some groups
appear collapsed.

Using the File Menu

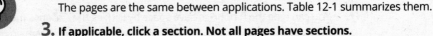

In each Office application, clicking the File tab opens the File menu, also known as *Backstage view.* Backstage view provides access to commands that have to do with the data file you're working with — commands such as saving, opening, printing, mailing, and checking the file's properties. The File tab is a different color in each application. In Excel, for example, it's green. To explore Backstage view, follow these steps:

1. **Click the File tab. Backstage view opens.**

2. **Click the desired page from the navigation pane at the left.**

The pages are the same between applications. Table 12-1 summarizes them.

3. **If applicable, click a section. Not all pages have sections.**

4A. **Click the desired command, as shown in Figure 12-9.**

OR

4B. **Click the back arrow or press Esc to leave Backstage view without making a selection.**

TABLE 12-1   **Pages on the File Menu in Word, Excel, and PowerPoint**

Page	What You Can Do
Info	See and edit file properties
	Password-protect the file and restrict editing
	Inspect the file for privacy, accessibility, and compatibility
	Recover unsaved versions
New	Start a new file using a template
Open	Open an existing file
Save	Save the active file for the first time, or save changes to an existing file using the same settings
Save As	Save changes to an existing file using different settings
Print	Print the active file
Share	Invite others to view or edit the file online
	Send the file via email to others
	Present online (Word and PowerPoint only)
	Publish slides (PowerPoint only)
	Post to blog (Word only)
Export	Create a PDF or XPS version
	Change the file type
	Create a video (PowerPoint only)
	Package a presentation for CD (PowerPoint only)
	Create handouts (PowerPoint only)
Account	View and change the active Microsoft account
	Change the background and theme for the application window
	Connect to online services (OneDrive, YouTube, Facebook)
	Manage updates and subscriptions
Options	Control application settings
Close	Close the active document

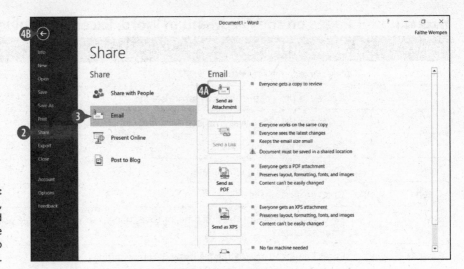

FIGURE 12-9:
After clicking File,
click a page and
choose the
command to
issue.

Creating a New Document

When you start an application, a Start screen appears. From there, you can choose a template on which to base a new document. (We're using *document* generically here to refer to a Word document, Excel workbook, or PowerPoint presentation file.) If you just want a blank file with default settings, press Esc to start one without having to choose a template. (Choosing the Blank template is the same as pressing Esc.)

You can also create additional new files without exiting and restarting the application. If you want an additional blank file with default settings, the easiest way is to press Ctrl+N. If you want a new file based on a template, follow these steps:

1. **Click the File tab and click New.**

   A gallery of templates appears.

2A. **Type a keyword in the Search for Online Templates box and press Enter.**

   OR

2B. **Click any template you want, as shown in Figure 12-10, and then skip to step 4.**

3. **In the search results shown in Figure 12-11, click the desired template to see details about it.**

4. **Click Create to download the template and start a new file based on it, as shown in Figure 12-12.**

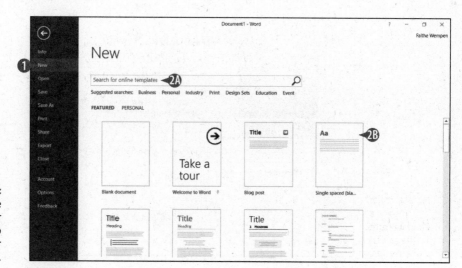

FIGURE 12-10:
Select a template thumbnail, or type a keyword to search for templates.

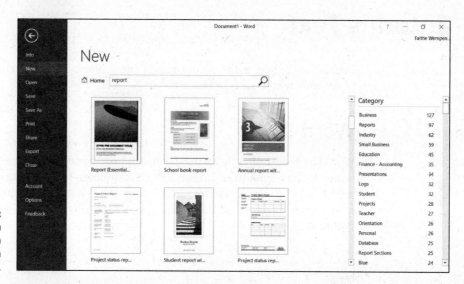

FIGURE 12-11:
Choose a template from the search results.

Depending on the template you choose, the document might not behave exactly like a blank document would. There might be pre-entered content, special formatting, or text placeholders. You're not locked into any of the content or formatting that comes with a template. You can delete any content that you don't want, and make any changes as desired.

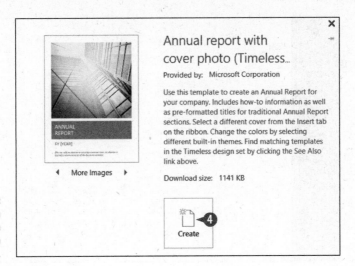

FIGURE 12-12:
Choose a
template from
the search
results.

Entering Text

Because of the layout differences among Excel, Word, and PowerPoint, the process of entering text in each program differs.

Word

Word places text directly on the document page (unless you happen to be using a template that employs text boxes, which is common for complicated layouts, like newsletters). To type text in a Word document, just start typing. The *insertion point* (a flashing vertical line) shows where the text you type will appear. (See Figure 12-13.)

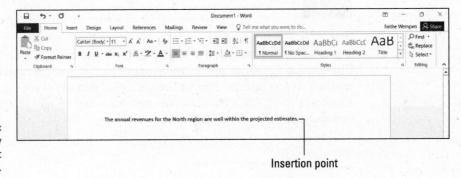

FIGURE 12-13:
Type text directly
on the document
page in Word.

Press Enter to start a new paragraph. (You don't have to press Enter at the end of each line, because Word wraps text to the next line automatically as needed.)

To edit text, press Backspace to erase the character to the left of the insertion point or press Delete to erase the character to its right. You can also select text (see "Selecting Text" in Chapter 13) and then press either of those keys to delete the selection or type new text to replace the selection.

Excel

Excel stores text in *cells*, which are boxes at the intersections of rows and columns. To type text in an Excel cell, click the desired cell to make that cell active, and then type.

TIP

It's okay if the text is so long that it doesn't fit in the cell. The text can spill over into cells to the right if they're empty. In Chapter 15 you learn how to format an Excel worksheet to correct cell width problems.

When you're finished typing in that cell, click a different cell or press an arrow key on the keyboard to move one cell in the direction of the arrow, or press Enter to move to the cell below the active one.

If you need to edit the text in a cell, double-click the cell to move the insertion point into it, or click the cell to select it and then make your edits in the formula bar, which lies between the Ribbon and the column headings. (See Figure 12-14.)

Formula bar

FIGURE 12-14: Type text and numbers into cells in Excel.

Insertion point

PowerPoint

PowerPoint places text in movable, resizable boxes on slides. Different slide layouts come with different placeholder boxes, and you can change layouts if you want a slide to have different placeholders. You can create your own text boxes, but you can't type text directly onto the slide. Everything has to be in some sort of box or frame. To place text in a placeholder, click inside it and start typing. At that point, text editing is the same as in Word. (See Figure 12-15.)

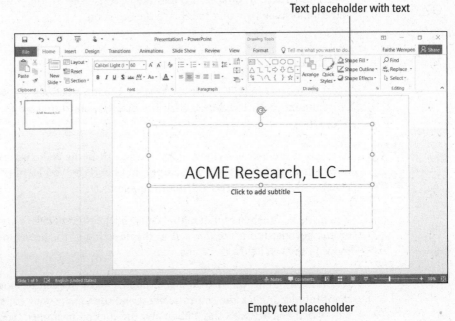

Text placeholder with text

Empty text placeholder

FIGURE 12-15:
Type text into
placeholders
on a slide in
PowerPoint.

Moving Around in an Application

As you work in one of the Office applications, you may add so much content that you can't see it all onscreen at one time. You might need to scroll through the document to view different parts of it. The simplest way to scroll through a document is by using the *scroll bars* with the mouse.

REMEMBER

Scrolling through a document with the scroll bars doesn't move the insertion point, so what you type or insert doesn't necessarily appear in the location that shows onscreen.

You can also get around by moving the insertion point. When you do so, the document view scrolls automatically so that you can see the newly selected location. You can move the insertion point by either clicking where you want it or using keyboard shortcuts.

Figure 12-16 provides a look at how to move around in a file using the scroll bar:

(A) Click a scroll arrow to scroll a small amount in that direction. In Excel, that's one row or column; in other applications, the exact amount varies per click.

(B) Click to one side or another of the scroll box (or above or below it on a vertical scroll bar) to scroll one full screen in that direction if the file is large enough that there's undisplayed content in that direction.

(C) Drag the scroll box to scroll quickly in the direction you're dragging.

(D) Hold down the left mouse button as you point to a scroll arrow to scroll continuously in that direction until you release the mouse button.

FIGURE 12-16:
You can use a scroll bar to move through a file.

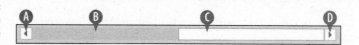

Figure 12-17 summarizes the ways you can move around by using the keyboard:

(A) Press an arrow key to move the insertion point or cell cursor in the direction of the arrow. The exact amount of movement depends on the application; for example, in Excel, one arrow click moves the cursor by one cell. In Word, the up and down arrows move the cursor by one line, and the right and left arrows move it by one character.

(B) Press Page Up or Page Down to scroll one full screen in that direction.

(C) Press Home to move to the left side of the current row or line.

(D) Press End to move to the right side of the current row or line.

(E) Hold down Ctrl and press Home to move to the upper-left corner of the document.

(F) Hold down Ctrl and press End to move to the lower-right corner of the document.

FIGURE 12-17:
You can use keyboard controls to move through a file.

Changing the View

All Office applications have zoom commands that make the data appear larger or smaller onscreen. Zoom is measured in percentage; 100 percent is the baseline. A lower number makes everything appear smaller and farther away; a higher number zooms in for a closer look at a smaller portion of the file.

Figure 12-18 shows how the zoom controls work:

(A) Click Zoom Out to decrease the zoom.

(B) Drag the slider to change the zoom quickly.

(C) Click Zoom In to increase the zoom.

(D) Click the current percentage to open the Zoom dialog box.

(E) Use the Zoom dialog box to select a preset zoom amount.

(F) Use the Zoom dialog box to select an exact numeric zoom value.

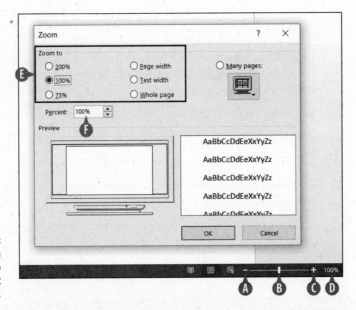

FIGURE 12-18: Each application enables you to zoom in and out on your data.

In addition, depending on what you're doing to the data in a particular application, you may find that changing the view is useful. Some applications have multiple viewing modes you can switch among; for example, PowerPoint's Normal view is suitable for slide editing, and its Slide Sorter view is suitable for rearranging the slides.

To change the view, use the buttons on the View tab, in the Views group. The views are different for each application. Figure 12-19 shows them for Word:

(A) The Views group contains buttons for the available views.

(B) Turn optional screen elements on or off with the check boxes in the Show group.

(C) The Zoom group provides an alternative method of controlling zoom.

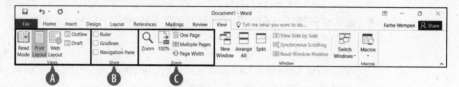

FIGURE 12-19:
Choose a view from the View tab.

Saving Your Work

As you work in an application, the content you create is stored in the computer's memory. This memory is only temporary storage. When you exit the application or shut down the computer, whatever is stored in memory is flushed away forever — unless you save it.

Each Office application has its own data file format. For example:

>> **Word:** Document files, `.docx`

>> **Excel:** Workbook files, `.xlsx`

>> **PowerPoint:** Presentation files, `.pptx`

>> **Outlook:** Outlook data files, `.pst`

Word, Excel, and PowerPoint use a separate data file for each project you work on. Every time you use one of these programs, you open and save data files. Outlook uses just one data file for all your activities. This file is automatically saved and opened for you, so you usually don't have to think about data file management in Outlook.

Each application has three important file types:

>> **Default:** The default format in each application supports most Office 2007 and higher features except macros. The file extension ends in the letter *X* for each one: Word is `.docx`; Excel is `.xlsx`; PowerPoint is `.pptx`.

» **Macro-enabled:** This format supports most Office 2007 and higher features, including macros. The file extension ends in the letter *M* for each one: `.docm`, `.xlsm`, and `.pptm`.

Macros are recorded bits of code that can automate certain activities in a program, but they can also carry viruses. The default formats don't support macros for that reason. If you need to create a file that includes macros, you can save it in a macro-enabled format.

» **97–2003:** Each application includes a file format for backward compatibility with earlier versions of the application (Office versions 97 through 2003). Some minor functionality may be lost when you save in this format. The file extensions are `.doc`, `.xls`, and `.ppt`.

The first time you save a file, the application prompts you to enter a name for it. You can also choose a different save location and/or file type. When you resave a previously saved file, the Save As dialog box doesn't reappear; the file saves with the most recent settings. If you want to change the settings (such as the location or file type) or save under a different name, choose File ➪ Save As.

Follow these steps to save a file for the first time:

1. Click the File tab, and click either Save or Save As (as shown in Figure 12-20).

Because you have not previously saved this file, the Save As page displays regardless of which you choose.

2. Click the general location in which to save:

- *This PC:* Saves to your own computer.

- *OneDrive:* Saves to your online OneDrive storage, which is a free Microsoft-provided online storage space associated with your Microsoft account.

3A. Click one of the recently used folders on the right side of the screen. These are all specific folders within the general location you chose in step 2.

OR

3B. Click Browse to open the location you chose in step 2 to its default folder.

4. Type the desired file name in the File name box, replacing the generic name there.

5. (Optional) Change the file type by choosing from the Save As Type drop-down list.

6. **(Optional) Change the save location, if desired.** See "Changing Locations When Saving or Opening Files," later in this chapter, for details.

7. **Click Save, as shown in Figure 12-21.**

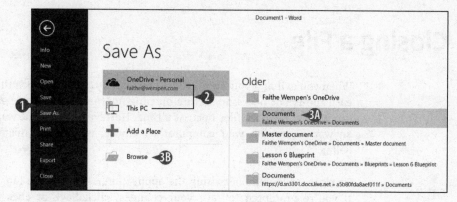

FIGURE 12-20: Choose File ⇨ Save As, and then select a general location in which to save.

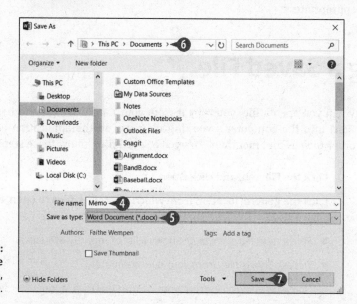

FIGURE 12-21: Specify a file name, location, and file type.

When you save your work on an already saved file, you can use File ⇨ Save or the Ctrl+S keyboard shortcut if you want to save using the same name, location, and file type. If you want to change any of those things, you must use File ⇨ Save As so that the Save As dialog box reopens.

TIP

If you want the Save As dialog box to appear immediately when you choose File⇨Save As, rather than show the general locations first on the Save As page, choose File⇨Options. Then in the Options dialog box, click Save on the left and then mark the Don't Show the Backstage When Opening or Saving Files check box.

Closing a File

When you exit an application, you automatically close any open files in it. Closing each file is not necessary before opening another file, because each application can have many data files open at a time. However, you might want to close files anyway to free up your computer's memory, which may make it run a little better.

To close a file without exiting the application, click the File tab and click Close. If you're prompted to save your changes, click Save or click Don't Save, as appropriate.

Opening a Saved File

When you open a file, you copy it from your hard drive (or another storage location) into the computer's working memory, so the application can access it in order to view and modify it. To open a saved file, follow these steps:

1. Click the File tab, and click Open.

2. Click the general location from which to browse files to open, as shown in Figure 12-22:

- *Recent (selected by default):* Shows a list of recently used files.

- *This PC:* Shows files from your own computer.

- *OneDrive:* Shows files from your online OneDrive storage.

3A. If you chose Recent in Step 2, click one of the files on the list. Skip the rest of the steps.

OR

3B. If you chose This PC or OneDrive in Step 2, click one of the location shortcuts that appear, or click Browse.

4. If needed, browse to a different folder. See "Changing Locations When Saving or Opening Files," later in this chapter.

5. Click the desired file name in the Open dialog box.

6. Click Open, as shown in Figure 12-23.

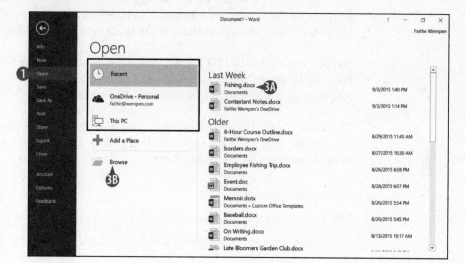

FIGURE 12-22: Select a location from which to browse available files to open.

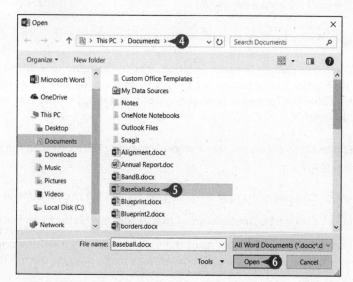

FIGURE 12-23: Choose the file to open and then click Open.

Changing Locations When Saving or Opening Files

Office 2016 uses the current Windows user's OneDrive as the default storage location. OneDrive is a secure online storage area hosted by Microsoft. Anyone who registers for the service, or who logs into Windows 8 or later with a Microsoft ID, is given a certain amount of free storage space, and can purchase more.

You can also save your files locally, where the default location is your Documents personal folder. In Windows, each user has her own, separate Documents folder (based on who is logged in to Windows at the moment).

To understand how to change save locations, you should first understand the concept of a file path. Files are organized into folders, and you can have folders *inside* folders. For example, you might have

>> A folder called Work

>> Within that folder, another folder called Job Search

>> Within that folder, a Word file called Resume.docx

The path for such a file would be

```
C:\Work\Job Search\Resume.docx
```

When you change the save location, you're changing to a different path for the file. You do that by navigating the file system via the Save As dialog box. The Save As dialog box provides several ways of navigating, so you can pick the one you like best.

Figure 12-24 points out some ways of changing the location in the Save As or Open dialog box.

(A) Click one of the right arrows on the address bar to open a menu of locations.

(B) Click the Up One Level arrow to go up one level in the folder hierarchy.

(C) The Quick Access list holds shortcuts to commonly used locations; you can place your own favorite locations here too by dragging them here.

(D) To browse your OneDrive from the top level, click OneDrive.

(E) To browse the local PC from the top level, click This PC.

(F) Click a location in the navigation pane to jump to that location.

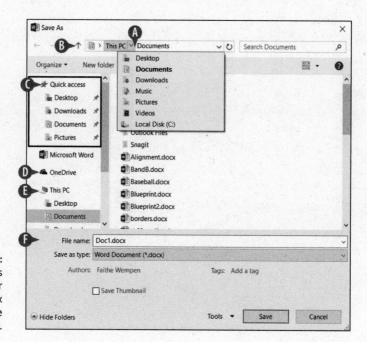

FIGURE 12-24:
Use the controls
in the Save As or
Open dialog box
to change
locations.

IN THIS CHAPTER

» Starting a new Word document

» Selecting and formatting text

» Applying themes and style sets

» Checking spelling and grammar

» Emailing a document to others

» Sharing a document in other formats

» Printing your work

Chapter **13**

Creating a Word Document

Microsoft Word is the most popular of the Office applications because nearly everyone needs to create text documents of one type or another. With Word, you can create everything from fax cover sheets to school research papers and from grocery lists to family holiday letters.

In this chapter, we explain how to create, edit, format, and share simple documents. If you read to the end of this chapter, you'll have a good grasp of the entire process of document creation, from start to finish, including how to share your work with others via print or email. Later chapters build on this knowledge, adding in the fancier aspects such as using styles, graphics, and multiple sections.

The type of formatting covered in this chapter is commonly known as *character formatting* (formatting that can be applied to individual characters). Character formatting includes fonts, font sizes, text attributes (such as italics), character spacing (spacing between letters), and text color. You can apply each type of character formatting individually, or you can use style sets or themes to apply multiple types of formatting at one time.

Starting a New Document as Word Starts

When you start Word, a Start screen appears, as shown in Figure 13-1. From there you can

(A) Click one of the shortcuts to recently used documents to reopen one.

(B) Click Blank Document to create a new, blank document. You can also press Esc to do this.

(C) Click one of the template thumbnails to start a new document with that template.

(D) Click in the Search for Online Templates box, type a keyword, and press Enter to look for more templates.

The Start screen shown in Figure 13-1 appears only when Word starts up; you can't get back to it without exiting Word and restarting. However, you can access all its features in other locations in Word at any time. You can choose File ⇨ New to start a new document (covered in Chapter 12) or press Ctrl+N to start a new blank document based on the default settings. Or, to access the list of recently used documents, choose File ⇨ Open.

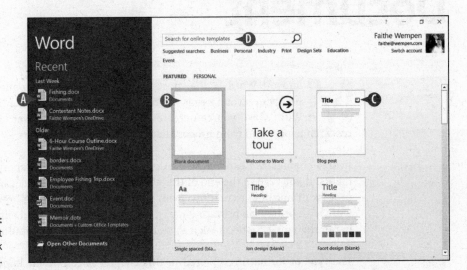

FIGURE 13-1:
From Word's Start screen, click Blank Document.

Even when you start a blank document, you're still (technically) using a template — a template called Normal. The *Normal template* specifies certain default settings for a new blank document, such as the default fonts (Calibri for body text and Cambria for headings), default font sizes (11 point for body text), and margins (1 inch on all sides).

TIP

If you stick with the default values for the Normal template's definition, the Normal template doesn't exist as a separate file. It's built into Word itself. You won't find it if you search your hard drive for it. However, if you make a change to one or more of the Normal template's settings, Word saves them to a file called `Normal.dotm`. If Word at any point can't find `Normal.dotm`, it reverts to its internally stored copy and goes back to the default values. That's useful to know: If you ever accidentally redefine the Normal template so that it produces documents with unwanted settings, or if it ever gets corrupted, all you have to do is find and delete `Normal.dotm` from your hard drive and you go back to a fresh-from-the-factory version of the default settings for new, blank documents. The template is stored in `C:\Users\user\AppData\Roaming\Microsoft\Templates`, where *user* is the signed-in username.

Selecting Text

When you apply formatting, it affects whatever is selected. Selecting blocks of text before you issue an editing or formatting command allows you to act on the entire block at one time. For example, you can select multiple paragraphs before choosing a certain text font, size, or color.

Here are some mouse methods of selecting text:

(A) Drag across the text with the mouse (with the left mouse button pressed) to select any amount of text, as shown in Figure 13-2.

FIGURE 13-2:
Select text by dragging across it.

(B) Double-click a word to select it (as shown in Figure 13-3, or triple-click within a paragraph to select the entire paragraph.

FIGURE 13-3:
Double-click a word to select it.

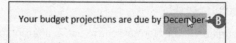

(C) Click to the left of a line to select that line (as shown in Figure 13-4); drag upward or downward from there to select additional lines.

FIGURE 13-4:
Click to the left of
a line to select it.

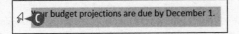
Your budget projections are due by December 1.

Here are some keyboard methods of selecting text:

>> Press Ctrl+A to select the entire document.

>> Move the insertion point to the beginning of the text and then hold down the Shift key while you press the arrow keys to extend the selection.

>> Press the F8 key to turn on Extend mode, and then use the arrow keys to extend the selection.

Choosing Between Manual and Style-Based Text Formatting

In the next several sections, you will learn various ways of applying manual formatting to text, such as changing the font, size, color, and effects. But are you sure that's what you really want to do? Give us a moment of your time to convince you that style-based formatting should be the norm and that manual formatting should be done only occasionally.

Word works best when you allow it to use its Styles feature to consistently format text based on the style applied to it. Later in this chapter, in the section "Changing the Style Set," we cover styles in detail, but here's a quick preview: A style is a named collection of formatting settings. The default style is called Normal, and in new, blank documents, it uses a font called Calibri. If you want to change the font used in your document, you can do it in one of these ways:

>> Select all the text and then manually apply a different font choice.

>> Redefine Normal style to use a different font, which you can do in any of these ways:

- Choose a different style set.

- Change the definition of the Normal style to use a different font.

- Apply a different theme that defines the Normal style differently.

>> Apply a different set of theme fonts that define the Normal style differently.

It might seem like you get the same result any way you go. However, as you start using other Word features that work using styles, you will realize that they aren't really the same.

Manual formatting overrides any formatting that comes from the style, so if you apply a font manually to a paragraph, that formatting will not change when you redefine the paragraph's style in a way that would otherwise change it. Therefore, if you try to do style-based formatting later with a document that you've manually formatted, you may find that your style-based formatting is not working as planned, perhaps in unexpected and frustrating ways.

Does that mean you should never use manual formatting? No. Manual formatting can be quite useful sometimes. For example, you might want to emphasize a particular word or phrase by making it bold, italic, or a different color. And, if you're creating a very short memo or letter and you're in a hurry, you might find that manual formatting is right for the situation.

However, if you're creating a multipage document that is going to hang around for a while, take a look at what style-based formatting has to offer. We cover applying different themes and changing style sets later in this chapter.

Removing Manually Applied Formatting

If you apply manual formatting to some text and then later decide that you would rather allow the formatting to be determined by the style, you can easily remove it. Just follow these steps:

1. **Select the text to affect.**

2. **Choose Home ⇨ Clear All Formatting (as shown in Figure 13-5). You can also press Ctrl+spacebar.**

FIGURE 13-5:
Remove manually applied formatting.

Changing the Text Font

The text in the document appears using a certain style of lettering, also called a *font* or a *typeface*. Office comes with dozens of typefaces, so you're sure to find one that meets the needs of whatever project you create. To change a font, follow these steps:

1. **Select the text to affect.**

   See the earlier section "Selecting Text" to learn some ways of selecting text.

2. **On the Home tab, click the down arrow to the right of the Font box. The Font list opens.**

   You can point at a font to see the selected text previewed in it before clicking to make your selection in Step 3.

   TIP

3. **Click the desired font.**

Notice that the Theme Fonts section in Figure 13-6 contains a (Headings) font and a (Body) font. These are the fonts that the document currently defines as the default heading and body fonts, respectively, based on the theme or style set in use. If you apply fonts from the Theme Fonts section, you aren't really applying the listed fonts manually; you're applying the placeholder. If the style definitions change, any text you have formatted using the choices in the Theme Fonts section will also change.

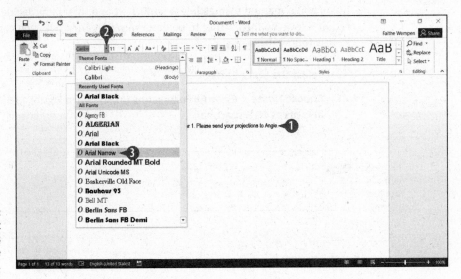

FIGURE 13-6:
Choose a font from the Fonts list on the Home tab.

Changing the Text Size

Each font is available in a wide variety of sizes. The sizes are measured in *points*. (The size it appears onscreen depends on the display zoom. You learn about zoom in Chapter 12.) Text sizes vary from very small (6 points) to very large (100 points or more). An average document uses body text that's between 10 and 12 points and headings between 12 and 18 points. To change the text size, follow these steps:

1. **Select the text to affect.**

2. **On the Home tab, click the down arrow to the right of the Size box, as shown in Figure 13-7.**

    The Size list opens.

3. **Click the desired size.**

Here are a few points to remember about changing text size:

(A) Instead of completing Steps 2 and 3, you can alternatively click in the Size box and type a number directly. This is useful if you want a size that's not on the list. Word accepts decimal points in font sizes, so you can have 10.5-point text, for example.

(B) Clicking Increase Font Size increases the font size by one setting from the Size list. Depending on the size, that might be more than 1 point. For example, notice that the list jumps from 36 straight to 48.

(C) Clicking the Decrease Font Size button decreases the font size by one setting from the Size list.

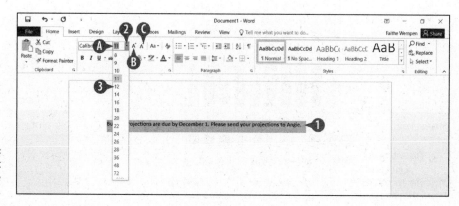

FIGURE 13-7: Choose a font size from the Size list.

Selecting Colors from a Palette

When selecting a color in Word or any other Office application (for text, borders, shapes, and so on), it's important that you understand how Office applications handle color. Take a moment to review this information, because you'll need it elsewhere in this book.

Every document, workbook, or presentation has a theme. Even plain blank ones have a theme (the default theme). One of the theme's duties is to define a set of color placeholders.

When you're choosing the color for an object, if you choose a color from one of these placeholders, that color choice is dependent upon the theme. If a different theme is applied that defines the colors differently, the object changes color.

As an alternative, Word also offers a set of colors it calls *standard* colors, which are fixed choices no matter which theme is applied.

When you make a color choice, you work with a palette like the one shown in Figure 13-8. Here are a few things to note about selecting colors:

(A) Click Automatic to return the selection to the default. On a white or light-colored background, Automatic is black; on a dark background, it's white.

(B) Click one of the theme colors, or a variant of one, to select a color that may change if the theme changes.

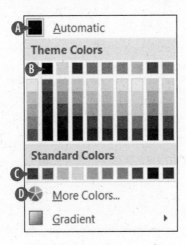

FIGURE 13-8: Select an appropriate color from the palette.

(C) Click a color from the Standard Colors area to choose a fixed color that will not change.

(D) Click More Colors to choose from a wider variety of standard colors.

If you choose More Colors, the Colors dialog box opens. This dialog box has two tabs: Standard and Custom.

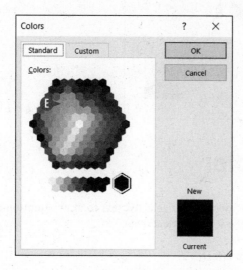

FIGURE 13-9:
The Standard tab
of the Color
dialog box.

(E) The Standard tab, as shown in Figure 13-9, contains swatches of common colors. Click the one you want.

(F) The Custom tab, as shown in Figure 13-10 contains a color grid. Click anywhere on the grid to select a color.

(G) The chosen color appears here.

(H) Drag this slider up or down to change the color's lightness.

(I) If you want a specific color that has a numeric value in a particular color model, select the color model here and then enter the numeric values.

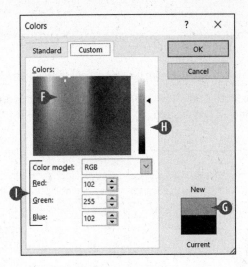

FIGURE 13-10:
The Custom tab
of the Color
dialog box.

Changing Text Color

You can choose a specific color for selected text to draw attention to it, or to dress up a document to make it more attractive.

1. **Select the text to affect.**

2. **On the Home tab, click the down arrow to the right of the Font Color button. A palette appears.**

TIP

To apply the color already shown on the face of the Font Color button, click the button face. Opening the palette is necessary only if you want a different color.

3. **Click the desired color, as shown in Figure 13-11.**

See "Selecting Colors from a Palette," earlier in this chapter, for guidance.

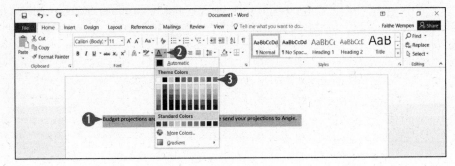

FIGURE 13-11:
Choose a
font color.

Applying Text Effects

Word supports two kinds of text effects. The basic ones, such as bold, italic, and underline, are supported by just about any word processing program you might work with. Stick to these if you're going to share the document with others who might not have a recent version of Word. The more advanced set, such as glow and outline, work only in Word 2007 and later. Figures 13-12 and 13-13 show the effects available of each kind.

FIGURE 13-12:
Basic effects, which work in almost any document format.

Bold	~~Double Strikethrough~~
Italic	Superscript[1]
Underline	Subscript[2]
Double Underline	SMALL CAPS
~~Strikethrough~~	ALL CAPS

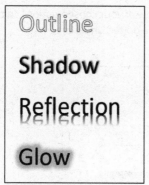

FIGURE 13-13:
Advanced effects, which may not translate well into other document formats.

Certain basic effects are available on the Home tab, in the Font group. To apply one of these, select the text and click its button. Figure 13-14 points out the available effects:

(A) Bold

(B) Italic

(C) Underline

(D) Strikethrough

(E) Subscript

(F) Superscript

FIGURE 13-14:
Some basic
effects can be
applied from the
Home tab on the
Ribbon.

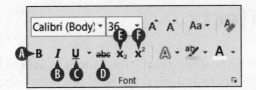

Other basic effects are available only in the Font dialog box. To open it, click the dialog box launcher in the Font group or press Ctrl+D. Figure 13-15 shows the Font dialog box:

(G) More underline styles are available from the drop-down list.

(H) You can use a different color for the underline than for the text.

(I) Double-strikethrough runs two horizontal lines through the text.

(J) Small caps make all letters capital style but retain their uppercase/lowercase statuses by the size of the letters.

(K) All caps makes all letters uppercase and the same height.

(L) The Preview area shows a preview of your chosen options. In this case, it shows small caps and italic with a dotted underline.

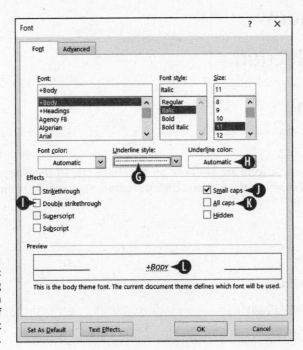

FIGURE 13-15:
The Font dialog
box provides a
complete set of
basic effect
options.

(M) To apply the effects shown earlier, in Figure 13-13, you must use the Effects button's menu, as shown in Figure 13-16. Point to an option on the menu to open its submenu, and then make your selection.

(N) For quick formatting, click one of these preset combinations of the various effects.

(O) Each menu option opens a submenu.

(P) Click the Options command at the bottom of the submenu to open a task pane where you can fine-tune the settings.

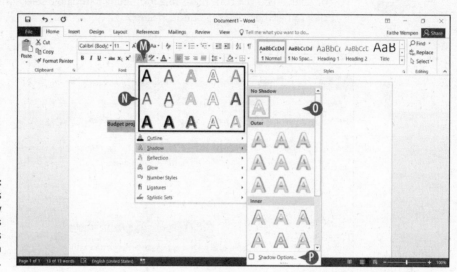

FIGURE 13-16: Use the Effects button to apply special effects such as the ones shown in Figure 13-13.

TIP

The Number Styles, Ligatures, and Stylistic Sets commands in Figure 13-16 affect the typesetting of the text in subtle ways; these options are rarely used except by publishing professionals.

Copying Formatting with Format Painter

It might take several different operations to get some text exactly the way you want it. Once it's perfect, you can copy its formatting to other text by using

Format Painter. This not only saves time but also ensures consistency. To format text with Format Painter, follow these steps:

1. **Select the text that already has the formatting you want to copy.**

2. **Click Format Painter, as shown in Figure 13-17.**

The mouse pointer appears as a paintbrush.

3. **Drag across the text that should receive the formatting.**

TIP

After Step 3, Format Painter shuts itself off automatically. If you want it to stay on so that you can copy that same formatting to multiple selections, double-click rather than click the button in Step 2.

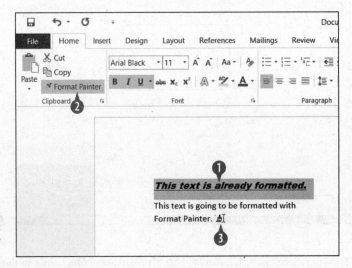

FIGURE 13-17:
Use Format Painter to copy formatting.

Changing the Style Set

In the section "Choosing Between Manual and Style-Based Text Formatting," earlier in this chapter, you see that each document has default definitions of the formatting. Formatting can be manually applied, or it can be indirectly changed by making a change to the underlying style applied to that text.

One way to change a document's look without manually tampering with individual paragraph settings is to apply a different style set. A *style set* is a collection of definitions for the most commonly used styles in a document, such as Normal, Heading 1, Heading 2, and so on. When you apply a different style set, you redefine these styles without having to manually do so.

1. **Start with a document that already has some text typed in it.**

   If you just want some dummy text to practice with and don't know what to type, type =RAND(5) and press Enter to generate five sample paragraphs.

2. **On the Design tab, roll the mouse over several of the samples in the Style Sets gallery to see the different formatting available.**

3. **Click the sample that best represents what you want.**

   Click More for more choices. (See A in Figure 13-18.)

FIGURE 13-18:
Apply a style
set from the
Design tab.

Applying a Different Theme

A *theme* is a named collection of settings for three types of formatting: fonts (one for headings and one for body), colors (one for each of 12 placeholders), and graphical object formatting effects. Themes are useful for ensuring document-wide consistency, but they go even further than that. Applying the same theme to multiple documents can ensure consistency across your entire library of work, including work you do in other Office applications, like Excel and PowerPoint.

Each document starts with a default theme applied, which it inherits from the template on which it's based. The Normal template by default uses a theme called Office. Follow these steps:

1. **On the Design tab, click Themes.**

2. **Click the desired theme, as shown in Figure 13-19.**

You can modify each of the theme's three aspects separately by choosing a color, font, or effect set from the Design tab. These sets do not correspond one-to-one with the themes on the Themes button's list; there are more color, font, and effect sets than there are themes (as shown in Figure 13-20):

(C) Click Colors and choose a different color set.

(D) Click Fonts and choose a different font set.

(E) Click Effects and choose a different effect set.

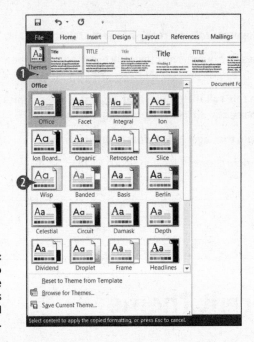

FIGURE 13-19:
Apply a theme to
affect the
document's
colors, fonts, and
effects.

FIGURE 13-20:
Change one
aspect of a theme
individually from
the Design tab.

Checking Spelling and Grammar

Word automatically checks spelling as you type, comparing each word to its dictionaries. If you type a word that doesn't appear, it places a wavy red (nonprinting) underline on it, flagging it for your attention.

You can right-click a red-underlined word to see spelling suggestions, as shown in Figure 13-21:

(A) Click a suggestion to change to it.

(B) Click Ignore All to mark this word as correct in the current document only.

(C) Click Add to Dictionary to mark this word as correct in this and all other documents.

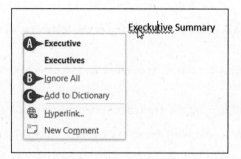

Grammar errors are similar, except that they appear with a wavy blue underline. A grammar error might be a usage error such as *is* versus *are* or a punctuation error such as too many spaces between words, as shown in Figure 13-22:

(D) Click a suggestion to change to it.

(E) Click Ignore Once to ignore this error but not errors similar to it.

(F) Click Grammar to open the Grammar task pane, which is explained next.

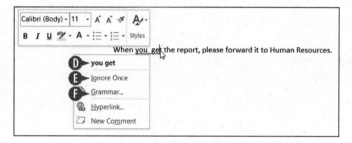

In a long document, you may find it easier to use the full Spelling and Grammar tool in Word rather than handle each underlined item individually. Here's how to use it:

1. **On the Review tab, click Spelling & Grammar, as shown in Figure 13-23.**

A task pane opens. It's either the Spelling task pane or the Grammar task pane, depending on which type of error it encounters first.

2. **In the Spelling task pane, you can do any of the following, as shown in Figure 13-24:**

   (A) Click Ignore to ignore this instance only but mark other instances in the same document.

   (B) Click Ignore All to mark this word as correct in the current document only.

   (C) Click Add to mark this word correct in this and all other documents.

   (D) Click a suggestion and then click Change to change this one instance to the selected word.

   (E) Click Change All to change all instances in the current document to the selected word.

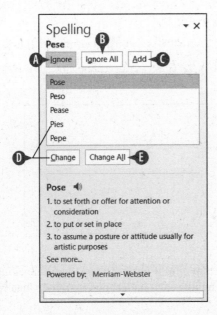

FIGURE 13-24:
Choose what to
do with a spelling
error.

3. **In the Grammar pane (shown in Figure 13-25), you can**

   (F) Click Ignore to mark this instance as correct.

   (G) Click the desired correction and then click Change.

4. **Keep working through the spelling and grammar errors that Word finds until you see a message that the check is complete.**

5. **Click OK, as shown in Figure 13-26.**

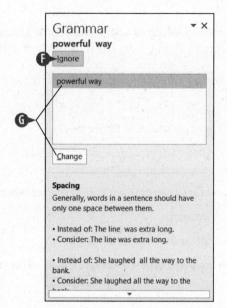

FIGURE 13-25:
Choose what to
do with a
grammar error.

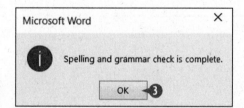

FIGURE 13-26:
Click OK to close
the message box.

TIP

To customize how the spelling and grammar are checked, choose File ⇨ Options and click the Proofing tab. You can add and remove words from custom dictionaries, ignore certain spelling and grammar errors, and set up automatic corrections for words you frequently mistype.

Emailing a Document to Others

Email can be an efficient way of delivering a document to other people. You don't have to leave Word in order to send it, as long as you have a compatible email application already configured on your computer, such as Microsoft Outlook.

(Word doesn't support web–based email applications such as Gmail and Yahoo! Mail for sending documents.) To email a document with Word, follow these steps:

1. **Click File, and click Share.**

2. **Click Email.**

3. **Click Send as Attachment (as shown in Figure 13-27).**

   A new email opens in your default email application. The file is already attached.

4. **Click in the To box and type the email address of the recipient.**

5. **Change the subject, if desired.**

   The default is the name of the file being attached.

6. **Click in the message body and type a message, if desired (as shown in Figure 13-28).**

7. **Click Send.**

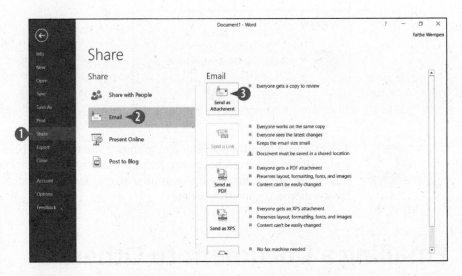

FIGURE 13-27: Choose to send a file as an attachment.

TIP

If the file is saved on a sharable drive, such as OneDrive, the Send a Link button is available, and in Step 3 you can choose to send a link rather than the attachment. Linking rather than attaching ensures that the recipient sees the latest version.

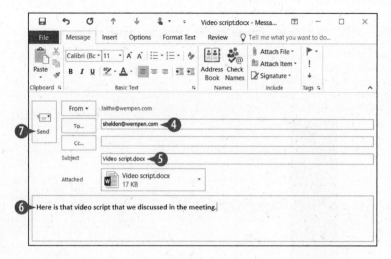

FIGURE 13-28:
Compose the
email message.

Saving a Document in Other Formats

When you share a document with other people, you're assuming that they have Microsoft Word or another application that opens Word files. These days, that's actually a pretty safe bet, with all the options available for opening Word files. WordPad, which comes free with Windows, opens Word documents, and the Word Online program at office.live.com is free to anyone with a Microsoft account.

Nevertheless, you might still want to convert a Word document to another format in some cases. For example, you could save a document in Word 97–2003 format for backward compatibility with early versions of Word, or you could save in Rich Text Format (.rtf) for compatibility with just about any word processing program in the world.

Here's how to save a document in another format:

1. **Click File ⇨ Export.**

2. **Click Change File Type.**

3. **Click the desired file type, as shown in Figure 13-29.**

4. **Click Save As.**

   The Save As dialog box opens.

   TIP

   Instead of Steps 1–4, you can choose File ⇨ Save, click Browse, and then change the setting in the File Type drop-down list.

5. **Navigate to the desired save location.**

6. If desired, change the filename, as shown in Figure 13-30.

The Save As Type setting should match what you chose in Step 3.

7. Click Save.

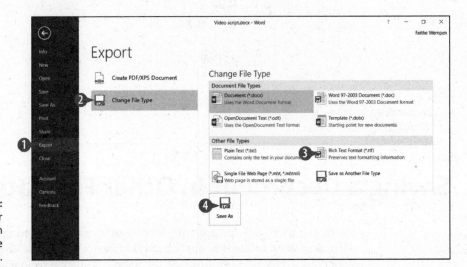

FIGURE 13-29:
Choose another
format in which
to save the
document.

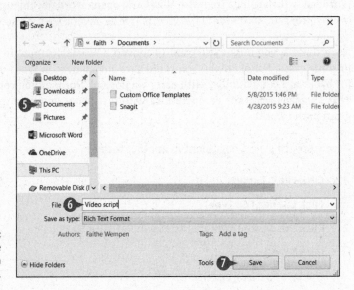

FIGURE 13-30:
An alternative
way of choosing a
Save format.

Creating a PDF or XPS Version of Your Document

You can also save your document in PDF or XPS format. These are both page layout formats, and files in this format are designed to show pages exactly as they will print. They are not designed to be easily editable. You might save a contract in this format, for example, or a ready-to-print brochure.

PDF stands for Page Description Format. It's a very popular format by Adobe. Anyone with the free application Adobe Reader can read PDF files. XPS is the Microsoft equivalent; it has similar features and properties, and can be opened using the XPS Reader application that comes with Windows Vista and later.

To create a PDF or XPS version of your document, follow these steps:

1. **Click File ⇨ Export.**

2. **Click Create PDF/XPS Document, as shown in Figure 13-31.**

3. **Click Create PDF/XPS.**

The Publish as PDF or XPS dialog box opens.

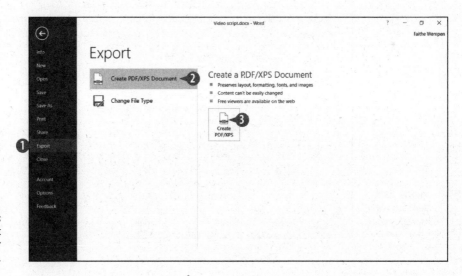

FIGURE 13-31:
Save a document as a PDF or XPS file.

4. **Change the filename in the File Name box (as shown in Figure 13-32), if desired.**

5. **Open the Save As Type drop-down list and choose PDF or XPS Document.**

6. **In the Optimize For section, click Standard or Minimum Size.**

In Step 5, use Standard in most cases. Minimum Size decreases the resolution of the file as it decreases its size. The smaller size may be useful when sending a document via email, as long as the document's quality (resolution) is not important.

After Step 6 you can click the Options button to see a dialog box containing even more options for the resulting PDF or XPS file.

7. **Mark or clear the Open File after Publishing check box.**

If marked, this option opens the PDF or XPS file in an appropriate reader application, outside of Word, after you save.

8. **Click Publish.**

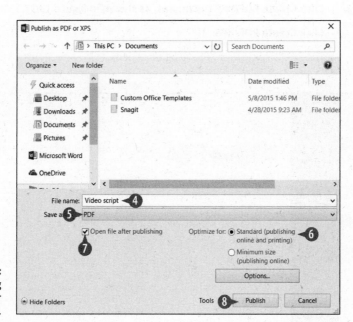

FIGURE 13-32:
Specify saving options for your PDF or XPS file.

Printing Your Work

To print a hard copy of your work, first make sure you have a printer set up in Windows. Follow the instructions that come with a new printer to set it up, or use the Add Printer Wizard in Windows to install a driver for an existing printer. (See the Devices and Printers section of the Control Panel.)

After the printer is set up and ready, follow these steps.

1. **(Optional) If you want to print only a certain part of the document, select the part you want to print.**

2. **Click File, and click Print.**

3. **In the Printer section, make sure the correct printer name appears. If needed, open the drop-down list and choose a different printer, as shown in Figure 13-33).**

4. **In the Copies box, type the number of copies you want, or use the up or down increment arrows to change the setting.**

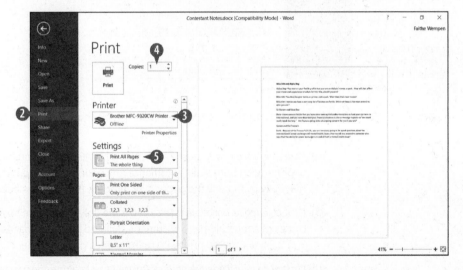

FIGURE 13-33:
Check the printer name and other settings.

5. **In the Settings section, if you don't want to print the entire document, do any of the following:**

    (A) Open the drop-down list and choose Print Selection. If you didn't select anything in Step 1, this option is not available.

(B) Open the drop-down list and choose Print Current Page.

(C) Type page numbers in the Pages box. You can specify a contiguous range with a hyphen, like this: 13-15. You can specify individual pages by separating them with commas, like this: 2, 4, 5. Specifying a page range automatically sets the drop-down list setting to Custom Print, as shown in Figure 13-34.

FIGURE 13-34:
Set the print range if you don't want to print the entire document.

6. **Set any other printing options you want, as shown in Figure 13-35. For example:**

(A) *Print one-sided or two-sided:* When you click this button, you have the option of printing on both sides automatically (if your printer supports it) or manually by flipping the paper over after the first side has been printed.

(B) *Print collated or uncollated:* This is an issue only when printing multiple copies of a multiple-page document. Collated prints the pages in sets (1, 2, 3, 1, 2, 3); uncollated prints all copies of each page together (1, 1, 2, 2, 3, 3).

(C) *Portrait or landscape orientation:* Portrait prints along the narrow edge of the paper; landscape prints along the wide edge.

(D) *Paper size:* Change this setting to correspond to the actual paper size you're using.

(E) *Margins:* Change to a preset such as Wide or Narrow, or choose Custom Margins to enter your own settings.

(F) *Pages per sheet:* The default is 1, but you can print multiple pages per sheet, shrinking each page so that they all fit. You probably won't be able to read each page very well, though.

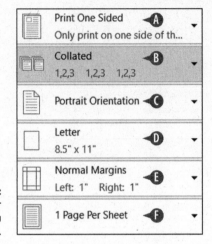

7. **When all the settings are the way you want them, click Print, as shown in Figure 13-36.**

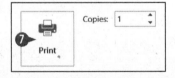

Word has a Quick Print feature that enables you to print with the default settings with a single click. It's not readily available by default, though. To add it to the Quick Access toolbar:

1. **Click the Customize Quick Access Toolbar arrow.**

2. **Choose Quick Print, as shown in Figure 13-37.**

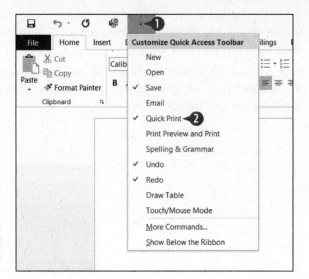

FIGURE 13-37:
Add Quick Print
to the Quick
Access toolbar.

IN THIS CHAPTER

» **Changing a paragraph's horizontal alignment**

» **Indenting a paragraph**

» **Adjusting a paragraph's vertical spacing**

» **Creating a bulleted or numbered list**

» **Setting the margins**

» **Setting page size and orientation**

» **Creating page headers and footers**

» **Creating page breaks**

» **Setting up multicolumn documents**

» **Adding line numbers**

Chapter **14**

Formatting Paragraphs, Sections, Pages, and Documents

aragraphs are essential building blocks in a Word document. Every time you press Enter, you start a new paragraph. If you've ever seen a document where the author didn't use paragraph breaks, you know how important paragraphs can be. They break up the content into more easily understandable chunks, which helps the reader both visually and logically.

Paragraph formatting is formatting that affects whole paragraphs and cannot be applied to individual characters. For example, line spacing is a type of paragraph formatting, along with indentation and alignment.

If you apply paragraph formatting when no text is selected, the formatting affects the paragraph in which the insertion point is currently located. If you apply paragraph formatting when text is selected, the formatting affects every paragraph included in that selection, even if only one character of the paragraph is included. Being able to format paragraphs this way is useful because you can select multiple paragraphs at a time and then format them as a group.

Some types of formatting cannot be applied to individual words or paragraphs, but only to entire pages and sections at a time. For example, you can't set the paper size or orientation for individual paragraphs.

In this chapter, you learn how to apply various types of formatting to paragraphs, pages, and documents.

Changing a Paragraph's Horizontal Alignment

The horizontal alignment choices are Align Text Left, Center, Align Text Right, and Justify. Figure 14-1 shows an example of each of the alignment types. Each of these is self-evident except the last one: *Justify* aligns both the left and right sides of the paragraph with the margins, stretching out or compressing the text in each line as needed to make it fit. The final line in the paragraph is exempt and appears left-aligned.

This paragraph is left-aligned. Each line begins at the left margin. This paragraph is left-aligned. Each line begins at the left margin. This paragraph is left-aligned. Each line begins at the left margin. This paragraph is left-aligned. Each line begins at the left margin.

This paragraph is centered. Each line is centered at the midpoint between the margins. This paragraph is centered. Each line is centered at the midpoint between the margins. This paragraph is centered. Each line is centered at the midpoint between the margins.

This paragraph is right-aligned. Each line ends at the right margin, and begins in whatever position is required for that to happen. This paragraph is right-aligned. Each line ends at the right margin, and begins in whatever position is required for that to happen.

This paragraph is justified. Its lines are stretched so that they align with both the left and right margin. This happens for every line except the final one, which is left-aligned. This paragraph is justified. Its lines are stretched so that they align with both the left and right margin. This happens for every line except the final one, which is left-aligned.

FIGURE 14-1:
Example of horizontal alignment.

TIP

If you apply Justify alignment to a paragraph that contains only one line, it looks like it's left-aligned. However, if you then type more text into the paragraph so that it wraps to additional lines, the Justify alignment becomes apparent.

To affect a single paragraph, click anywhere in the paragraph and then set the alignment. To affect multiple paragraphs, select the paragraphs first.

Use the alignment buttons in the Paragraph group on the Ribbon's Home tab (see Figure 14-2) to set an alignment for one or more paragraphs. You can also use the keyboard shortcut for a button:

(A) Left (Ctrl+L)

(B) Center (Ctrl+E)

(C) Right (Ctrl+R)

(D) Justify (Ctrl+J)

FIGURE 14-2:
Use the alignment buttons on the Home tab.

Indenting a Paragraph

The *indentation* of a paragraph refers to the way its left and/or right sides are inset. In addition to a left and right indent value, each paragraph can optionally have a special indent for the first line. If the first line is indented more than the rest of the paragraph, it's known as a *first-line indent*. (Clever name.) If the first line is indented less than the rest of the paragraph, it's called a *hanging indent*. Take a look at some examples in Figure 14-3. You should also look at the indentation controls in Figure 14-4. Here are some things to remember about indenting paragraphs:

(A) When a paragraph has no indentation, it's allowed to take up the full range of space between the left and right margins.

(B) When you set indentation for a paragraph, its left and/or right sides are inset by the amount you specify. Many people like to indent quotations to set them apart from the rest of the text for emphasis, for example.

(C) First-line indents are sometimes used in reports and books to help the reader's eye catch the beginning of a paragraph. In layouts with vertical space between paragraphs, however, first-line indents are less useful because it's easy to see where a new paragraph begins without that help.

(D) Hanging indents are typically used to create listings. In a bulleted or numbered list, the bullet or number hangs off the left edge of the paragraph, in a hanging indent. However, in Word, when you create bulleted or numbered lists (covered later in this lesson), Word adjusts the paragraph's hanging indent automatically, so you don't have to think about it.

To increase or decrease a paragraph's left indent:

(E) Click the Decrease Indent button to move the paragraph's left indentation a half-inch to the left.

(F) Click the Increase Indent button to move the paragraph's left indentation a half-inch to the right.

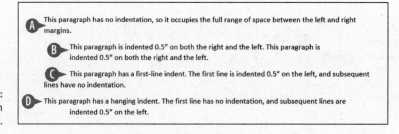

FIGURE 14-3:
Indentation examples.

A — This paragraph has no indentation, so it occupies the full range of space between the left and right margins.

B — This paragraph is indented 0.5" on both the right and the left. This paragraph is indented 0.5" on both the right and the left.

C — This paragraph has a first-line indent. The first line is indented 0.5" on the left, and subsequent lines have no indentation.

D — This paragraph has a hanging indent. The first line has no indentation, and subsequent lines are indented 0.5" on the left.

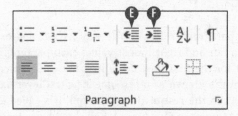

FIGURE 14-4:
Controls for changing indentation on the Ribbon.

Paragraph

You can also change indentation by dragging indent markers on the ruler.

TIP

If the ruler doesn't appear, select the Ruler check box on the View tab.

Select the paragraphs to affect and then drag a marker (see Figure 14-5), as follows:

(G) The upper triangle on the left is the First Line Indent marker. Drag it to affect only the first line.

(H) The lower triangle on the left is the Hanging Indent marker. Drag it to affect all except the first line.

(I) The square on the left is the Left Indent marker. Drag it to affect all lines on the left. If you drag it when the First Line Indent and Hanging Indent markers are set to different values, it moves them both, maintaining the relative distance between them.

(J) The triangle on the right is the Right Indent marker. Drag it to affect the right indent (all lines).

(K) The margins for the entire document are indicated by the spot where gray meets white on the ruler. You can drag that spot to change the margins for the whole document (not just the selected paragraphs).

FIGURE 14-5: Drag markers on the ruler to change indents.

You can also create a first-line indent by positioning the insertion point at the beginning of a paragraph and pressing the Tab key. Normally this would place a half-inch tab at the beginning of the paragraph, but the Word AutoCorrect feature immediately converts it to a real first-line indent for you.

To set left and/or right indents with precise numeric values, use the Left and Right text boxes on the Layout tab, in the Paragraph group (see Figure 14-6). For each of these, enter a number or use the increment buttons:

(L) Left indent.

(M) Right indent.

FIGURE 14-6: You can use the Layout tab's Paragraph group to control left and right indentation.

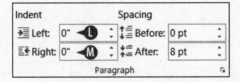

For the ultimate in indent control, follow these steps to use the Paragraph dialog box (shown in Figure 14-7):

1. Select the paragraph(s) to affect.

2. Click the dialog box launcher in the Paragraph group on either the Home or Layout tab.

3. **Set left and right indents in the Left and Right text boxes, respectively (see Figure 14-8).**

4. **(Optional) Open the Special drop-down list and choose First Line or Hanging.**

5. **Enter the amount of first-line or hanging indent in the By box.**

6. **Click OK.**

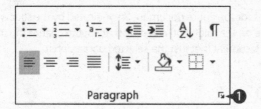

FIGURE 14-7:
Click the dialog
box launcher.

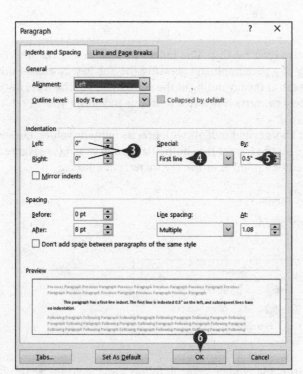

FIGURE 14-8:
Set up indents in
the Paragraph
dialog box.

Adjusting a Paragraph's Vertical Spacing

Vertical spacing refers to the amount of space (also known as the *leading*) between each line. A paragraph has three values you can set for its spacing:

>> **Line spacing:** The space between the lines within a multiline paragraph

>> **Before:** Extra spacing added above the first line of the paragraph

>> **After:** Extra spacing added below the last line of the paragraph

Adjust line spacing within the paragraph

To change the line spacing, follow these steps:

1. Select all the paragraphs to affect.

2. On the Home tab, in the Paragraph group, click the Line and Paragraph Spacing button to open its menu.

3. Click a number that represents the line spacing you want: 1.0 is single-spaced, 2.0 is double-spaced (one blank line between each line), and so on (see Figure 14-9).

   The exact amount of space in points depends on the font size used.

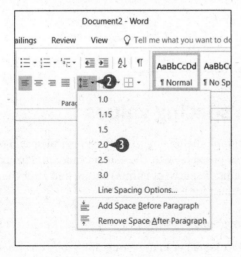

FIGURE 14-9: Choose a line spacing amount for the selected paragraphs.

Adjust spacing before or after the paragraph

To change the spacing before or after the paragraph(s), follow these steps:

1. **Select all the paragraphs to affect.**

2. **On the Home tab, in the Paragraph group, click the Line and Paragraph Spacing button to open its menu.**

3. **Click the Add Space or Remove Space command for before or after the paragraph as needed (see Figure 14-10).**

   The default amount of space before a paragraph is 12 points, and the default amount after a paragraph is 8 points, both regardless of font size.

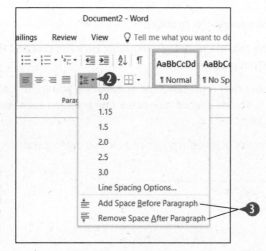

FIGURE 14-10:
Turn the spacing before and/or after the paragraph on or off.

Use custom spacing values

You can use the Paragraph dialog box to control vertical spacing for much more precise control than is possible with the Ribbon method. For example, you can specify a certain amount of space (in points) before and after the paragraph, and you can use custom values for line spacing.

1. **Select all the paragraphs to affect.**

2. **Click the dialog box launcher in the Paragraph group on either the Home or Layout tab (see Figure 14-11).**

3. **In the Spacing section, change the values in the Before and After boxes as desired (see Figure 14-12).**

4. **Open the Line spacing drop-down list and choose a unit of measurement:**

   - *Single:* No extra space between lines.

   - *1.5 lines:* One-half a line of extra space between lines. The actual amount of space depends on the largest font size used in the paragraph.

   - *Double:* One line of extra space between lines. The actual amount of space depends on the largest font size used in the paragraph.

   - *At least:* Sets the minimum line height to a precise amount for each line of the paragraph. Depending on the largest font size used in the paragraph, the actual amount of space each line occupies may be greater than the setting.

   - *Exactly:* Sets a precise line height for each line of the paragraph and does not take font size into consideration.

WARNING

     If you aren't sure what font sizes you will be using in the final version of your document, don't use Exactly. If you specify a line height that is smaller than needed for the font size you have chosen, some letters may appear cut off at the top or bottom.

   - *Multiple:* Like Double except that you specify the multiplier. For example, entering 3 results in triple-spacing (two blank lines between each line). You can use decimal places in the number, such as 3.25.

5. **Enter the measurement in the At box if a measurement is required for the setting you chose in Step 4.**

6. **Click OK.**

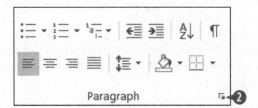

FIGURE 14-11:
Click the dialog
box launcher.

Paragraph

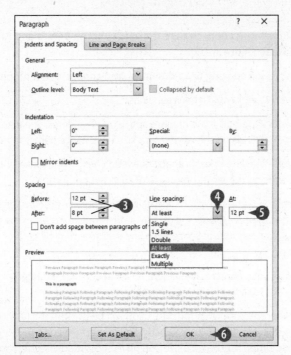

FIGURE 14-12:
Adjust line
spacing in
the Paragraph
dialog box.

Creating a Bulleted or Numbered List

Use a bulleted list for lists where the order of items isn't significant and the same "bullet" character (such as · or ⇨) is used in front of each item. You might use a bulleted list for a packing list for a trip, for example, or a to-do list.

Use a numbered list for lists where the order of items is significant and where a sequential step number is used to indicate order. A numbered list might contain the steps for a recipe or a meeting agenda.

Word makes it easy to create bulleted and numbered lists in your documents. You can create a list from existing paragraphs, or you can turn on the list feature and type the list as you go.

Convert text to a list

To convert existing text to a list, follow these steps:

1. **Select the paragraphs to convert to a list.**

2. **On the Home tab, in the Paragraph group, click the Bullets button or the Numbering button (see Figure 14-13).**

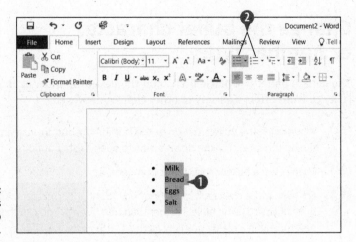

Type a new list

To enter new text into a list format, follow these steps:

1. **Position the insertion point at the desired location.**

2. **On the Home tab, in the Paragraph group, click the Bullets button or the Numbering button.**

3. **Type the first list item, and then press Enter.**

4. **Repeat Step 3 until the list is complete.**

5. **Press Enter twice in a row, or click the Bullets button or Numbering button again, to turn off the list feature (see Figure 14-14).**

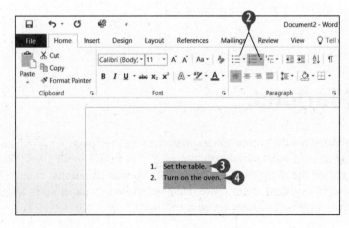

Change the bullet character or number type

The default bullet is a black circle, and the default number is an Arabic numeral (1, 2, 3). Word offers a variety of other choices, however.

(A) When using the Bullets button or the Numbering button, instead of clicking the button face, click the down arrow to open a list of options.

(B) Then select a bullet character or number type.

(C) For even more choices, click Define New Number Format (or Define New Bullet if you're using bullets rather than numbering). You can then set up a new format in a dialog box (see Figure 14-15).

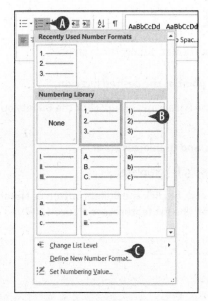

FIGURE 14-15: Choose a different numbering type.

Setting Margins

Margins are the empty spaces on each side of the page. A normal amount of margin (or at least what Word calls "Normal") is 1 inch on all sides. You might want to change the margins to accommodate special situations, though. (*Helpful hint:* If you're a student, don't try to make your research paper seem longer by increasing the margins. Teachers are wise to that trick.)

Word comes with several margin presets, such as Narrow (half–inch all around) and Wide (1 inch at the top and bottom and 2 inches on the left and right). You can also set custom margins, where you get to specify an exact number for each side of the page individually.

1. On the Layout tab, click the Margins button.

2A. Click one of the presets (see Figure 14-16). You're done.

OR

2B. Click Custom Margins to open the Page Setup dialog box to the Margins tab (see Figure 14-17).

3. Enter a value in the Top, Bottom, Left, and Right boxes.

TIP

The Gutter and Gutter Position settings are for situations where you're printing a double-sided publication that will be bound like a book. The margin closest to the binding should be somewhat larger than the rest to accommodate the binding; depending on whether it's an odd- or even-numbered page, that extra gutter amount should be either on the left or right side of the page. Using the Gutter setting ensures that each page has the gutter on the correct side.

4. Click OK.

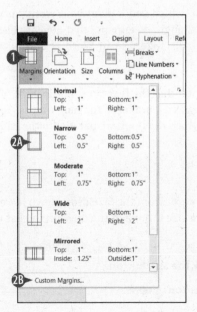

FIGURE 14-16: Choose a margin preset from the Margins button's drop-down list.

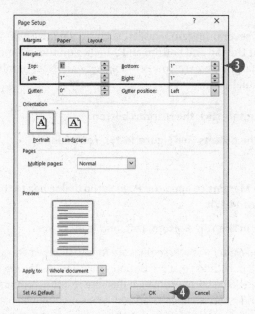

FIGURE 14-17:
Set custom
margins in the
Page Setup dialog
box, on the
Margins tab.

Setting Page Size and Orientation

Page size is the paper size on which you'll print your work. You have a page size even if you aren't printing, though; documents that appear onscreen have a page size too, of course. The default page size in Word is Letter, which is 8.5-x-11 inches.

Page orientation is the direction that the text runs on the page. The default is *portrait*, in which the lines of text are parallel to the narrower edge of the paper. The alternative is *landscape*, in which the lines are parallel to the wider edge.

Set page size

You can choose a page size preset from the Size drop-down list on the Layout tab, or you can set a custom page size if none of the ones on the list matches the page size you want.

1. On the Layout tab, click the Size button.

2A. Click one of the presets. You're done.

   OR

2B. Click More Paper Sizes to open the Page Setup dialog box to the Paper tab.

3A. Open the Paper size drop-down list and choose a preset (see Figure 14-18).

This list of presets is more extensive than the list on the Size button.

OR

3B. Enter the paper's measurements in the Width and Height text boxes (see Figure 14-19).

TIP

If you don't know what the paper size is called, it may be difficult to locate it by name on the list in Step 3A. You may find it quicker to enter its measurements in Step 3B.

4. Click OK.

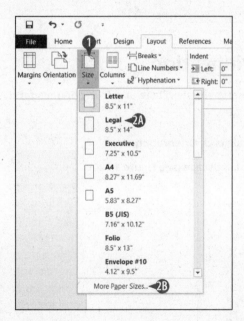

FIGURE 14-18: Choose a paper size preset from the Size button's drop-down list.

TIP

When printing a multipage document, you might want the first page to pull paper from a different paper tray in your printer. For example, it's common in multi-page business letters for the first page to be on letterhead and subsequent pages to be on plain paper. In the Paper Source area of the dialog box (refer to Figure 14-19), you can choose a different paper source for the first page and for other pages.

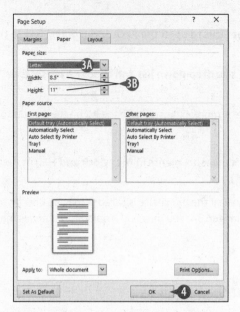

FIGURE 14-19:
Choose a custom
paper size in
the Page Setup
dialog box, on the
Paper tab.

Set page orientation

Page orientation is pretty simple: There aren't any options for it. Here's how you do it:

1. **On the Layout tab, click Orientation.**

2. **Click Portrait or Landscape (see Figure 14-20).**

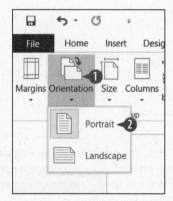

FIGURE 14-20:
Switch between
portrait and
landscape
orientations.

Adding Page Headers and Footers

Headers and footers contain content that repeats at the top and bottom of each page, respectively, outside of the top and bottom margins. Every document has a header and footer area, which are both empty by default. The header and footer appear in Print Layout view, Read Mode, and Web Layout view, and also on the printed page. (If you're in Draft view, you might want to switch to Print Layout view to follow along in this section more easily.)

You can place text in the header and footer that repeats on every page, and you can insert a variety of codes in them that display information such as page numbers, dates, and times.

Number the pages

Have you ever dropped a stack of papers that needed to stay in a certain order? If the pages were numbered, putting them back together was fairly simple. If not, what a frustrating, time-consuming task.

Fortunately, Word makes it easy to number your document pages. And you can choose from a variety of numbering styles and formats. When you number pages in Word, you don't have to manually type the numbers onto each page. Instead, you place a code in the document that numbers the pages automatically. Sweet!

When you use the Page Number feature in Word, it automatically inserts the proper code in either the header or the footer so that each page is numbered consecutively.

TIP

Page numbers are visible only in Print Layout view, Read mode, Print Preview, and on the printouts themselves. You don't see the page numbers if you're working in Draft view or Web Layout view, even though they're there.

To number pages, follow these steps:

1. **On the Insert tab, click Page Number.**

   A menu appears.

2. **Point to Top of Page or Bottom of Page, depending on where you want the page numbers (see Figure 14-21).**

   A submenu appears.

3. **Click one of the presets.**

   The document enters Header/Footer mode, and the new page number appears in either the header or footer.

The Plain Number 1, 2, and 3 presets are identical except for the placement of the page number, on the left, center, or right, respectively.

4. **If you want to further edit the header or footer, do so. Otherwise, double-click in the main part of the document to exit from Header/Footer mode.**

In Step 4 you can also click Close Header and Footer on the Header & Footer Tools Design tab to return to normal editing.

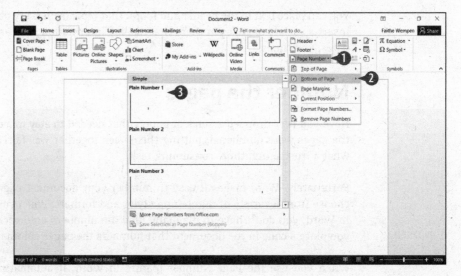

FIGURE 14-21:
Choose a page number position.

Here are some additional things you can do with page numbers in Word from the Page Number button's list (refer to Figure 14-21):

>> Point to Page Margins for a selection of presets in which the page numbers appear in the right or left margin area.

>> Point to Current Position for a selection of presets that enable you to place the page number code in the body of the document rather than in the header or footer.

>> Click Format Page Numbers to open a dialog box in which you can select a page number format. *Format* in this context does not mean font, size, or color; instead, it means the numbering format, like Arabic numerals (1, 2, 3) versus Roman numerals (I, II, III).

>> Click Remove Page Numbers to remove all page numbering codes.

Type text in the header or footer area

In addition to a page number, you can put other content in the header and footer areas of your document. For example, if you're typing the minutes of a club meeting, you might want to put the club's name in the header so that it appears across the top of each page.

Here are two ways to put content into them: You can use presets to insert codes and formatting, or you can type text and insert codes manually into the headers and footers.

To use a preset, follow these steps:

1. On the Insert tab, click the Header button, or click the Footer button.

2. Click one of the presets that appears on the list (see Figure 14-22).

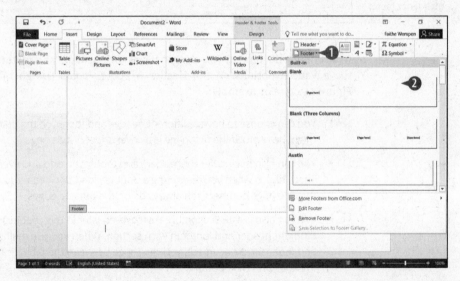

FIGURE 14-22: Choose a header or footer preset.

To create your own header or footer, follow these steps:

1A. In Page Layout view, double-click the top or bottom margin area of the page.

OR

1B. On the Insert tab, click the Header button or the Footer button and then choose Edit Header or Edit Footer from the menu that appears.

The Header & Footer Tools Design tab appears on the Ribbon.

2. **Position the insertion point where you want the header or footer text to appear.**

TIP

The header and footer have preset tab stops: a center tab stop in the center and a right-aligned tab stop at the right. So, in Step 2, if you want to place something in the center, press Tab once; if you want to place something on the right, press Tab twice.

3. **Type the text that you want to appear.**

4. **(Optional) If you want to switch between the header and footer, click Go to Header or Go to Footer.**

5. **Click Close Header and Footer (see Figure 14-23).**

FIGURE 14-23:
Type text into the
header or footer
area.

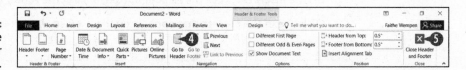

In a complex document, you can get fancy with headers and footers using some of the advanced options on the Header & Footer Tools Design tab, as shown in Figure 14-24. For example:

(A) You can choose to have a different header and footer on the first page. That might be useful if the first page is a cover sheet or title page.

(B) You can also have different headers and footers on odd and even pages. That's handy when you're printing a double-sided booklet, for example, so that the page numbers can always be on the outside edges.

(C) You can also create section breaks (covered later in this chapter) and have a different header and footer in each section. When you use multiple headers and footers in a document, you can move between them by clicking the Previous and Next buttons.

(D) To adjust the header and footer size and positioning, use the settings in the Position group. You can specify a Header from Top and Footer from Bottom position there. For example, if you want a taller header section, increase the Header from Top setting.

FIGURE 14-24:
Use the Header &
Footer Tools
Design tab to set
options for
headers and
footers.

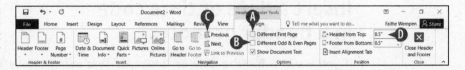

Insert a page number code in a header or footer

If you already have the header or footer open for editing (Steps 1 and 2 of the procedure in the preceding section), you can easily insert a page number code at the insertion point's current position by following these steps:

1. On the Header & Footer Tools Design tab, click Page Number.

2. Click Current Position (see Figure 14-25).

3. Click Plain Number.

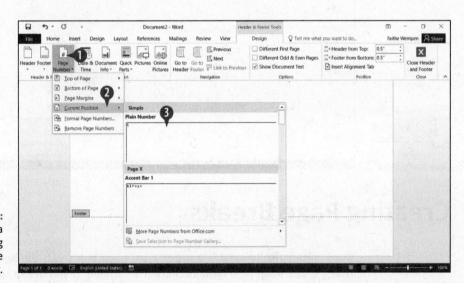

FIGURE 14-25:
You can insert a
page numbering
code at the
insertion point.

Insert a date or time code in a header or footer

If you want to insert a date or time code that automatically updates, follow these steps:

1. **On the Header & Footer Tools Design tab, click Date & Time.**

2. **Click the desired format.**

3. **Mark the Update Automatically check box (see Figure 14-26).**

4. **Click OK.**

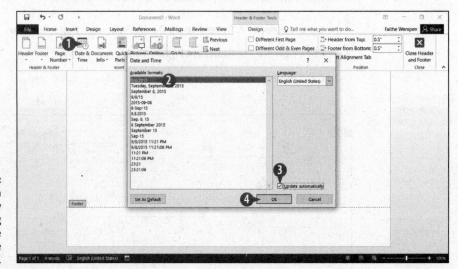

Creating Page Breaks

Word automatically creates a page break when you reach the bottom of a page. That's called a *soft page break* because it's variable. If you delete some content on the previous page, the page break point changes. You can also create *hard page breaks*, which are manually created breaks that don't change when the document content changes. For example, you might insert a hard page break to start a new chapter of a story on a new page.

The easiest way to create a hard page break is to press Ctrl+Enter. That way, you don't even have to take your hands off the keyboard. You can also choose Layout, Breaks, Page.

To delete a hard page break, move the insertion point to the top of the page that follows the break and then press Backspace.

TIP

If you have a hard time finding the page break to delete it, switch to Draft view.

Setting Up a Multicolumn Document

You can create two kinds of multicolumn layouts in Word: tabular and newspaper-style.

A *tabular* layout is a table that's used for text positioning. Create a table, as you can see in Chapter 15, and remove the borders from all cells. The text lines up neatly in the table columns, and your audience is none the wiser that you used a table to make the layout. A tabular layout can coexist in a document with normal text without using section breaks. Tabular layouts are good for aligning the entries in multiple columns with one another, such as a grid of names and addresses.

Newspaper columns, which we cover here, are entirely different: Text snakes down a narrow column from top to bottom and then starts up again at the top of the next column. To use varying numbers of newspaper-style columns in different parts of a document, you have to employ section breaks. Newspaper columns are good for creating newsletters, brochures, and other graphical publications.

Follow these steps to use multiple newspaper-style columns:

1A. To affect only certain paragraphs, select them.

OR

1B. Position the insertion point within the section that you want to affect.

If the document has no section breaks, the setting will apply to the entire document.

2. On the Layout tab, click Columns.

3. Click the number of columns you want.

(A) The Left and Right settings in Figure 14-27 represent 2-column layouts where one column is wider than the other.

(B) If you want more control over the column widths, choose More Columns from the menu, and then specify exact column widths in the Columns dialog box.

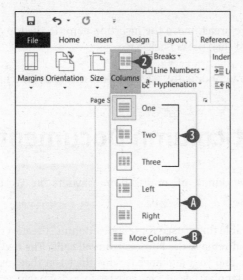

FIGURE 14-27:
Select a number
of columns.

If you selected certain paragraphs in Step 1A, Word creates two new section breaks in Step 3: one at the beginning of the selected text and one at the end of it. The setting you choose in Step 3 applies only to the section between those two breaks.

To return a section to using only one column, repeat the steps, selecting One as the number of columns.

Adding Line Numbers

Line numbering can help people refer to specific locations in the document more easily when they're collaborating on drafts. Some legal documents also make use of line numbers.

Line numbering is a document-wide setting (although you can apply it on a section-by-section basis, as with most other document formatting).

You can enable line numbering at a basic level by choosing a setting from the Line Numbers button's drop-down list on the Layout tab, as shown in Figure 14-28. Turn off line numbering by choosing None from this list (see Figure 14-28).

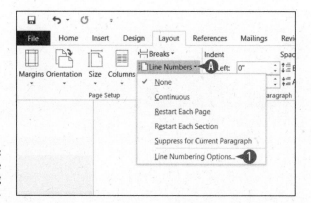

FIGURE 14-28:
Choose a line
numbering
setting.

For additional numbering options, follow these steps:

1. **On the Layout tab, click Line Numbers, and then click Line Numbering Options.**

   The Page Setup dialog box opens to the Layout tab.

2. **Click the Line Numbers button (see Figure 14-29).**

3. **Mark the Add Line Numbering check box.**

4. **Set any line numbering options you want.**

5. **Click OK.**

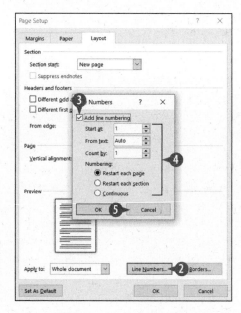

FIGURE 14-29:
Access the
Line Numbers
button from the
Layout tab.

» Moving between cells

» Selecting cells and ranges

» Entering and editing text in cells

» Using AutoFill to fill cell content and Flash Fill to extract content

» Copying and moving data between cells

» Inserting and deleting rows, columns, and cells

» Creating and managing multiple worksheets

Chapter **15**

Creating Basic Excel Worksheets

Excel has many practical uses. You can use its orderly row-and-column worksheet structure to organize multicolumn lists, create business forms, and much more. Excel provides more than just data organization, though: It enables you to write formulas that perform calculations on your data. This feature makes Excel an ideal tool for storing financial information, such as checkbook register and investment portfolio data.

In this chapter, we introduce you to the Excel interface and teach you some of the concepts you need to know. You learn how to move around in Excel, how to type and edit data, and how to manipulate rows, columns, cells, and sheets.

Understanding the Excel Interface

Let's start out with some basic terminology. A *spreadsheet* is a grid composed of rows and columns. *Spreadsheet* is a generic term, not an Excel-specific one. Excel calls each spreadsheet a *worksheet*. An excel file is a *workbook*. Here are a few other things to remember about the Excel interface:

(A) A workbook can have multiple worksheets. Each worksheet has a tab at the bottom of the screen; you can click a tab to switch to that sheet.

(B) At the intersection of each row and column is a *cell*. You can type text, numbers, and formulas into cells to build your spreadsheet (see Figure 15-1).

(C) The active cell has a thicker green outline around it called the *cell cursor*. Whatever you type is entered into the active cell.

(D) The content of the active cell appears in the formula bar. When the cell contains text or a fixed number, the formula bar content is the same as what you see in the cell. However, when the cell contains a formula, the cell shows the results of the formula, and the formula bar shows the formula itself.

(E) A cell's *address* consists of its column letter and row number. The active cell's address appears in the *Name box*.

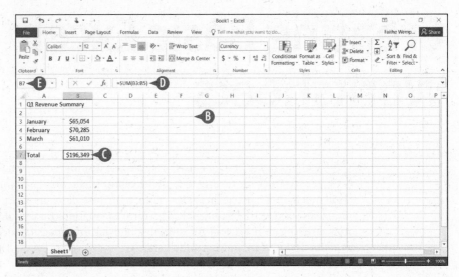

FIGURE 15-1: Cells are at the intersections of rows and columns.

Excel is very much like Word in many ways (see Figure 15-2). Here are some parts that might seem familiar from earlier chapters:

(F) The *Ribbon* is a multitabbed toolbar of commands to issue. Click a tab to switch to it.

(G) The *Zoom slider* controls the magnification of the work area. Drag the slider left or right to zoom out or in.

(H) Clicking File opens *Backstage view,* where you can save, open, and print files.

(I) *Scroll bars* enable you to move around in the worksheet.

(J) The *Quick Access toolbar* provides shortcuts to a few commonly used commands.

(K) Type in the Tell Me What You Want to Do box to ask a question if you don't know how to do something.

Now that you know what you're looking at, check out the next several sections, which tell you what you can do with it.

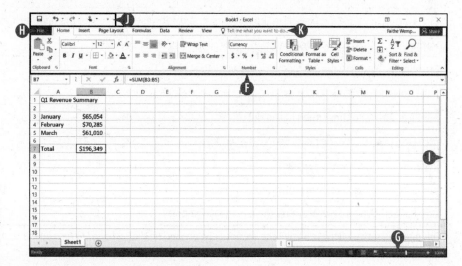

FIGURE 15-2:
Excel has a similar interface to that of other Office applications.

Moving Between Cells

To type in a cell, you must first make that cell active by moving the cell cursor there. As shown earlier, in Figure 15-1, the cell cursor is a thick green outline. You can move the cell cursor by pressing the arrow keys on the keyboard, by clicking the desired cell, or by using an Excel keyboard shortcut. Table 15-1 provides some of the most common keyboard shortcuts for moving the cell cursor.

REMEMBER

Scrolling with the scroll bar doesn't change which cell is active; it only changes which cells are visible, but it does not move the cell cursor. One common beginner mistake is to scroll to place the desired cell in view and then start typing without first clicking it to make it active.

TABLE 15-1   ## Cell Cursor-Movement Shortcuts

Press This	To Move Here
Arrow keys	One cell in the direction of the arrow
Tab	One cell to the right
Shift+Tab	One cell to the left
Ctrl+arrow key	To the edge of the current data region (the first or last cell that isn't empty) in the direction of the arrow
End*	To the cell in the lower-right corner of the window
Ctrl+End	To the last cell in the worksheet, in the lowest used row of the rightmost used column
Home	To the beginning of the row containing the active cell
Ctrl+Home	To the beginning of the worksheet (cell A1)
Page Down	One screen down
Alt+Page Down	One screen to the right
Ctrl+Page Down	To the next sheet in the workbook
Page Up	One screen up
Alt+Page Up	One screen to the left
Ctrl+Page Up	To the previous sheet in the workbook

This one works only when the Scroll Lock key has been pressed on the keyboard to turn on the Scroll Lock function.

Selecting Cells and Ranges

You might sometimes want to select a multicell *range* before you issue a command. For example, if you want to format all the text in a range a certain way, select that range and then issue the formatting command. Technically, a range can consist of a single cell; however, a range most commonly consists of multiple cells. Here are some things to note about cells and ranges:

(A)   In Figure 15-3, the range A1:F3 is selected. Range names are written with the upper-left cell address, a colon, and the lower-right cell address.

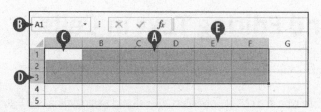

FIGURE 15-3:
The range A1:F3
is selected.

(B) The active cell is A1. The active cell's address appears in the Name box.

(C) The active cell within the range appears in white, and all other cells in the selected range are gray.

This points out the difference between the active cell and a multicell range. The active cell is significant when doing data entry; when you type text, it goes into the active cell only. The selected range is significant when you're issuing a command, such as applying formatting.

(D) To select a row, click its column letter. Drag across multiple column letters to select multiple columns.

(E) To select a column, click its row number. Drag across multiple row numbers to select multiple rows.

A range is usually *contiguous*, or all the cells are in a single rectangular block, though they don't have to be. You can also select *noncontiguous* cells in a range by holding down the Ctrl key while you select additional cells.

When a range contains noncontiguous cells, the pieces are separated by commas, like this: A1:C3,E3:E5. This range name tells Excel to select the range from A1 through C3, plus the range from E3 through E5. Figure 15-4 shows that range.

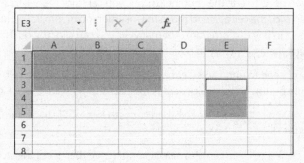

FIGURE 15-4:
A noncontiguous
range.

Entering and Editing Text in Cells

Here are some tips for entering and editing text:

(A) To type in a cell, simply select the cell and begin typing (see Figure 15-5). If you make a mistake when editing, you can press the Esc key to cancel the edit before you leave the cell.

(B) Notice that if you type an entry that is wider than the cell, it hangs into the next column. The solution to that is to widen the column using the Column Width dialog box. (Choose Format ⇨ Column Width to access this dialog box.)

When you finish typing, you can leave the cell in any of these ways:

- *Press Enter:* Moves you to the next cell down.

- *Press Tab:* Moves you to the next cell to the right.

- *Press Shift+Tab:* Moves you to the next cell to the left.

- *Press an arrow key:* Moves you in the direction of the arrow.

- *Click in another cell:* Moves you to that cell.

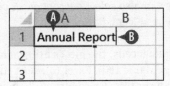

FIGURE 15-5:
Type directly into
a cell.

If you need to edit the content in a cell, you can click the cell to select it and then click the cell again to move the insertion point into it. Edit just as you would in any text program. Alternatively, you can click the cell to select it and then type a new entry to replace the old one.

(C) If you need to undo an edit immediately after you leave the cell, click the Undo button on the Quick Access toolbar, or press Ctrl+Z (see Figure 15-6).

(D) To clear a cell, select the cell; then choose Home ⇨ Clear ⇨ Clear Contents (see Figure 15-7).

To clear a cell, you can also select it and then either press the Delete key or right-click it and choose Clear Contents.

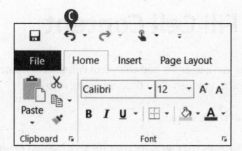

FIGURE 15-6:
Undo an edit.

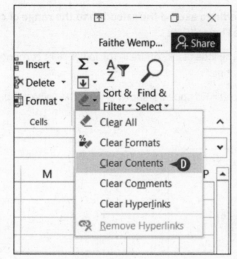

FIGURE 15-7:
Clear a cell's
content.

Don't confuse the Delete key on the keyboard (which issues the Clear command) with the Delete command on the Ribbon. The Delete command on the Ribbon doesn't clear the cell content; instead, it removes the entire cell. You find out more about deleting cells in the upcoming section "Insert and delete rows, columns, and cells."

And while we're on the subject, don't confuse Clear with Cut, either. The Cut command works in conjunction with the Clipboard. Cut moves the content to the Clipboard, and you can then paste it somewhere else. Excel, however, differs from other applications in the way this command works: Using Cut doesn't immediately remove the content. Instead, Excel puts a flashing dotted box around the content and waits for you to reposition the cell cursor and issue the Paste command. If you do something else in the interim, the cut-and-paste operation is canceled, and the content that you cut remains in its original location. You learn more about cutting and pasting in the section "Copying and Moving Data Between Cells," later in this chapter.

Using AutoFill to Fill Cell Content

When you have a lot of data to enter and that data consists of some type of repeat-able pattern or sequence, you can save time by using AutoFill.

To use AutoFill, follow these steps:

1. **Select the cell or cells that already contain an example of what you want to fill.**

2. **Drag the fill handle to extend the selection to the range of cells you want to fill (see Figure 15-8):**

(A) The *fill handle* is the little black square in the lower-right corner of the selected cell or range.

(B) As you drag, a ScreenTip appears, showing what the value will be in the final cell of the range.

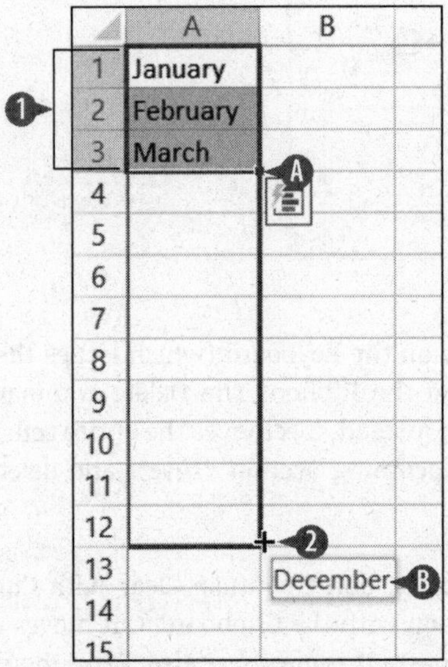

FIGURE 15-8:
Fill a range of cells by dragging the fill handle.

Depending on how you use it, AutoFill can either fill the same value into every cell in the target area or fill in a sequence (such as days of the month, days of the week, or a numeric sequence such as 2, 4, 6, 8). Here are the general rules for how it works:

(C) When AutoFill recognizes the selected text as a member of one of its preset lists (see Figure 15-9), such as days of the week or months of the year, it automatically increments those. For example, if the selected cell contains Monday, AutoFill places Tuesday in the next adjacent cell.

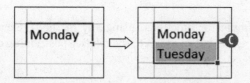

FIGURE 15-9:
AutoFill works on
commonly
occurring series.

(D) When AutoFill doesn't recognize the selected text, it fills the chosen cell with a duplicate of the selected text (see Figure 15-10).

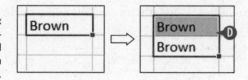

FIGURE 15-10:
AutoFill dupli-
cates the selected
text if it's not a
recognized series.

(E) When AutoFill is used on a single cell containing a number, it fills with a duplicate of the number (see Figure 15-11).

(F) You can click the AutoFill Options button to open a menu of other choices.

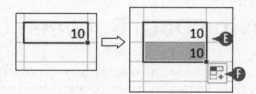

FIGURE 15-11:
AutoFill dupli-
cates a single
number.

(G) When Auto Fill is used on a range of two or more cells containing numbers, AutoFill attempts to determine the interval between them and continues filling using that same pattern (see Figure 15-12). For example, if the two selected cells contain 2 and 4, the next adjacent cell would be filled with 6.

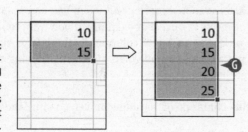

FIGURE 15-12:
AutoFill deter-
mines the interval
between multiple
selected numbers
and repeats that
pattern.

When you copy formulas or functions (using any method), Excel automatically adjusts the cell references in the copies to the relative positioning of the new locations (see Figure 15-13). For example:

(H) If you have =A1+A2 in cell A3 . . .

(I) . . . and you copy A3's formula into B3 . . .

(J) . . . the resulting formula in B3 will be =B1+B2.

This is called *relative referencing*, and it's covered in more detail in Chapter 16.

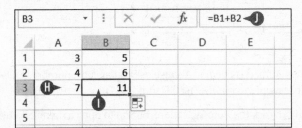

FIGURE 15-13: AutoFill works when copying formulas and functions.

Copying and Moving Data Between Cells

When you're creating a spreadsheet, it's common not to get everything in the correct cells on your first try. Fortunately, moving content between cells is easy.

Here are the two methods you can use to move content: Drag it with the mouse or cut/copy and paste using the Clipboard.

Copy and move using the mouse

Moving or copying with the mouse works well when you can see both the source and the destination locations at once. For example, if you want to move a range of cells a few rows up or down, or a few columns to the left or right, this is the method for you. It's not a good method when moving or copying between different worksheets or workbooks.

To move or copy the contents of a range of cells using the mouse, follow these steps:

1. **Select the range of cells to be moved or copied.**

2. **Position the mouse pointer at the dark outline around the selected range.**

The mouse pointer changes to a 4-headed arrow with a white arrow pointer on top of it.

3. **(Optional) If you want to copy (not move), hold down the Ctrl key and keep it down until you're finished with Step 4.**

   If you do this, the mouse pointer changes to a white arrow pointer with a small plus sign (+) on it.

4. **Drag the selection outline to the new location (see Figure 15-14).**

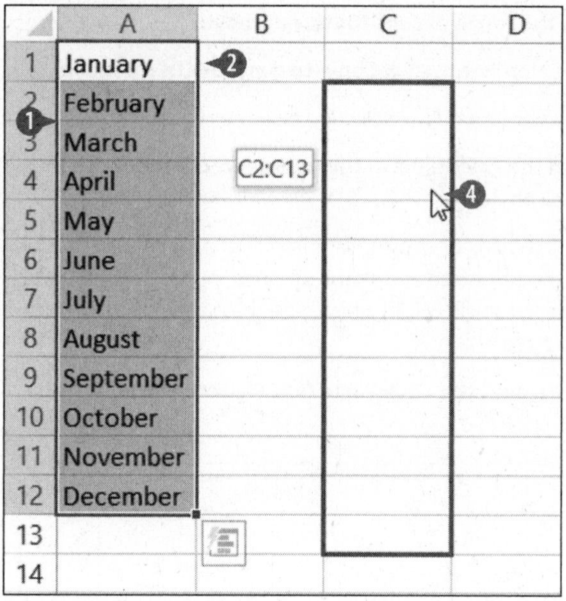

FIGURE 15-14:
Drag a selected range to a new location using the mouse.

Copy and move using the Clipboard

The *Clipboard* is a temporary holding area in Windows, designed for moving and copying content from one location to another. That statement is intentionally very broad because the Clipboard works with just about any type of content. You can use it to move files from one folder to another, or to move a selection of data in an application (like Excel) from one spot to another in the same data file or a different one.

You can think of the Clipboard like a real-life clipboard: You place something on it for temporary holding, and then when you get to the desired location, you retrieve the item.

The Clipboard works via a combination of the following commands:

>> **Cut:** Removes the item from its original location and places it on the Clipboard.

>> **Copy:** Places a copy of the item on the Clipboard, leaving the original in place.

>> **Paste:** Places a copy of whatever is on the Clipboard in the active location.

To copy, you use a combination of Copy and Paste; to Move, use Cut and Paste:

1. **Select the range of cells to copy or move.**

2. **On the Home tab, click Copy (to copy) or Cut (to move).**

   The border around the selection becomes dashed temporarily.

3. **Click in the cell that is in the upper-left corner of the area into which you want to paste.**

TIP

   If you're moving or copying a multicell range with the Clipboard, you can either select the same size and shape of range for the destination in Step 3 or you can select a single cell, in which case the paste occurs with the selected cell in the upper-left corner.

4. **On the Home tab, click Paste (see Figure 15-15).**

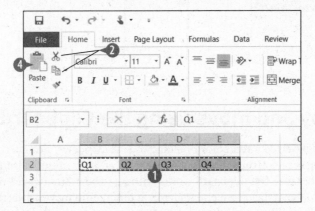

FIGURE 15-15:
Cut or copy, and then paste.

Because the Clipboard is a popular tool, there are many ways to use it. Table 15-2 summarizes the different ways to issue each of the three basic Clipboard commands.

TABLE 15-2

Methods of Cutting, Copying, and Pasting with the Clipboard

Action	Right-click Method	Keyboard Method	Ribbon Method
Cut	Right-click selection and click Cut.	Ctrl+X	Home ⇨ Cut
Copy	Right-click selection and click Copy.	Ctrl+C	Home ⇨ Copy
Paste	Right-click at the destination and click Paste.	Ctrl+V	Home ⇨ Paste

Inserting and Deleting Rows, Columns, and Cells

Even if you're a careful planner, you'll likely decide that you want to change your worksheet's structure. Maybe you want data in a different column, or certain rows turn out to be unnecessary. Excel makes it easy to insert and delete rows and columns to deal with these kinds of changes.

Insert rows or columns

When you insert a new row or column, the existing ones move to make room for it.

1. Select one or more existing rows or columns adjacent to where you want the inserted ones.

For example, if you want two new columns, select two adjacent existing columns. See "Selecting Cells and Ranges," earlier in this chapter, for help if needed.

TIP

There is no limit on the number of rows or columns you can insert at once.

2. On the Home tab, click Insert (see Figure 15-16).

FIGURE 15-16:
Insert rows or columns with the Insert command.

Delete rows or columns

When you delete rows or columns, whatever they contained is lost, so be careful with this command. Delete is not the same as Cut. Cut moves the content to the Clipboard, but Delete just destroys it.

TIP

If you accidentally delete something you meant to keep, use Undo (Ctrl+Z) to undo commands until you get it back. This works only if you haven't closed the application or the data file since you made the deletion.

1. **Select one or more existing rows or columns to delete.**

   See "Selecting Cells and Ranges," earlier in this chapter, for help if needed.

   TIP

   There is no limit on the number of rows or columns you can delete at once.

2. **On the Home tab, click Delete (see Figure 15-17).**

FIGURE 15-17:
Delete rows or
columns with the
Delete command.

Insert or delete cells and ranges

You can also insert and delete individual cells or even ranges that don't neatly correspond to entire rows or columns. When you do so, the surrounding cells shift. In the case of an insertion, cells move down or to the right of the area where the new cells are being inserted. In the case of a deletion, cells move up or to the left to fill in the voided space.

REMEMBER

Deleting a cell is different from clearing a cell's content, and this becomes apparent when you start working with individual cells and ranges. When you clear the content, the cell itself remains. When you delete the cell itself, the adjacent cells shift.

When shifting cells, Excel is smart enough that it tries to guess which direction you want existing content to move when you insert or delete cells. If you have content immediately to the right of a deleted cell, for example, Excel shifts it left. If you have content immediately below the deleted cell, Excel shifts it up. You can still override that, though, as needed.

To insert cells, follow these steps:

1. **Select a range the size and shape of the range of cells you want to insert, adjacent to where you want to insert them (see Figure 15-18).**

   To insert a single cell, select a single cell.

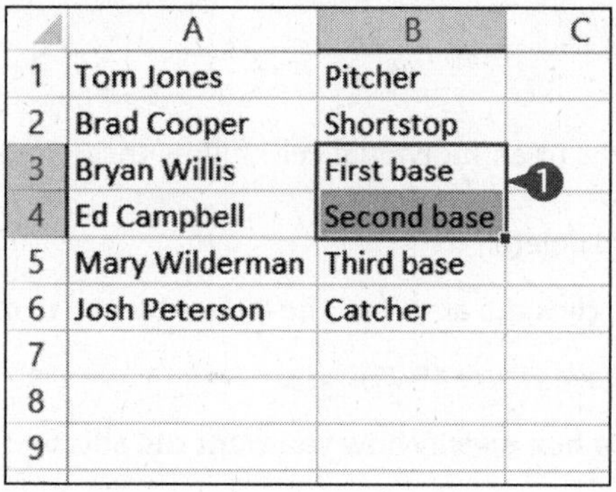

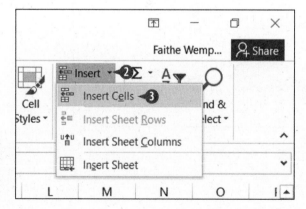

FIGURE 15-18:
Select a range
where you want
to insert cells.

2. **On the Home tab, click the arrow on the Insert button to open its menu.**

3. **Click Insert Cells (see Figure 15-19).**

4. **In the Insert dialog box, specify how you want the adjacent cells to move (see Figure 15-20).**

5. **Click OK.**

FIGURE 15-19:
Choose Insert
Cells from
the Insert
button's menu.

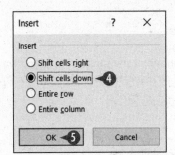

To delete a range of cells or an individual cell, follow these steps:

1. **Select the cell(s) to delete.**

2. **On the Home tab, click the arrow on the Delete button to open its menu.**

3. **Click Delete Cells (see Figure 15-21).**

4. **In the Insert dialog box, specify how you want the adjacent cells to move (see Figure 15-22).**

5. **Click OK.**

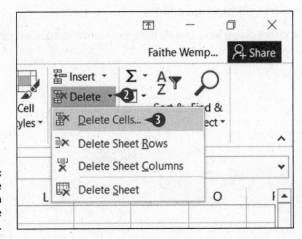

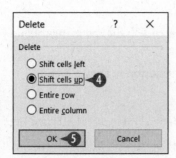

Using Flash Fill to Extract Content

The Flash Fill feature enables you to extract data from adjacent columns intelligently by analyzing the patterns in that data. Suppose that you have a list of email addresses in one column, and you want the usernames (that is, the text before the @ sign) from each email address to appear in an adjacent column. You would extract the first few yourself by manually typing the entries into the adjacent column, and then you would use Flash Fill to follow your example to extract the others. You could also use Flash Fill to separate first and last names that are entered in the same column.

To use Flash Fill, follow these steps:

1. **Make sure there are enough blank columns to the right of the original data to hold the extracted data.**

    See "Inserting and Deleting Rows, Columns, and Cells," earlier in this chapter, if you need help.

2. **In the first row of the data, create an example of the separation you want by typing in the empty column(s) (see Figure 15-23).**

	A	B	C	D	E
1	Tom Jones	Tom	Jones	Pitcher	
2	Brad Cooper			Shortstop	
3	Bryan Willis			First base	
4	Ed Campbell			Second base	
5	Mary Wilderman			Third base	
6	Josh Peterson			Catcher	
7					
8					

3. In the second row of the data, click in the cell in the column you want to populate.

4. On the Home tab, click the Fill button to open a menu.

5. Click Flash Fill.

    The data in the column you selected in Step 3 is filled in (see Figure 15-24).

6. Repeat steps 3–5 as needed to populate additional columns.

FIGURE 15-24:
The Flash Fill command populates the columns with data using your example.

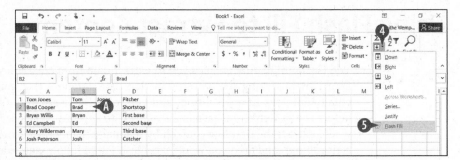

TIP

Step 6 is necessary because you can use Flash Fill to fill only one column at a time. If you want to split out data from multiple columns at once, use the Data ⇨ Text to Columns command. Use the Help system in Excel to find out how to use that command.

Creating and Managing Multiple Worksheets

Each new workbook starts with one sheet: Sheet1. (It's not the most interesting name, but you can change it.) Each worksheet is represented by a tab at the bottom of the Excel window; you can click a tab to switch to that sheet.

You can add or delete worksheets, rearrange the worksheet tabs, and apply different colors to the tabs to help differentiate them from one another, or to create logical groups of tabs.

Add a worksheet

Adding a worksheet gives you an additional page on which to enter data without having to start a new data file. To add a worksheet, follow these steps:

1. **Click the tab that the new worksheet's tab should appear to the** *right* **of.**

If your current workbook has only one sheet in it, this is a non-issue.

It's kind of a non-issue anyway because you can easily reorder the tabs later. See "Reorder worksheet tabs," later in this chapter.

TIP

2. **Click the New Sheet button (+) to the right of the existing sheet tabs at the bottom of the Excel window (see Figure 15-25).**

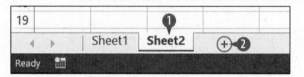

FIGURE 15-25:
Add a worksheet.

Remove a worksheet

Be careful when removing worksheets; whatever was on that sheet is lost when you do so, and you can't use Undo to get it back. If you're deleting a blank sheet, Excel offers no warning, but if the sheet contains anything, you must confirm the deletion.

To delete a worksheet:

1. **Right-click the worksheet's tab at the bottom of the screen.**

2. **Click Delete (see Figure 15-26).**

3. **If a deletion-confirmation dialog box appears, click Delete (see Figure 15-27).**

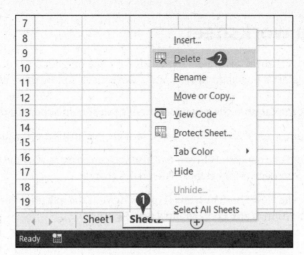

FIGURE 15-26:
Delete a
worksheet.

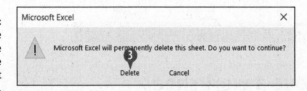

FIGURE 15-27:
Confirm the
deletion if the
sheet you're
deleting is not
empty.

Rename a worksheet

As we mention earlier in this chapter, the default sheet names are not terribly useful (Sheet1, Sheet2). You will probably want to rename each sheet's tab to help you remember what is stored on that sheet.

1. **Double-click the worksheet tab to place the name in Editing mode.**

    Alternatively, you can right-click the tab and choose Rename.

2. **Edit the name or type a new name (see Figure 15-28).**

3. **Click away from the tab to accept the new name.**

FIGURE 15-28:
Edit the tab's
name.

Reorder worksheet tabs

The tab for a new worksheet is always placed to the right of whichever worksheet is active when you create it. You can easily reorder the worksheet tabs, though.

(A) Drag a tab to the right or left to move it **(see Figure 15-29)**.

(B) A small black triangle shows where the worksheet tab will be dropped when you release the mouse button.

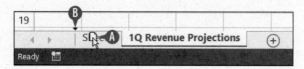

FIGURE 15-29:
Drag a tab to the
right or left.

Change the worksheet tab color

If you have a lot of worksheets in a workbook, it can get confusing when you're trying to find the one you want. You can make it easier by color-coding the tabs: gold for management, blue for medical, red for security, and so on. (Yes, those are the *Star Trek* colors. Use your own scheme.)

To change a tab's color, follow these steps:

1. **Right-click the tab.**

2. **Point to Tab Color.**

3. **Click the desired color (see Figure 15-30).**

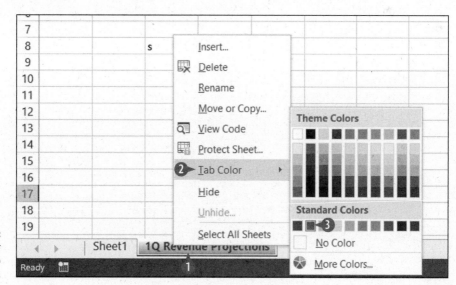

FIGURE 15-30:
Assign a color
to a tab to
categorize it.

» Copying and moving formulas

» Inserting functions

» Showing the current date or time
with a function

» Calculating loan terms

» Performing math calculations

» Evaluating a condition with an IF
function

» Referring to named ranges

» Using the Quick Analysis feature

Chapter **16**

Creating Excel Formulas and Functions

M ath. Excel is really good at it, and it's what makes Excel more than just
data storage. Even if you hated math in school, you might still like Excel
because it does the math for you.

In Excel, you can write math formulas that perform calculations on the values in
various cells, and then, if those values change later, you can see the formula
results update automatically. You can also use built-in functions to handle more
complex math activities than you might be able to set up yourself with formulas.
This capability makes it possible to build complex worksheets that calculate loan
rates and payments, keep track of your bank accounts, and much more.

In this chapter, we show you how to construct formulas and functions in Excel, how to move and copy formulas and functions (there's a trick to it), and how to use functions to create handy financial spreadsheets.

Writing Basic Formulas

A *formula* is a math calculation, like 2+2 or 3*(4+1). In Excel, a formula can perform calculations with fixed numbers or cell contents.

In Excel, formulas are different from regular text in two ways:

>> Formulas begin with an equal sign, like this: =2+2.

>> Formulas don't contain text (except for function names and cell references). They contain only symbols that are allowed in math formulas, such as parentheses, commas, and decimal points.

REMEMBER

Excel also has an advantage over some basic calculators (including the one in Windows): It easily does exponentiation. For example, if you want to calculate 5 to the 8th power, you would write it in Excel as =5^8.

Create formulas that calculate numeric values

To create a basic formula that performs math calculations on numbers, follow these steps:

1. In the desired cell, begin typing the formula to create (see Figure 16-1), starting with an equal sign (=).

2. Type the formula to calculate. Use these math operators:

- + for addition

- – for subtraction

- * for multiplication

- / for division

- ^ for exponentiation

3. **Press Enter.**

   The formula result appears in the cell, and the cell cursor moves down into the next row.

4. **(Optional) To see the formula in the cell, click the cell.**

   Its formula appears in the formula bar (see Figure 16-2).

FIGURE 16-1:
Type a formula into a cell.

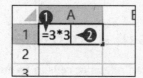

FIGURE 16-2:
The formula result appears in the cell, and the formula itself appears in the formula bar.

Formula appears in formula bar

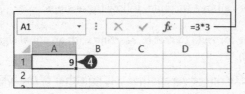

Control the order of math precedence

Just as in basic math, formulas are calculated by an order of precedence. Table 16-1 lists the order.

TABLE 16-1

Order of Precedence in a Formula

Order	Item	Example
1	Anything in parentheses	=2*(2+1)
2	Extrapolation	=2^3
3	Multiplication and division	=1+2*2
4	Addition and subtraction	=10−4

Here are a few additional examples. Work through them yourself and see whether you come up with the same results; if you do, you understand order of precedence:

3*3+4/2 = 11

3*(3+4)/2= 10.5

3*3+4^2= 25

Reference other cells in a formula

One of Excel's best features is that it can reference cells in formulas. When a cell is referenced in a formula, whatever value it contains is used in the formula. When the value changes, the result of the formula changes too.

To reference another cell in a formula, follow these steps:

1. **Begin typing the formula to create, starting with an equal sign (=) (see Figure 16-3).**

2. **When you need to reference another cell, do either of the following:**

   (A) Type the cell's address directly into the formula (for example, A1).

   (B) Click the cell to fill in its address in the formula being typed.

3. **Continue creating the formula normally, adding numbers and math operators as needed. When you're finished, press Enter.**

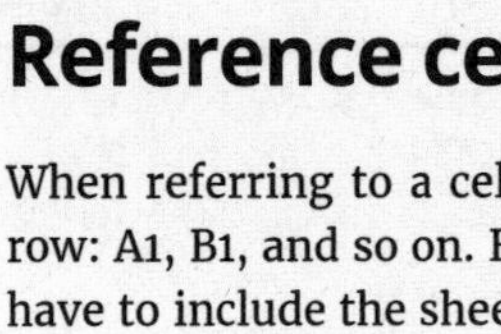

FIGURE 16-3:
Type a formula that includes references to other cells by their column letter and row number.

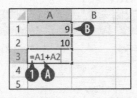

Reference cells on other worksheets

When referring to a cell on the same sheet, you can simply use its column and row: A1, B1, and so on. However, when referring to a cell on a different sheet, you have to include the sheet name in the formula.

The syntax for doing this is to list the sheet name in single quotes, followed by an exclamation point, followed by the cell reference, like this:

```
='Sheet1'!A2
```

You can also select cells on another sheet by first clicking the sheet tab and then the desired cell as you're creating the formula, as in the following steps:

1. **Begin typing the formula to create, starting with an equal sign (=).**

2. **When you need to reference a cell on another sheet, click the worksheet's tab (see Figure 16-4).**

3. **Click the desired cell on that sheet (see Figure 16-5).**

4. **Press Enter to return to the sheet containing the formula you began in Step 1.**

   Excel assumes that the formula is complete at this point and moves out of that cell.

5. **If the formula is not yet complete, click the cell containing the formula and edit it in the formula bar.**

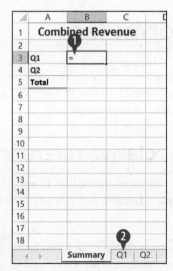

FIGURE 16-4: Click a tab while typing a formula to reference a cell on that sheet.

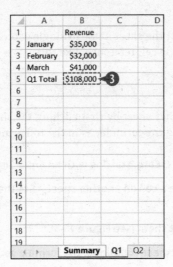

FIGURE 16-5:
Click the desired
cell to reference
and press Enter.

REMEMBER

As you may have noticed in the preceding steps, one drawback to selecting a cell in this way is that Excel ends the formula after you select it. It's not a big deal to edit the formula, but if you would prefer to not have to do so, you can use the typing method instead of the selecting method.

Copying and Moving Formulas

When it comes to copying formulas, beware of a few "gotchas." The following sections explain relative and absolute referencing in formulas and how you can use them to get the results you want when you copy.

Refer to cells with relative referencing

When you move or copy a formula, Excel automatically changes the cell references to work with the new location. That's because cell references in formulas are, by default, *relative references.*

In Figure 16-6, suppose that you want to copy the formula from F2 into F3. The new formula in F3 should refer to values in row 3, not in row 2; otherwise, the formula wouldn't make much sense. So, when F2's formula is copied to F3, it becomes =B3+C3+D3+E3 there.

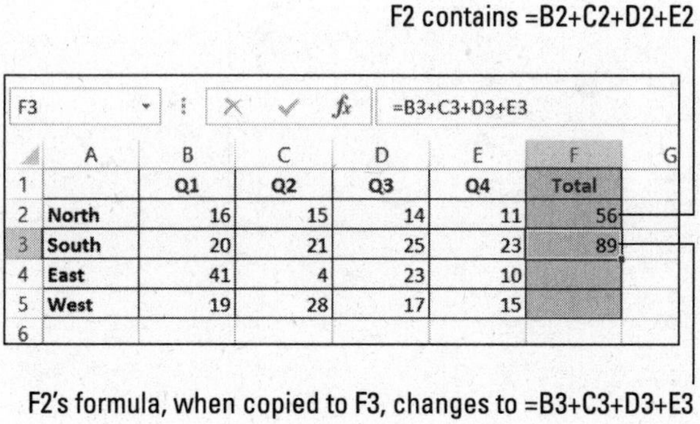

F2 contains =B2+C2+D2+E2

F3		▼ :	✕ ✓	fx	=B3+C3+D3+E3	
▲	A	B	C	D	E	F	G
1		Q1	Q2	Q3	Q4	Total	
2	North	16	15	14	11	56	
3	South	20	21	25	23	89	
4	East	41	4	23	10		
5	West	19	28	17	15		
6							

FIGURE 16-6:
Most of the time when you copy a formula, you want its cell references to change.

F2's formula, when copied to F3, changes to =B3+C3+D3+E3

You don't have to do anything special to move copy with relative referencing. It's the default when you move or copy.

Refer to cells with absolute referencing

You might not always want the cell references in a formula to change when you move or copy it. In other words, you want an *absolute reference* to that cell. To make a reference absolute, you add dollar signs in front of the column letter and in front of the row number. For example, an absolute reference to cell B1 would be =B1.

Figure 16-7 shows a sample scenario in which an absolute reference would be appropriate:

(A) Cell B4 contains the formula =A4*B1. This calculates the tax on the amount in A4, where the tax rate appears in B1.

(B) If you copy this formula to the range B5:B17, you want the reference to the purchase price to change for each row (A5, A6, A7, and so on).

(C) However, you want the reference to the tax rate to stay the same for each row.

The dollar signs in the reference B1 ensure that the cell reference will remain static when copied.

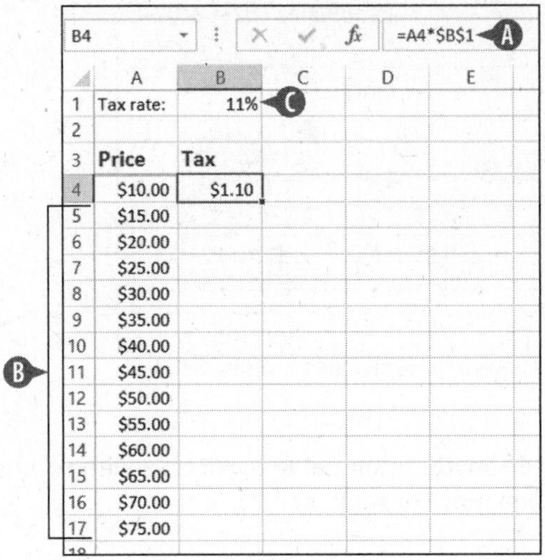

FIGURE 16-7:
An absolute
reference
ensures that
the cell reference
will not change
when copied.

If you want to lock down only one dimension of the cell reference, you can place a dollar sign before only the column or only the row. For example, =$C1 would make only the column letter fixed, and =C$1 would make only the row number fixed. This is called a *mixed reference*.

To create an absolute or mixed reference, you can type the dollar signs directly into the cell where they're needed. Alternatively, you can press F4 to cycle through all the available combinations of relative, mixed, and absolute references.

Inserting Functions

In Excel, a *function* refers to a named type of calculation. Functions can greatly reduce the amount of typing you have to do to create a particular result:

(A) For example, instead of using this formula:

```
=B2+B3+B4+B5+B6+B7+B8+B9+B10+B11
```

you could use the SUM function like this: =SUM(B2:B11).

(B) With a function, you can represent a range with the upper-left corner's cell reference, a colon, and the lower-right corner's cell reference. In the case of B2:B11, there is only one column, so the upper-left corner is cell B2, and the lower-right corner is cell B11.

Range references cannot be used in simple formulas — only in functions. For example, =A6 : A9 would be invalid as a formula because no math operation is specified in it. You can't insert math operators within a range. To use ranges in a calculation, you must use a function (see Figure 16-8)

	A	B	C
1	Date	Revenue	
2	12/21/2017	$2,500	
3	12/22/2017	$2,200	
4	12/23/2017	$2,100	
5	12/24/2017	$1,800	◄B
6	12/25/2017	$1,700	
7	12/26/2017	$2,400	
8	12/27/2017	$1,900	
9	12/28/2017	$1,200	
10	12/29/2017	$3,000	
11	12/30/2017	$2,800	
12	Total	=sum(B2:B11)	◄A
13			
14			

FIGURE 16-8:
You can specify a range as one of the function's arguments.

An *argument* is a placeholder for a number, text string, or cell reference. Each function has one or more arguments, along with its own rules about how many required and optional arguments there are and what they represent. For example, the SUM function requires at least one argument: a range of cells. So, in the preceding example, B2 : B11 is the argument. The arguments for a function are enclosed in a set of parentheses.

(C) You don't have to memorize the sequence of arguments (the *syntax*) for each function. Excel prompts you for them (see Figure 16-9). When you type a function directly into a cell, a ScreenTip prompts you for that function's arguments.

FIGURE 16-9:
Excel prompts you for arguments when you type a function.

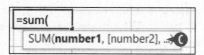

Use the SUM function

The SUM function is by far the most popular function; it sums (that is, adds) a data range consisting of one or more cells, like this:

```
=SUM(D12:D15)
```

You don't *have* to use a range in a SUM function; you can specify the individual cell addresses, if you want. Separate them by commas, like this:

```
=SUM(D12, D13, D14, D15)
```

If the data range is not a contiguous block, you need to specify the individual cells that are outside the block. The main block is one argument, and each individual other cell is an additional argument, like this:

```
=SUM(D12:D15, E22)
```

The SUM function is so frequently used that it has its own button on the Home tab, in the Editing group. Here's how to use it:

1. Select the cell into which you want to insert the SUM function.

2. On the Home tab, click Sum (see Figure 16-10):

   (A) The SUM function is placed in the cell.

   (B) Excel attempts to guess the range you want to sum and places a dashed outline around it (see Figure 16-11).

   (C) It also fills the range into the SUM function's argument. The range is highlighted so that it can be easily removed.

3A. If the range is correctly selected, press Enter to accept it.

   OR

3B. Drag across the correct range to make a different selection, and then press Enter.

REMEMBER

When you press Enter to complete a function, as in Step 3, Excel automatically adds a closing parenthesis to the function if one was not already entered. You don't have to worry about typing one.

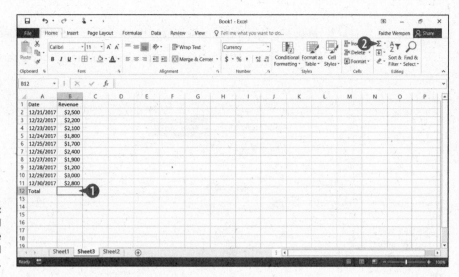

FIGURE 16-10:
Select the cell
to hold the
function and
then click Sum.

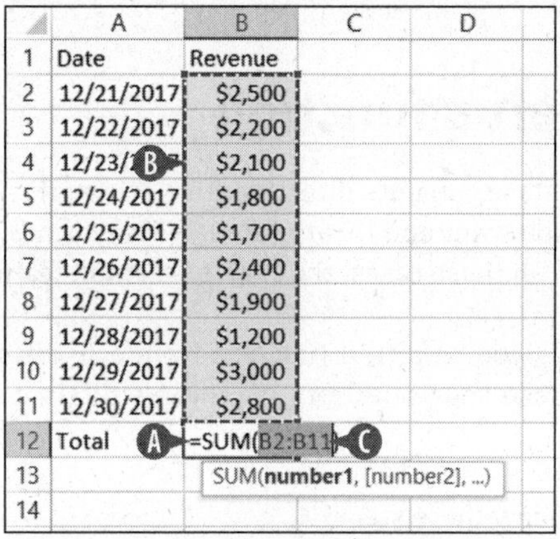

FIGURE 16-11:
Excel tries to
complete the
function for you.

Use AVERAGE, COUNT, MAX, and MIN functions

Perhaps you noticed that the Sum button on the Home tab has an arrow on it. Click the arrow for a list (see A in Figure 16-12). From this list, you can select one of several other common functions to use instead of SUM:

(B) **Average:** Provides the average of the numeric values within the selected range; ignores blank and non-numeric values

(C) **Count Numbers:** Counts within the selected range the number of cells that contain numeric values

(D) **Max:** Finds and returns the largest numeric value within the selected range

(E) **Min:** Finds and returns the smallest numeric value within the selected range

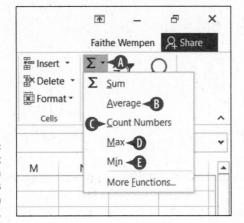

Find and insert a function

Typing a function and its arguments directly into a cell works fine if you happen to know the function you want and its arguments. Many times, though, you may not know these details. In those cases, the Insert Function feature can help you.

Insert Function enables you to pick a function from a list based on descriptive keywords. After you make your selection, it provides fill-in-the-blank prompts for the arguments.

To insert a function, follow these steps:

1. **Select the cell in which to insert the function.**

2. **In the formula bar, click the Insert Function button (see Figure 16-13) to open the Insert Function dialog box.**

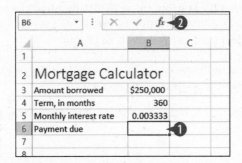

FIGURE 16-13:
Click Insert
Function in the
formula bar.

3. In the Search for a Function box, describe what you want to do (see Figure 16-14).

4. In the Select a Function box, click a function and then read about it below the list.

5. When the appropriate function is selected, click OK.

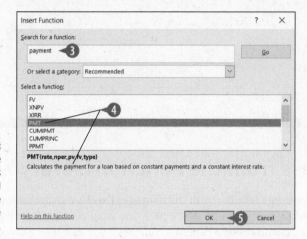

6. In the Function Arguments dialog box, type the number or enter the cell reference for each argument (see Figure 16-15).

Here are some things to remember about this dialog box:

(A) You can type directly into any of the argument text boxes.

(B) You can click in an argument's box and then click a cell on the worksheet behind the dialog box to fill in that cell reference.

(C) You can click the Collapse Dialog button for any argument to temporarily shrink the dialog box so that you can see which cell you want to choose.

(D) Arguments in bold are required.

(E) Arguments that are not in bold are optional.

(F) The Formula Result area previews the formula's result.

7. Click OK to complete the function.

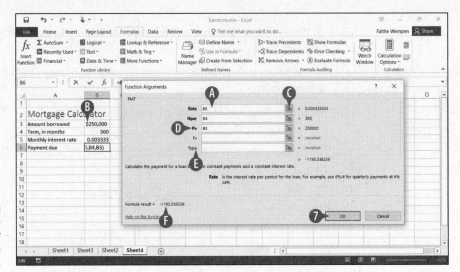

FIGURE 16-15:
Fill in the
arguments for
the chosen
function.

Choose from the Function Library

Once you become familiar with the names of Excel's most common functions, you don't need to look them up every time you need one, as described in the earlier section "Find and insert a function." Instead, you can take a shortcut in the process, by either typing them directly into the cell or choosing them from the Function Library group on the Formulas tab.

The Formulas tab's Library group organizes functions by their general purpose. There is a separate drop-down list button for each category. There are also extra buttons for AutoSum, which is the same as the Sum button on the Home tab, and Recently Used.

To select a function from the library, follow these steps:

1. **Select the cell in which to insert the function.**

2. **On the Formulas tab, click the button for the category of function you want.**

3. **Scroll through the list and click the desired function.**

   You can point at a function on the list to see a pop-up box describing it (see A in Figure 16-16).

4. **Pick up the steps at Step 6 in the earlier section "Find and insert a function" to complete the function.**

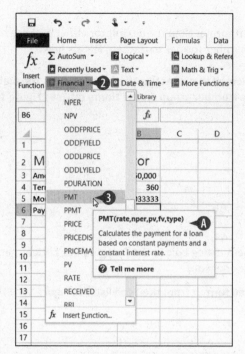

FIGURE 16-16:
Choose a
function from the
category list.

Showing the Current Date or Time with a Function

You can use functions to show the current date or time in a cell and have that value be updated automatically every time you open the worksheet. (You can also update the field manually at any time by pressing F9 or choosing Formulas ➪ Calculate Now.) The functions to do this are

» NOW: Reports the current date and time

» TODAY: Reports the current date

Even though neither uses any arguments, you still have to include the parentheses, so they look like this when you use them:

```
=NOW( )
=TODAY( )
```

If you want a different format than the default for either of those results, you need to apply a different number format to the cell. Here's how:

1. **With the cell selected that contains the function, click the dialog box launcher for the Number group on the Home tab (see Figure 16-17).**

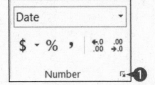

2. **In the Format Cells dialog box, in the Category list, click either Date or Time, whichever you want.**

3. **Select the desired format from the Type list (see Figure 16-18).**

4. **Click OK.**

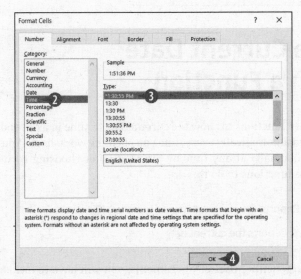

TIP

You can combine the NOW or TODAY function with a formula to get results that are in the past or future. For example, =TODAY( )+7 returns the date that is 7 days in the future. Use decimal points to indicate times. For example, =NOW( )-0.5 returns the time that is 12 hours (50 percent of one day) in the past.

Many other date and time functions are available. Check out the functions on the Date & Time button's menu on the Formulas tab.

Calculating Loan Terms

One of the most common calculation tasks in Excel is to determine the terms of a loan — a set of functions is designed specifically for this task. Each function finds a different part of the loan equation, given the other parts:

>> PV: Short for present value; finds the amount of the loan

>> NPER: Short for number of periods; finds the number of payments (the length of the loan)

>> RATE: Finds the interest rate per period

>> PMT: Finds the amount of the payment per period

Each of those functions uses the other three pieces of information as its required arguments. For example, the arguments for PV are rate, nper, and pmt.

Let's say that you want to know the length of a loan in which you borrow $20,000 at 5 percent interest per year (0.417 percent per month) if you make a monthly payment of $350. You can use the NPER function to figure that out. Here's how:

1. **In Excel, create the labels needed for the structure of the worksheet, as shown in Figure 16-19.**

Fill in the information you already know about the loan.

	A	B
1		
2	Loan Calculator	
3	Amount borrowed	$20,000
4	Term, in months	
5	Monthly interest rate	0.417%
6	Payment due	$300.00
7		

2. **Type =NPER(into the cell where the function should be placed.**

A ScreenTip reminds you of the arguments to use and their proper order (see Figure 16-20).

3. **Click or type the cell that contains the interest rate, and then type a comma.**

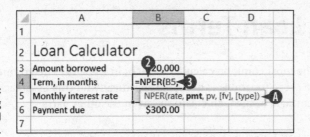

FIGURE 16-20:
Begin entering
the function and
its arguments.

4. **Click or type the cell that contains the payment amount, and then type a comma (see Figure 16-21).**

5. **Click or type the cell that contains the loan amount, and then press Enter to complete the formula.**

   The closing parenthesis is automatically added for you. If you complete the example correctly, the loan term will show as –58.95187.

FIGURE 16-21:
Add the
remaining
arguments,
separating them
with commas.

Besides these four simple functions, dozens of other financial functions are available in Excel. For example, IPMT is like PMT except that it returns only the amount of interest in the payment, and PPMT returns only the amount of principal. Explore on your own the functions on the Financial button's menu on the Formulas tab.

TIP

The result of the calculation is negative if the present value (the loan amount) is a positive number. If you want the term to show as a positive number, change the amount borrowed to a negative number, or enclose the function within the ABS function (absolute value), like this: =ABS(NPER(B5,B6,B3)). ABS is short for absolute value.

TIP

Since the number of payments must be a whole number, you might choose to use the ROUNDUP function to round up that value to the nearest whole. The ROUNDUP function has two arguments: the number to be rounded and a number of decimal places. For a whole number, use 0 for the second argument. The finished formula would then look like this: =ROUNDUP(ABS(NPER(B5,B6,B3)),0).

Performing Math Calculations

Technically, all formulas perform math calculations, but there's a specific category of functions called Math & Trig for functions that deal directly with familiar math calculations like finding the square root (SQRT), tangent (TAN), sine (SIN), or cosine (COS) of a number. The ABS and ROUNDUP functions we mention at the end of the earlier section "Calculating Loan Terms" fall into this category also. Check out the Math & Trig category list on the Formulas tab for a complete list of math functions.

Most of the math-related functions are fairly simple, with just one or two arguments. For example, the SQRT function takes only one argument: the number to be calculated. SQRT(A1) finds the square root of the number in cell A1.

Evaluating a Condition with an IF Function

The IF function determines whether a condition is true and then performs different actions based on that answer (see Figure 16-22). IF is only one of many logical functions that Excel provides; see the list on the Logical button on the Formulas tab for others. For example:

(A) Suppose that a customer gets a 10 percent discount if he spends more than $50. You could use the IF function to determine whether his order amount qualifies.

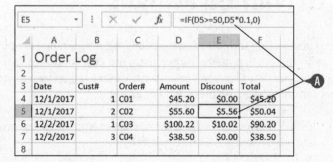

FIGURE 16-22:
The amount of discount is determined using an IF function.

An IF function typically contains three arguments: condition, value_if_true, and value_if_false. Like all arguments, they're separated by commas (see Figure 16-23).

(B) The condition in this example is D5>=50. In other words, is the value in D5 greater than or equal to 50?

(C) The value_if_true in this example is calculated by multiplying D5 by 0.1 (in other words, calculating 10 percent of it).

(D) The value_if_false in this example is zero (0).

FIGURE 16-23:
An IF function
with three
arguments.

The condition argument is the only required one. If you omit the value_if_true argument, the function returns 1 if the condition is true and 0 if the condition is false. If you omit the value_if_false argument, a value of 0 is assumed for it. Therefore, in this example, technically we did not have to include the value_if_false argument, because we wanted zero for it anyway.

TIP

If you want to combine a SUM operation with an IF condition, you can use the SUMIF function, which does both at once. It sums a range of data if the condition you specify in its argument is true. You'll find it on the Math & Trig button's list rather than under the Logical category.

Referring to Named Ranges

When constructing formulas and functions, naming a range can be helpful because you can refer to that name rather than the cell addresses (see Figure 16-24). Therefore, you don't have to remember the exact cell addresses, and you can construct formulas based on meaning. For example:

(A) Instead of remembering that the number of employees is stored in cell B2, you could name the cell B2 *Employees*.

(B) Then in a formula that used B2's value, such as =B2*3, you could use the name instead: =Employees*3.

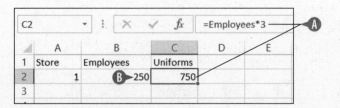

FIGURE 16-24:
You can use range names in formulas.

You can name individual cells, as in this example, but in some cases it may be more advantageous to name multicell ranges. For example, you might name multiple cells in a column that contains the same kind of information. When you then use the range name in a formula or function, Excel assumes that you mean the cell within that range that corresponds to the row or column in which you're typing:

(C) In Figure 16-25, the named range of Employees encompasses B2:B7.

(D) The same formula is used in every cell in column C: =Employees*3.

(E) In each row, Excel assumes that you mean the cell in that same row.

C7	▼	⋮	✕ ✓	*fx*	=Employees*3		
	A	B	C	D	E		
1	Store	Employees	Uniforms				
2	1	250	750				
3	2	300	900				
4	3	200	600				
5	4	250	750				
6	5	200	600				
7	6	100	300				
8							

FIGURE 16-25:
When a multicell range is named, references to that range are relative to the cell in which the formula is entered.

Excel is rather intelligent about deducing what you mean when you refer to named ranges. When you refer to a range in a calculation like the one shown in Figure 16-25, the reference is to an individual cell in the range. However, if you use the range name in a formula where it makes sense to be referring to the entire range, Excel does so.

For example, =SUM(Employees) would return the sum of *all* values within that range (see F in Figure 16-26).

You can name a range in three ways, and each has its pros and cons.

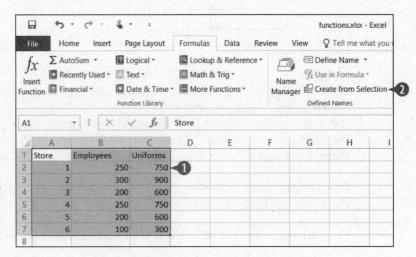

B8			×	✓	f_x	=SUM(Employees)	

◢	A	B	C	D	E
1	Store	Employees	Uniforms		
2	1	250	750		
3	2	300	900		
4	3	200	600		
5	4	250	750		
6	5	200	600		
7	6	100	300		
8	Total	1300			
9					

FIGURE 16-26:
When you refer to a multicell range in a context that infers the entire range, Excel interprets it that way.

Create range names by selection

If default names are okay to use, you may find automatic naming useful. With this method, Excel chooses the name for you based on text labels it finds in adjacent cells (above or to the left of the current cells). This method is fast and easy, and it works well when you have to create a lot of names at once and when the cells are well labeled with adjacent text:

1. **Select the range to name.**

   If you want to create multiple named ranges, each referring to a different column or row, select the entire range, including the cells containing the names to use (see Figure 16-27).

2. **From the Formulas tab, click Create from Selection.**

FIGURE 16-27:
Allow Excel to automatically create ranges with names defined by labels in adjacent cells.

3. In the Create Names from Selection dialog box, mark or clear check boxes as needed to indicate where the labels are (see Figure 16-28).

4. Click OK.

The range names are created.

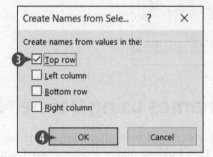

FIGURE 16-28:
Confirm that
Excel has
correctly guessed
where the labels
are.

TIP

If you aren't sure whether the ranges were correctly created, click the Name Manager button on the Formulas tab to see a list of all named ranges and their definitions.

Create range names using the Name box

With this fast-and-easy method, you get to choose the name yourself. However, you have to complete each range separately; you can't do a big batch at a time. Follow these steps:

1. Select the cells to include in the named range.

Make sure that you select only the cells that contain actual data, not the cell containing text (like the column header).

2. Click in the Name box and type the new range name (see Figure 16-29).

3. Press Enter.

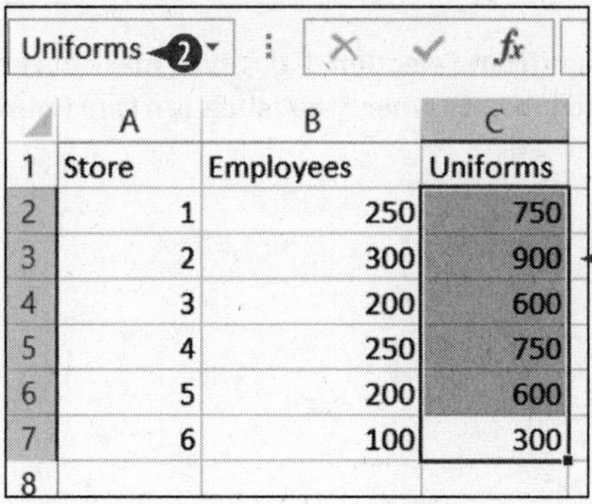

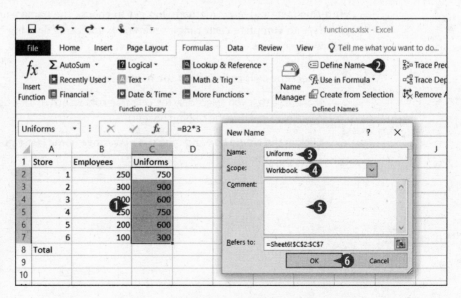

FIGURE 16-29:
Type a range name into the Name box.

Create range names using Define Name

If you want to more precisely control the options for the name, you can use the Define Name command. This method opens a dialog box from which you can specify the name, the scope, and any comments you might want to include:

1. **Select the cells to include in the named range.**

Make sure that you select only the cells that contain actual data, not the cell containing text (like the column header).

2. **On the Formulas tab, click Define Name (see Figure 16-30).**

3. **In the New Name dialog box, type the desired name in the Name box.**

FIGURE 16-30:
Define a range using the Define Name command.

4. **(Optional) To limit the scope of the name to just the active worksheet, change the Scope setting to a particular sheet (such as** Sheet1**).**

5. **(Optional) Type any comments in the Comment box.**

This step can help you remember why you created the range.

6. **Click OK.**

Using Quick Analysis Features

Here are some points to keep in mind about Quick Analysis:

(A) When you select a range of cells, a small icon appears in the lower-right corner of the selected area. This is the Quick Analysis icon, and clicking it opens a panel containing shortcuts to several types of common activities related to data analysis (see Figure 16-31).

(B) Click on the five headings to see the shortcuts available in that category (see Figure 16-32). Then hover the cursor over one of the icons in that category to see the result previewed on your worksheet.

(C) *Formatting:* These shortcuts point to conditional formatting options. For example, you could set up a range to make values under or over a certain amount appear in a different color or with a special icon adjacent.

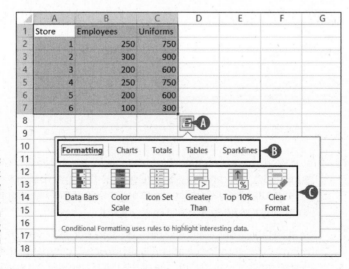

FIGURE 16-31: Open the Quick Analysis panel by clicking its icon. Then choose a category heading and click an icon for a command.

(D) *Charts:* These shortcuts generate common types of charts based on the selected data.

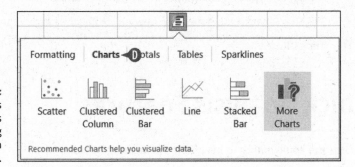

FIGURE 16-32:
Quick Analysis offers shortcuts for creating several common chart types.

(E) *Totals:* These shortcuts add the specified calculation to adjacent cells in the worksheet. For example, Sum adds a total row or column (see Figure 16-33).

(F) Notice that there are separate icons here for rows versus columns.

(G) Notice also that in this category there are more icons than can be displayed at once, so you can click right and left arrows to scroll through them.

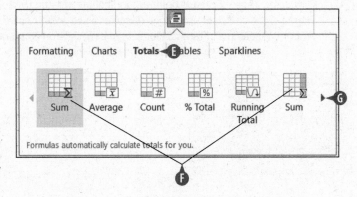

FIGURE 16-33:
You can use Quick Analysis to add summary rows or columns.

(H) *Tables:* You can convert the range to a table for greater ease of analysis (see Figure 16-34). You can also generate several different types of PivotTables via the shortcuts here. A *PivotTable* is a special view of the data that summarizes it by adding various types of calculations to it.

(I) The PivotTable icons aren't well differentiated, but you can point to one of the PivotTable icons to see a sample of how it will summarize the data in the selected range. If you choose one of the PivotTable views, it opens in its own, separate sheet.

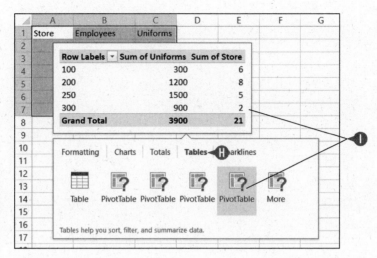

FIGURE 16-34:
You can convert the range to a table or apply one of several PivotTable specifications.

(J) *Sparklines:* Sparklines are minicharts placed in single cells (see Figure 16-35). They can summarize the trend of the data in adjacent cells. They're most relevant when the data you want to trend appears from left to right in adjacent columns.

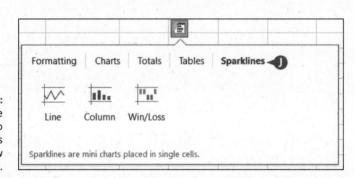

FIGURE 16-35:
Choose Sparklines to add minicharts that show overall trends.

Chapter **17**

Creating Charts in Excel

s a picture really worth a thousand words? Just ask anyone who has been faced with a spreadsheet full of numbers to analyze. Creating charts that summarize data is a quick way to make sense of data — or to present data to someone else.

In this chapter, you see how to create several types of charts and how to add and remove chart elements such as legends, data labels, and data tables. You learn how to move and resize charts, how to place a chart on its own, separate tabs in a workbook, and how to apply a variety of formatting to a chart.

Choosing the Correct Chart Type

Excel offers various chart types, each suited for a different type of data analysis. Here are some things to note about Excel's chart types:

(A) Pie charts (see Figure 17-1) are helpful in situations in which the relationship among the values being charted is the most significant thing. Suppose that

Bill sold 15 cars, Dave sold 7, and Tom sold 8. If the important factor is that Bill sold 50 percent of all the cars, a pie chart is ideal. Pie charts are limited in that they can handle only one data series.

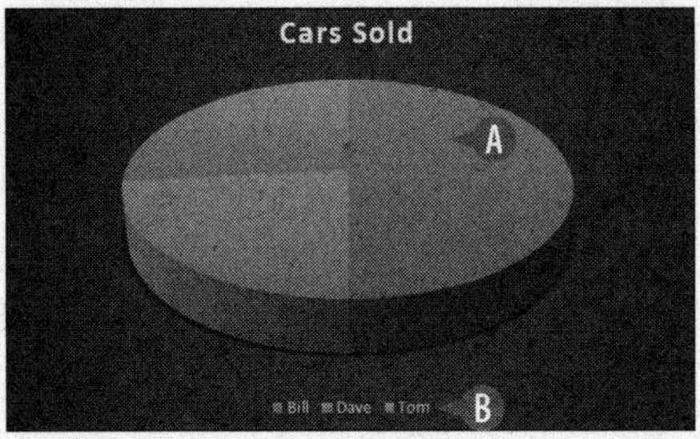

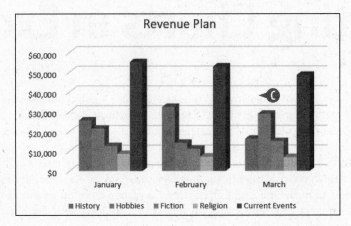

FIGURE 17-1:
A pie chart shows the relationship of each data point to the whole.

(B) The key that tells what each color represents is a *legend*.

(C) A column chart (see Figure 17-2) is useful for showing multiple data series on a 2-axis grid. This particular subtype is a *clustered* column chart; each data point has its own bar, and the bars are clustered together into groups.

FIGURE 17-2:
A column chart summarizes multiple data series.

(D) When a column chart is horizontal, it's called a *bar chart* (see Figure 17-3).

(E) The subtype shown here is called a *stacked chart;* instead of having a separate bar for each month, it combines all three months into a single bar, which makes it easier to see their cumulative value.

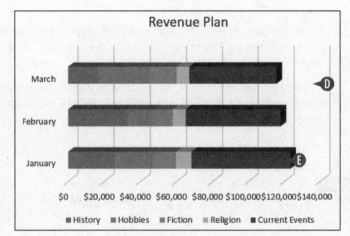

FIGURE 17-3:
A bar chart is a horizontal version of a column chart.

A few of the other chart types available include

>> **XY (Scatter):** Plots each data point as a small dot on a 2-dimensional (XY) grid, like in geometry class

>> **Stock:** Plots the high, low, open, and close prices of a stock on a particular day or range of dates

>> **Line:** Plots each data point as a small dot and then connects the dots of each series with a different line color

>> **Area:** Like a line chart, except that the area beneath each line is filled in solid with color

>> **Surface:** Like an area chart, only 3-dimensional

There are many other types, and you might want to explore them on your own. In the rest of this chapter, though, we stick with the basic column and pie charts for the examples.

Creating a Chart

Here's how to create a chart:

1. **Select the data to include.**

   Include any labels that go with that data, too. The labels will become label text on the chart.

To select noncontiguous cells, hold down Ctrl as you drag across them. For example, if the labels aren't contiguous with the data you want to include, you might need to use Ctrl to select the labels.

If there are total rows or columns in your data, don't include them in your selection in Step 1 unless you're charting *only* the total row or column (see A in Figure 17-4).

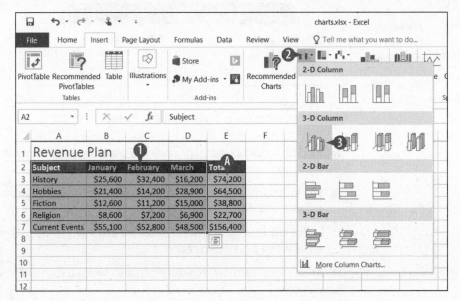

FIGURE 17-4:
Click a chart type, and then choose a subtype.

2. **On the Insert tab, in the Charts group, click the button for the chart type you want.**

   You can change the chart type later, if you change your mind.

3. **On the menu that appears, click the desired subtype.**

   A preview of the chart appears behind the menu as you move the mouse pointer over the various subtypes.

Moving and Resizing a Chart

After creating a chart, you can move it around on the worksheet or resize it by dragging it:

(A) Position the mouse pointer over any part of the chart except a selection handle so that the pointer becomes a 4-headed arrow, and drag it where you want it.

(B) To resize a chart (see Figure 17-5), drag one of the selection handles (white circles) on its border.

REMEMBER

Resizing a chart may change its *aspect ratio* (its ratio of height to width), and the chart may stretch or compress as you drag.

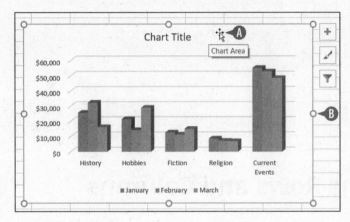

FIGURE 17-5:
Drag a chart to
move or resize it.

You can also place a chart on its own, separate sheet in the workbook. Here's how to do that:

1. **Select the chart.**

2. **On the Chart Tools Design tab, click Move Chart (see Figure 17-6).**

3. **Click New Sheet.**

4. **(Optional) Change the sheet name, if desired.**

5. **Click OK.**

To reverse that process, display the chart's sheet and repeat Steps 2–5, but in Step 3 choose Object In, and then choose the desired existing worksheet.

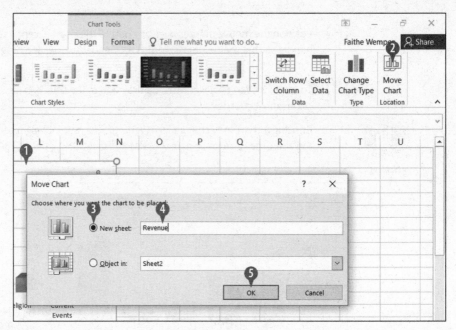

FIGURE 17-6:
Move a chart to
its own sheet.

Switching Rows and Columns

When you create a chart that includes multiple data series, the chart might not plot that data in the way you expect, by default. For example, take a look at the chart shown earlier, in Figure 17-5. What if you had intended for the different column colors to represent the different book categories, as in Figure 17-7?

On the Chart Tools Design tab, click Switch Row/Column to switch back and forth between the two ways of plotting the data (see A in Figure 17-8).

FIGURE 17-7:
This chart uses
the same data as
Figure 17-5 but
plots it by
columns rather
than by rows.

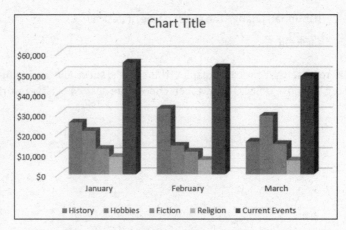

FIGURE 17-8:
Click Switch/Row/
Column to
change the plot
orientation.

Modifying the Data Range for a Chart

If you need the chart to plot different data than you originally chose, there are two ways to go. One is to delete the chart and start over. If you haven't invested much time in formatting and customizing the chart, this may be your quickest option.

The other method is to modify the data range for the chart:

1. **On the Chart Tools Design tab, click Select Data.**

2. **To select a different range for the chart:**

   (A) Click in the Chart Data Range box.

   (B) On the worksheet, drag to redefine the range (see Figure 17-9).

3. **Clear the check box for any series or category that you want to temporarily exclude.**

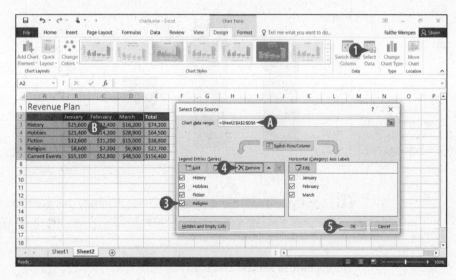

FIGURE 17-9:
Modify the data
range.

4. **Select any series that you want to remove permanently from the chart, and then click Remove.**

5. **Click OK.**

Changing the Axis Scale of a Chart

The *axis scale* is the numeric scale on the chart on which the values are plotted. In Figure 17-5, for example, the axis scale is $0 to $60,000.

Excel sets the axis scale automatically based on the values in the data range. However, you might sometimes want to adjust the axis scale strategically to give the audience a different impression of the data. For example, check out the following charts:

(A) In Figure 17-10, the axis scale is automatically set by Excel. The lower value is 16150, and the upper value is 16650. The differences among the bars are obvious.

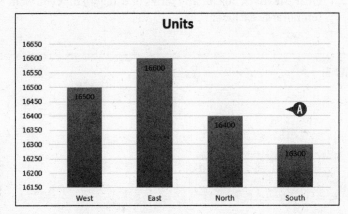

FIGURE 17-10:
With the default axis scale, the differences are clear.

(B) In Figure 17-11, the axis scale has been manually changed to 0 as the lower value and 16650 as the upper value. In this version, the values appear to be nearly identical.

Here's how to set the axis scale:

1A. **Click the vertical axis on the chart to select it.**

OR

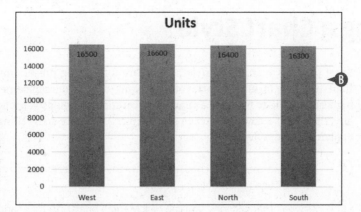

FIGURE 17-11:
You could manually modify the axis scale to make the differences seem less significant.

1B. On the Chart Tools Format tab, open the Select Object drop-down list and choose Vertical (Value) Axis.

2. On the Chart Tools Format tab, click Format Selection.

The Format Axis task pane opens.

3. Click the Axis Options text hyperlink if it isn't already selected.

4. Click the Axis Options icon.

5. Click the Axis Options heading to expand its options if it isn't already expanded.

6. In the Bounds area, change the Minimum and Maximum values as desired.

If you decide to go back to the default value, click Reset (see C in Figure 17-12).

7. Click Close to close the task pane.

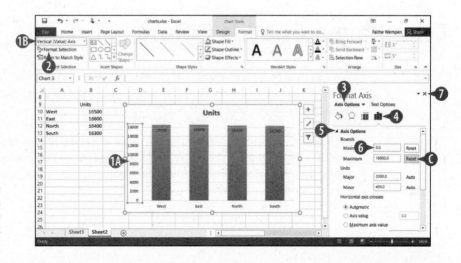

FIGURE 17-12:
Change the axis scale in the Format Axis task pane.

Applying a Chart Style

Excel provides many *chart styles*, which are formatting presets for charts. Rather than manually format a chart, you may want to save yourself some time by applying a chart style to improve a chart's appearance. (If you do want to format manually, though, it's covered later in this chapter.) Here are some things to note about applying chart styles:

(A) To apply a chart style, choose one from the Chart Styles gallery on the Chart Tools Design tab (see Figure 17-13).

(B) As with other galleries, you can click More to open up a list of additional choices.

Some chart styles have more or fewer chart elements (that is, helper objects such as titles, legends, labels, and so on). In the next section, you learn how to add and remove chart elements so that you aren't tied to the particular combination of elements that a particular chart style uses.

FIGURE 17-13:
Apply a chart style.

REMEMBER

Here's another way to apply a chart style. With the chart selected, click the Chart Styles button (the paintbrush button) to the right of the chart's frame. Then select a style from the palette that appears.

Changing a Chart's Colors

You can change, independently of the chart style, the colors used in the chart. To do so, click Change Colors on the Chart Tools Design tab, and then choose a different set of colors. (see A in Figure 17-14.)

Note that these aren't really different color schemes in the same sense as the overall color scheme for the entire workbook. The colors that appear on the Change Colors button's menu are just different combinations, tints, and shades of the overall workbook's colors.

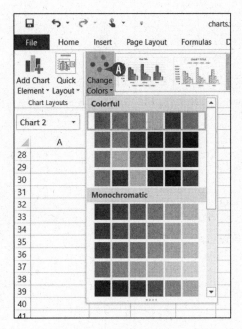

FIGURE 17-14:
Change the colors
used in the chart.

REMEMBER

Here's another way to change the colors. With the chart selected, click the Chart Styles button (the Paintbrush button) to the right of the chart's frame. At the top of the pane that appears, click Colors and then choose the desired colors.

If you want to change the overall colors of the workbook, do the following:

1. **On the Page Layout tab, click Colors.**

2. **Click the desired color scheme (see Figure 17-15).**

   This changes all the color placeholders for the workbook and also affects the chart colors.

If you want to individually customize a particular chart element, such as making a certain data series or data point a specific color, see "Formatting a Chart Element," later in this chapter.

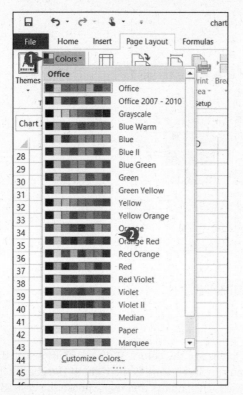

FIGURE 17-15:
Apply a different
color scheme to
the entire
workbook.

Adding or Removing Chart Elements

Chart elements refers to the individual parts of a chart that you can enable, adjust, and format separately. Figure 17-16 points out some of the most common chart elements. Most of these elements are optional and can be turned on or off.

TIP

In Figure 17-16, we have increased the size of some of the text-based chart elements so that you can see them better. To increase the size of a text-based element, such as data labels or a legend, select that element and then use the Grow Font button on the Home tab. Keep in mind, though, that if you manually change the size of some text, it won't change automatically any more if you resize the chart.

Here are some things to remember about chart elements:

(A) The *chart area* is the entire chart.

(B) A *chart title* describes the entire chart.

(C) The *plot area* is the section of the chart area that contains the actual plotted data. It's usually set to the same background color as the chart area, so it's not that noticeable; in Figure 17-16, however, we've made it a different color so that you can see it.

(D) The *legend* is a key that describes the meaning of each series color or pattern.

(E) A *data table* shows the data on which the chart is based; it can be helpful to use a data table if the chart isn't near the data.

(F) An *axis* contains the scale on which the data is plotted. When the axis contains numeric values, it's called the *value axis*. When the axis contains labels, like the months shown in Figure 17-16, it's called the *category axis*.

(G) An *axis label* explains the unit of measurement or the meaning of the axis values.

(H) *Data labels* report the exact value of each data point.

(I) An individual bar, column, slice, or other data marker is a *data point*.

(J) The set of bars, columns, or other data markers of a common color or pattern is a *data series*.

(K) A 3D-style chart, like the one in Figure 17-16, has *walls* behind the data series and a *floor* on which the bars sit. The walls and floor can be formatted separately from the chart or plot area and can even be formatted separately from one another.

(L) *Gridlines* appear behind the columns or bars to help make the height of the columns or bars easier to read on the axis.

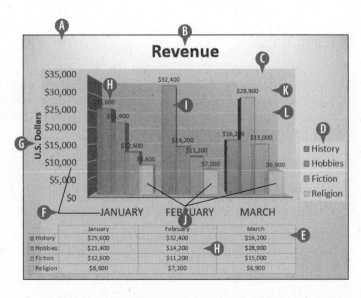

FIGURE 17-16:
Parts of a chart.

A few of the elements of a chart are fairly essential, like the data points and the value axis, and you couldn't remove them without the chart losing its meaning. Most of the other elements, however, are optional. A chart can still make sense without a data table, data labels, or even a legend, in some cases.

TIP

Some chart elements can be removed by selecting them (by clicking) and then pressing the Delete key on the keyboard. The chart title and legend are that way, for example.

To add or remove a chart element, follow these steps:

1. **Select the chart so that icons appear in its upper-right corner.**

2. **Click Chart Elements.**

   A menu of the optional chart elements appears.

3. **Mark or clear the check box for each element to turn it on or off (see Figure 17-17).**

4. **When you're finished, click Chart Elements again to close the menu.**

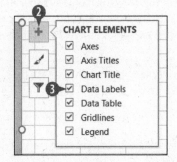

FIGURE 17-17:
Add or remove
chart elements.

Taking the route laid out in the preceding step list is the quickest and easiest way to enable or disable a certain element. However, if you're enabling an element, you might want a bit more control over how it appears. For some additional options, use the following method instead:

1. **Select the chart.**

2. **On the Chart Tools Design tab, click Add Chart Element.**

3. **Point to the desired chart element to see a submenu.**

4. **Click the desired option on the submenu.**

In Figure 17-17, if you hover the mouse pointer over one of the items on the menu, you see a right-pointing triangle. Click that, and a submenu appears that contains many of the same options as in Figure 17-18.

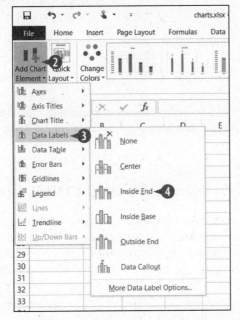

FIGURE 17-18:
Add a chart
element with
specific options.

Formatting a Chart Element

Now let's look at some ways to change a chart element's appearance.

Reposition a chart element

As you can see in Figure 17-18, each element has a submenu on the Add Chart Element button's menu. Some of these, like the ones for Legend and Chart Title, contain options for different positions within the chart area.

You can also drag-and-drop some of the chart elements to move them within the chart area:

1. **Select the chart element (see Figure 17-19) so that selection handles appear around that element.**

2. Position the mouse pointer over it so that the pointer turns into a 4-headed arrow.

3. Drag the element to a new location.

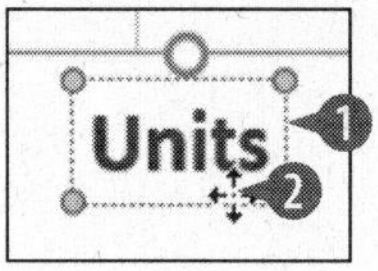

FIGURE 17-19:
Add a chart element with specific options.

Not all chart elements can be repositioned. For example, the data points and the axes are in fixed locations, and a data table can't appear anywhere other than below the chart.

Change the properties of a chart element

Each chart element has its own, unique customizable properties. It's hard to generalize about these, because they vary dramatically, depending on the element. For example, for a data series (a set of colored bars) in a 3D column chart, you can adjust the width of the bars, the gaps between them, and the shape of the bars (box, pyramid, cylinder).

To access an element's properties, do the following:

1A. Click the chart element to select it.

OR

1B. On the Chart Tools Format tab, open the Select Object drop-down list and choose the desired element.

2. On the Chart Tools Format tab, click Format Selection.

The Format task pane opens for that element.

3. Click the rightmost icon on the task pane. Its name and appearance vary, but this is the one that shows the properties that are specific to the chosen element type.

4. Adjust the properties as desired (see Figure 17-20).

5. Close the task pane.

TIP

While you're in the task pane, check out the other sections to see what else you can do to change the appearance of that element. Dozens of settings are available.

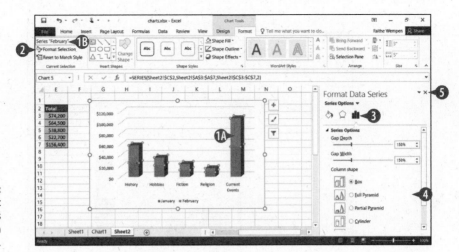

FIGURE 17-20:
Change the chart element's properties from its task pane.

Resize chart element text

To adjust the size of some text in a chart, do the following:

1. **Select the desired chart element.**

You can do this by clicking it or by using the Select Object drop-down list on the Chart Tools Format tab.

2A. **On the Home tab (see Figure 17-21), click the Increase Font Size or Decrease Font Size button to change the font size.**

OR

2B. **Open the Size drop-down list and select a specific size.**

Format chart element text

You can also change the attributes of the text (bold, italic, and so on). From the Home tab, use the buttons in the Font group, as shown in Figure 17-22, or use keyboard shortcuts:

(A) Bold (Ctrl+B)

(B) Italic (Ctrl+I)

(C) Underline (Ctrl+U)

To apply further special effects to the text, use the Text Effects settings in the element's task pane. Here's how:

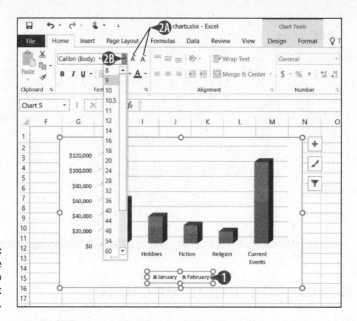

FIGURE 17-21:
Use the Home
tab controls to
change the text
size.

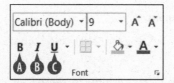

FIGURE 17-22:
Apply bold, italics,
or underline to a
text element on a
chart.

1. Select the desired chart element.

2. On the Chart Tools Format tab, click Format Selection to open the element's task pane.

3. At the top of the task pane, click the Text Options hyperlink.

4. Click the Text Effects icon.

5. Click an effect category to expand its settings.

6. Adjust the settings as desired (see Figure 17-23).

7. Repeat Steps 5–6 as needed, and then close the task pane.

Change a chart element's border and fill

Most of the chart elements have their own rectangular frames around them, although by default that frame may not have any border or fill, so the element blends in with the background behind it. For example, the plot area is its own, separate rectangular area, but you usually don't see it. The same is true for the legend, the axes, and the axis labels.

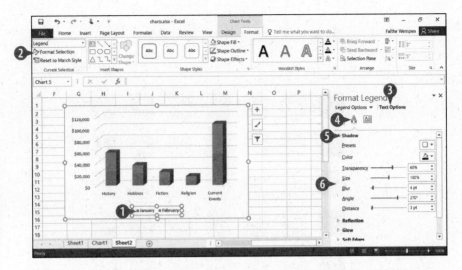

First, here's a quick way to apply border and fill combinations to a chart element — apply a shape style to it:

1. **Select the chart element.**

2. **On the Chart Tools Format tab, click the More button in the Shape Styles group to open the Shape Styles gallery (see Figure 17-24).**

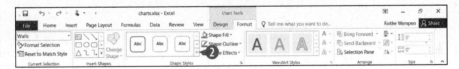

3. **Click one of the shape styles to apply it (see Figure 17-25).**

Want more control? To manually change the fill and/or border of an element, follow these steps:

1. **Select the chart element.**

2. **On the Chart Tools Format tab, open the Shape Fill button's menu.**

3. **Select a fill color (see Figure 17-26):**

   (A) Automatic allows Excel to choose the color based on the background color and is the default.

   (B) You can choose one of the theme colors.

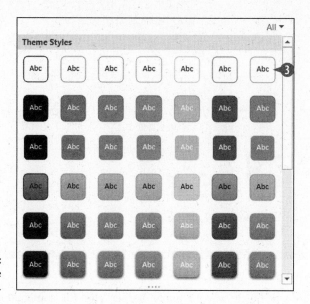

FIGURE 17-25:
Choose a shape style.

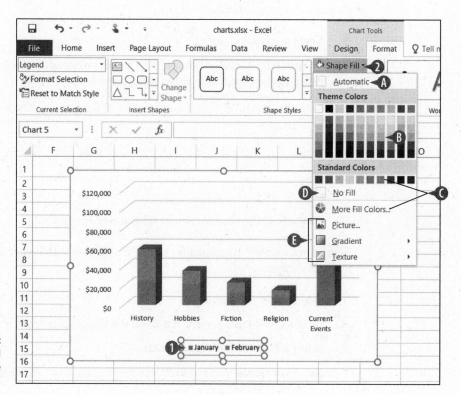

FIGURE 17-26:
Choose a fill effect for the selected element.

(C) You can choose a standard color. Click More Fill Colors for additional choices.

(D) To remove the fill, click No Fill.

(E) You can also choose a picture, gradient, or texture fill.

4. **Open the Shape Outline button's menu.**

5. **Select an outline color (see Figure 17-27):**

(F) Automatic allows Excel to choose the color based on the background color and is the default.

(G) You can choose one of the theme colors.

(H) You can choose a standard color.

(I) To remove the outline, click No Outline.

After selecting an outline color, you can, optionally, adjust the line style and thickness:

6. **Click the Shape Outline button again to reopen its menu.**

7. **If you want a different line thickness, point to Weight and select a line weight.**

8. **The default is a solid outline; if you want a dotted or dashed line, point to Dashes and select a line style.**

Apply special effects to a chart element

Special effects that you can add to an element include shadow, glow, soft edges, bevel, and 3D rotation. Most people don't take the time to apply such effects, but you may encounter situations where it's worthwhile to do so.

To apply an effect, follow these steps:

1. **Select the chart element.**

2. **On the Chart Tools Format tab, open the Shape Effects button's menu.**

3. **Point to an effect to open its submenu.**

4. **Click the desired effect.**

To remove an effect, click the selection in the No area of the menu, such as No Bevel for a bevel (see A in Figure 17-28).

5. **Repeat Steps 2–4 to apply any additional effects you want.**

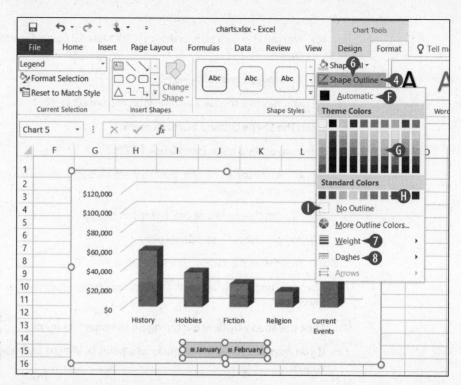

FIGURE 17-27:
Choose an outline color for the selected element.

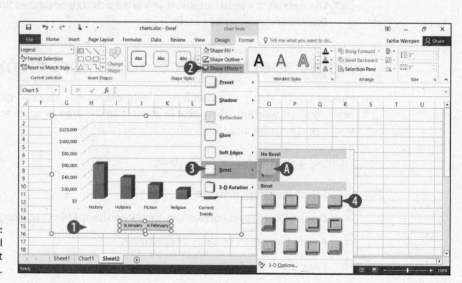

FIGURE 17-28:
Apply special effects to a chart element.

4

Communicating in Office 2016

Use Outlook as your email client.

Manage your contacts and tasks.

Make an impression with PowerPoint.

Chapter **18**

Managing Email with Outlook

O utlook is a multipurpose program. It's an address book, a calendar, a to-do list, and an email handling program, all in one. The most popular Outlook feature, though, is the email handling. Millions of people use Outlook as their primary email program, and for good reason! It's fast, full-featured, and easy to use and customize.

In this chapter, we show you how to set up an email account in Outlook and then how to use it to send and receive email messages.

Navigating the Outlook Interface

Outlook 2016 is like other Office 2016 applications in many ways. For example, it has a Ribbon, a File tab that opens Backstage view, and a status bar that shows status messages and provides a Zoom slider for changing the magnification of the application's content. The following sections explain what is unique about Outlook, and what you might not pick up on immediately on your own.

TIP

If you've never used Outlook before this, you might be prompted to set up an email address before Outlook starts working normally. See "Setting Up a Mail Account," later in this chapter, if you need help with the initial setup.

View the Mail section's layout

The Mail section consists of three panes, shown in Figure 18-1, from left to right:

(A) **Navigation:** Lists different locations you can click to make the active location. The default location is Inbox, where your incoming mail is located.

(B) **List:** Provides a list of emails stored in the active location.

(C) **Reading:** Shows a preview of whatever message is selected in the Mail list pane.

You can move the Reading pane to the bottom of the screen, or turn it off altogether. On the View tab, click Reading Pane, and then make your selection from the menu. (See D in Figure 18-2.)

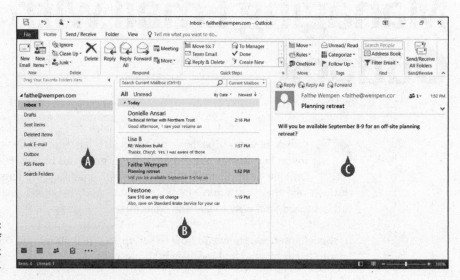

FIGURE 18-1:
The Mail area of the Outlook application.

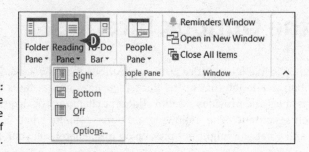

FIGURE 18-2:
Change the location of the Reading pane, if desired.

Switch between folders

In the navigation pane, you can click any folder to view its contents in the center (List) pane. The exact folders that appear depend somewhat on the type of email account you have set up and the folders on its server, but will probably include these:

(A)   **Inbox:** This is where incoming email arrives. You will probably spend most of your time in this folder.

(B)   **Drafts:** Any messages that you partially compose and then quit working on for some reason wait here for you to complete and send them.

(C)   **Sent Items:** Outlook saves a copy of every message you send in this folder, for your reference.

(D)   **Deleted Items (or Trash):** When you delete a message from any other folder, it goes here instead of being destroyed. To permanently delete a message, delete it from Deleted Items. For some mail accounts, this folder is called Trash.

(E)   **Junk Email:** If Outlook's junk mail filter identifies a message as potentially unwanted, it moves it here.

(F)   **Outbox:** Messages that you have sent but that have not yet been uploaded to the mail server wait here. If a message stays here for more than a few minutes, there may be a problem with your mail server or Internet connection.

(G)   **RSS Feeds:** *RSS* stands for Really Simple Syndication. It's a technology for aggregating updates from multiple websites in a single, easy-to-read location. It's no longer popular, but if you use this service, messages appear here.

(H)   **Search Folders:** If you have any saved searches, you can run them from here.

     You can also create your own mail folders, as you will learn later in this chapter. If you have done so, they appear in the Navigation pane also.

(I)   Notice where the top of the Navigation pane in Figure 18-3 says *Drag Your Favorite Folders Here.* You can drag a folder from the main section of the navigation pane and drop it there to create easily accessed shortcuts to the folders you use most often. This is not that big a deal if you have only a few folders, as shown in Figure 18-3, but if you start creating your own custom folders, over time you may have dozens of folders, with one inside another, and navigating to the correct folder may become not so simple any more.

(J)   If more than one email account is configured in Outlook, you might have multiple sections in the Navigation pane. At the top of each section is the email address to which it pertains. Other email accounts might have their own sections beneath that. Alternatively, all email accounts might use the same set of folders under a generic heading like Outlook or Mail, depending on how they're set up.

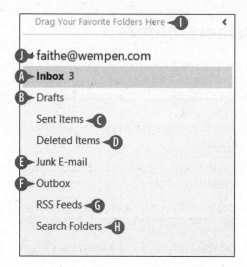

FIGURE 18-3:
Navigate among the available mail folders.

Navigate to other areas of the application

Outlook has several diverse areas, each providing a different service, and each area has a different interface. These areas are Mail, Calendar, People, Tasks, and Notes. (Two other items that are also listed aren't really separate areas: Folders and Shortcuts.)

Even though this lesson covers only the email component of Outlook, it's a good idea to familiarize yourself with the entire application so you can get an idea of how the areas fit together.

You click a button in the lower-left corner of the Outlook application window to switch to the area you want to work with, as shown in Figure 18-4:

(A) **Mail:** Send, receive, and manage email

(B) **Calendar:** Record and display appointments and events

(C) **People:** Store and retrieve information about people and businesses

(D) **Tasks:** Record and track the progress of to-do items

(E) **More:** Open a menu of other areas of Outlook, such as Notes

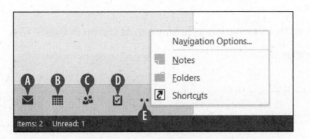

FIGURE 18-4:
Switch among the different Outlook areas using the buttons in the lower-left corner.

Setting Up a Mail Account

The first time you start Outlook, you're prompted to complete several setup operations. The most important of these is to set up your email account.

If you aren't prompted to set up a mail account, and Outlook simply opens up, your mail account may already be configured. If that's the case, you don't have to do anything other than start enjoying it. See the rest of this chapter to learn what to do.

If you aren't prompted but you also don't have a valid email account set up, *or* if you want to set up additional accounts, follow the steps in the next section, "Set up an account automatically." If you *are* prompted, jump into the steps at Step 3 in the next section.

Set up an account automatically

First, let Outlook try to configure your account automatically — if it works, you've just saved yourself some time and effort:

1. **In Outlook, click File to open Backstage view.**

2. **Click Add Account (see Figure 18-5).**

    The Add Account dialog box opens.

FIGURE 18-5:
Choose to add a new account.

3. Fill in the information as prompted, as shown in Figure 18-6.

4. Click Next.

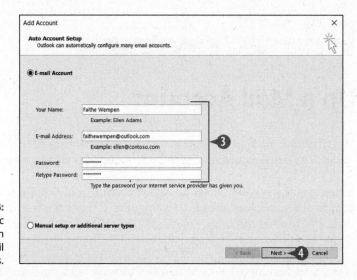

5. Wait for Outlook to attempt to configure the account. If it's successful, you see a Congratulations message. Click Finish and you're done.

TIP

Outlook is usually successful if you have a Microsoft Exchange account on the network to which your computer is connected, or if you're using an Outlook. com or Hotmail.com address. That's because those are Microsoft account types.

6. If the initial attempt failed, you might see the following:

An encrypted connection to your mail server is not available. Click Next to attempt using an unencrypted connection.

If you see that message, click Next to try the alternative, unencrypted method.

7. Wait for Outlook to try the alternative method.

You might see a success message, like the one shown in Figure 18-7, or another failure message.

8. If you see another failure message, mark the Let Me Set Up My Account Manually check box in the dialog box (see Figure 18-8), and then click Next.

9. Go on to the next section to continue your mail setup.

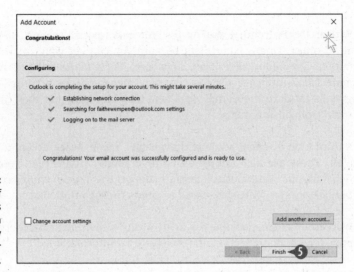

FIGURE 18-7:
Click Finish if
Outlook was
successful in
automatically
configuring your
mail account.

FIGURE 18-8:
Choose to change
the account
settings
manually.

Set up an account manually

If the preceding procedure didn't work out for you, you need to manually enter the settings for your account. That means you need to know a bit more *about* your email account.

There are different kinds of mail servers. You need to know which type you have before you start setting up your email account in Outlook. Ask your Internet service provider or IT department, if needed.

Outlook offers a few choices right at the beginning. If you have an Office 365, Outlook.com, or Exchange account, Outlook is happy to work within the Microsoft family to get you hooked up. Click the correct account type and go from there. Outlook also (probably grudgingly) offers to work with a Gmail account. If none of those applies to you, Outlook offers POP3 and IMAP options.

POP3 (Post Office Protocol 3) is the most common for home use and for most offices. With a POP3 account, mail is stored on the server until you retrieve it, and then it's downloaded to your PC (and deleted from the server). This is called a *store-and-forward* system.

With an IMAP (Internet Mail Access Protocol) account, the mail stays on the server at all times. This is convenient because you can get your email from anywhere (and review old messages from anywhere), but it's slower than POP3 to access and more labor-intensive for the company managing the server. Some companies provide IMAP to their employees who travel a lot so that they can retrieve their email from different PCs.

A third kind of email account is available: a web-based account, such as Yahoo! Mail. These are also known as HTTP accounts (HyperText Transfer Protocol). Generally speaking, Outlook doesn't support this type of email account. However, Outlook does support web-based accounts through Outlook.com.

TIP

Workarounds are available for many of the web-based email services. Check the provider's Support section on its website for information.

You need to know not only which kind of account you have but also the incoming and outgoing mail server addresses. An incoming email server might be something like `pop.provider.net` or `imap.provider.net`. An outgoing email server usually starts with *smtp* (Simple Mail Transfer Protocol), as in `smtp.provider.net`. Don't try to guess, though; get the information from the mail provider.

Depending on the account type and provider, you might also need to know the answers to these questions:

>> What kind of authentication does the outgoing mail server require?

>> What ports are used (numeric codes) for incoming and outgoing mail? For example, a mail server might use 110 for incoming and 3535 for outgoing mail.

When you have your info in hand, it's time to set up your account. Follow these steps:

1. **At the Choose Service screen, make your selection of an account type.**

2. **Depending on the account you pick, fill in the information about your email account using the data you gathered from your provider or IT department.**

   Outlook tries to handle its own accounts automatically, but the others require some work. Some of the important fields include:

   • Enter the incoming and outgoing mail servers.

   • Enter the password you were assigned for your email account.

- If you choose POP3 as the account type, you have a choice to use an existing Outlook data file or create a new one to store the received mail for this account. This choice isn't available for IMAP because IMAP stores messages on the server.

3. **Click Connect.**

   Some of the fields will be different depending on the account type.

REMEMBER

4. **Enter any other information Outlook requires.**

   The program tries to handle as much as it can automatically, but you may need to give it a little nudge here and there.

5. **If you've entered all the information correctly, Outlook gives you a confirmation messages and asks whether you want to set up Outlook Mobile on your phone as well.**

   We'll leave that decision up to you.

   If you encounter errors, keep modifying the information until you end up in a happier place.

Modify an account's settings

If an account isn't working right, check with your provider to make sure your settings haven't changed. For example, our email provider changed the default port for outgoing mail, and we didn't know until we suddenly couldn't send mail one day.

To modify an account's settings, follow these steps:

1. **Click File to open Backstage view.**

2. **Click Account Settings to open a menu, and then click Account Settings on the menu (see Figure 18-9).**

3. **Click the account you want to change (see Figure 18-10).**

4. **Click Change.**

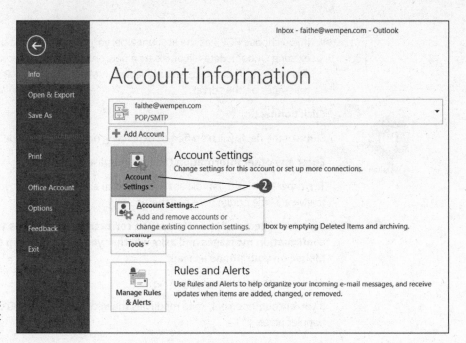

FIGURE 18-9:
Choose Account
Settings.

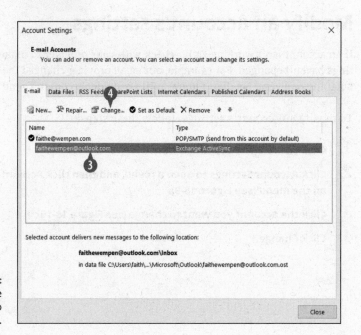

FIGURE 18-10:
Choose the
account to
change.

5. **Modify the account's settings (see Figure 18-11).**

You cannot change the account type (Exchange, POP3, IMAP), but you can change most other properties.

TIP

If you need to change the account type, remove and re-create the account in Outlook.

6. **Click Next.**

Outlook performs a test send-and-receive operation.

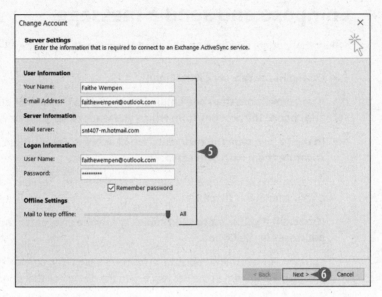

FIGURE 18-11:
Modify the
account settings.

7. **Click Close.**

8. **If the test was successful, click Finish. If not, return to Step 5.**

9. **Click Close to close the Account Settings dialog box (see Figure 18-12).**

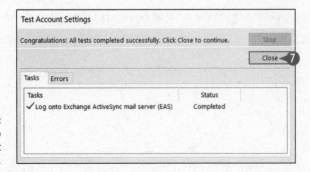

FIGURE 18-12:
Click Close to
accept the test
results.

Composing and Sending Email

You can send a new email message to anyone for whom you have an email address. Just fill in the recipient, subject, and message and then send it off.

If you have stored contacts in the People section of Outlook, you can look up recipients' email addresses from there. If you're on an Exchange server, you can also use the directory or address book provided on that system.

Compose and send a message

Follow these steps to compose and send a message (see Figure 18-13):

1. **On the Home tab, click New Email.**

2. **If you have more than one email account set up in Outlook, click From and choose the account from which you want to send this message.**

3. **In the To box, type the recipient's email address. For multiple recipients, separate them with semicolons.**

   Or, alternatively, look up addresses, as explained in the section "Address an email," later in this chapter.

4. **(Optional) If you want to send copies to anyone else, enter their email addresses in the Cc box.**

   You can also send blind copies (Bcc) from Outlook. To do so, click the Cc button and then enter them in the Bcc text box in the dialog box that appears.

   TIP

5. **In the Subject box, type the email subject.**

   This text will appear in the recipient's inbox.

6. **Type the body of your message.**

7. **If desired, format the text in the message body using the Basic Text group on the Message tab.**

   The controls are nearly the same as on Word's Home tab.

8. **Click Send.**

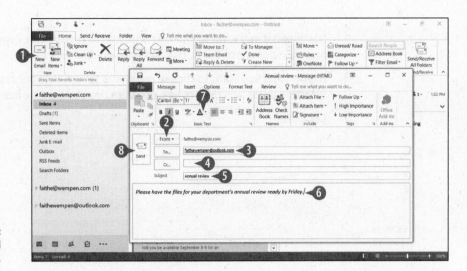

FIGURE 18-13:
Compose and
send an email.

Address an email

You can look up recipient email addresses as you compose a message. You can place recipients into one of three categories:

» **To:** Main recipients

» **Cc:** Recipients that should receive a courtesy copy

» **Bcc:** Recipients that should receive a courtesy copy without other recipients knowing about it

Follow these steps to select recipients in one or more of these categories from your company's address list on its mail server or from your own private list of addresses stored in the Contacts section of Outlook (covered in Chapter 19):

1. Click the To button in the message composition screen, shown in Figure 18-14.

2. Double-click the desired name. Repeat this as needed for additional recipients.

The name moves to the To line in the dialog box (see A in Figure 18-15).

If the names that appear on the list in the dialog box aren't the ones you expect, or if the list is empty, you might need to change which address book is shown. To do so, open the Address Book drop-down list and select another source (see B in Figure 18-15).

3. **(Optional) If you want to choose recipients to receive a Cc copy, move the insertion point into the Cc box and then double-click the desired name.**

4. **(Optional) If you want to choose recipients to receive a Bcc copy, move the insertion point into the Bcc box and then double-click the desired name.**

5. **Click OK.**

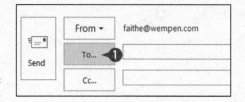

FIGURE 18-14:
Click To.

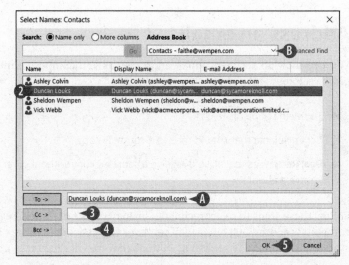

FIGURE 18-15:
Select names for
the To field and,
optionally, for Cc
and/or Bcc.

Attach a file to a message

You can attach a file to an email, such as a word processing document or a photo. There is no limit on the number of attachments you can add to an email, although some mail servers have a limit on the size of an email message being sent or received (usually somewhere between 2 and 10MB).

WARNING

For your safety, Outlook does not allow you to receive attachments with certain file extensions, such as exe, com, and vbs. That's because those executable formats can carry viruses. Other people's email programs may have the same restriction, so any files you send with those extensions might not be received. Therefore, if you need to send such files, compress them in a ZIP file or use a file sharing service such as OneDrive or Dropbox.

To attach a file as you're composing an email, follow these steps:

1. **From the message composition window, on the Message tab, click Attach file (see Figure 18-16).**

2. **From the menu that appears, click Browse This PC.**

3. **Navigate to and select the desired file to attach.**

4. **Click Insert (see Figure 18-17).**

5. **Finish sending the message as you normally would.**

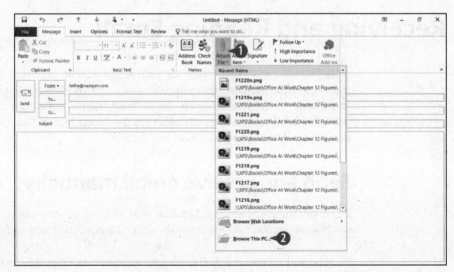

FIGURE 18-16: Click the Attach File button.

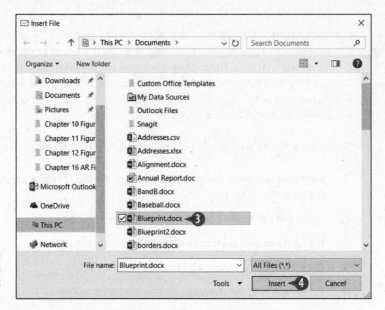

FIGURE 18-17:
Choose the file to
attach and click
Insert.

Receiving and Reading Email

After you configure your email account(s) in Outlook, receiving mail is an automatic process. Outlook automatically sends and receives mail when you start it and also at 30-minute intervals (by default) whenever Outlook is running. Your incoming mail comes automatically into the Inbox folder. You can also initiate a manual send/receive operation at any time.

Send and receive email manually

When you manually send and receive mail, Outlook connects to the mail server(s), sends any mail you have waiting to be sent, and downloads any waiting mail for you.

To send and receive manually, you can either press F9 or do one of the following (see Figure 18-18):

(A) On the Quick Access toolbar, click Send/Receive All Folders.

(B) On the Send/Receive tab, click Send/Receive All Folders.

FIGURE 18-18:
Perform a
manual send/
receive.

Change the send/receive automatic interval

If you would like to change the interval at which Outlook automatically sends and receives mail, or disable automatic send/receive altogether, do the following:

1. On the Send/Receive tab, click Send/Receive Groups.

2. Click Define Send/Receive Groups, as shown in Figure 18-19.

3. Select the default group name (All Accounts) if it's not already selected.

There might not be any other groups.

4. Increase or decrease the value in the Schedule an Automatic Send/Receive Every ___ Minutes box.

You can also turn off the automatic send/receive action altogether by clearing its check box (see A in Figure 18-20).

There are separate settings for when Outlook is offline; this might happen if you were on a dial-up connection that was not always on. Scheduling an automatic send/receive to occur when Outlook is offline would tell Windows to establish the dial-up connection each time, get the mail, and then disconnect (see B in Figure 18-20).

5. Click Close.

FIGURE 18-19: Select Define Send/Receive Groups.

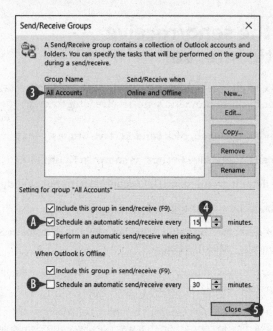

FIGURE 18-20:
Change the
interval for
automatic
sending and
receiving.

Read a received email

Got a new message in your inbox? Time to take a look!

(A) Unread messages appear with bold and blue subject lines in the Inbox.

(B) You can read the selected message in the Reading pane.

(C) You open a received message in its own, separate window by double-clicking
the message (see Figure 18-21).

Work with a received attachment

After receiving an attachment, you will want to do something with it, such as view
it or save it. Here are some tips for working with received attachments:

(A) If the received message has an attachment, a paperclip icon appears in the
message list.

(B) In the Reading pane, the attachment filename appears above the message.

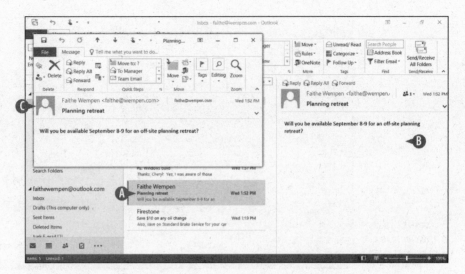

FIGURE 18-21:
Read a message.

(C) To open the attachment in whatever program is the default for its type on your system, double-click it. Doing so does not automatically save the attachment to your PC, although it remains available via the message in Outlook until you delete that message.

(D) To save the attachment to your PC, or to perform other actions on it such as printing or previewing, click the arrow on the filename in the reading pane (see Figure 18-22).

(E) Choose Quick Print to print a copy of the attachment on your default printer using default settings.

(F) If you choose Save As, the Save Attachment dialog box opens. Navigate to a storage location and click Save.

(G) If there are multiple attachments and you want to save them all to the same location, use Save All Attachments to save them all at once.

(H) Remove Attachment is not common because normally you would want to keep a record of having received the attachment. You might use it if the attachment contained sensitive information, or a virus.

(I) Copy places the attachment on the Windows Clipboard; you can then use Paste (press Ctrl+V) to paste it somewhere (such as in a location in File Explorer).

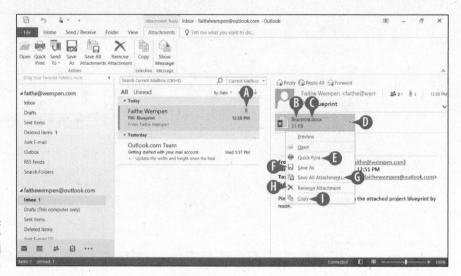

FIGURE 18-22:
You can save or
print a received
attachment.

Reply to a message

Email messages often consist of multiple back-and-forth exchanges. Rather than
start a new message each time, you can use the Reply feature. Here's how:

1. **To reply to a message, select the message and then click Reply on the
Home tab, as shown in Figure 18-23.**

Use Reply All if you want the reply to also go to anyone who was also a
recipient of the original message (see A in Figure 18-23). This doesn't include
Bcc recipients.

You can also use the Reply or Reply All button in the Reading pane (see B in
Figure 18-23)

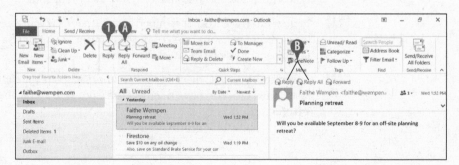

FIGURE 18-23:
Click Reply or
Reply All.

TIP

When you reply to a message, the original attachments are not included. That's
because the original recipient probably doesn't want to get her attachment back.

The reply message begins in the Reading pane by default, but you can pop it out into its own window, if you want, by clicking Pop Out (see C in Figure 18-24).

The recipient is already filled in, based on the sender of the original message (see D in Figure 18-24).

The subject is already filled in; it's the original subject with RE: at the beginning (see E in Figure 18-24).

2. **Type your reply in the message body.**

The original message appears quoted. You can delete any portion of it that you don't want to include in your reply (see F in Figure 18-24).

3. **Click Send when you finish composing the reply.**

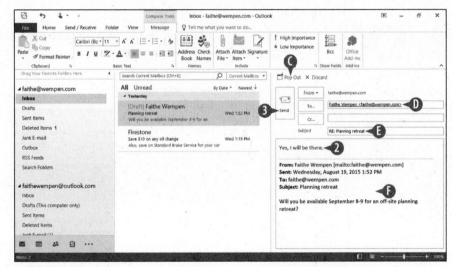

FIGURE 18-24: Compose your reply.

Forward a message

Forwarding is mostly the same as replying (see the earlier section "Reply to a message") except that the recipient isn't filled in automatically for you.

To forward a message, follow these steps:

1. **To forward to a message, select the message and then click Forward on the Home tab.**

You can also use the Forward button in the Reading pane (see A in Figure 18-25).

FIGURE 18-25:
Click Forward to
begin forwarding
a message.

2. **Enter the recipient(s) in the To box, or click To and select them.**

3. **(Optional) Type any comments or notes you want to include in the message body.**

4. **Click Send.**

TIP

Unlike when replying, forwarding (see Figure 18-26) includes any attachments that the original contained in the forwarded copy.

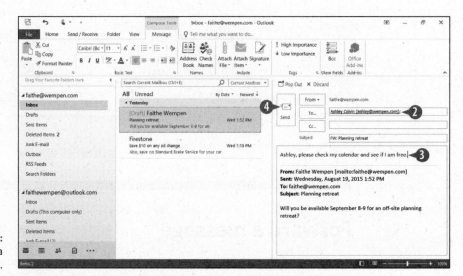

FIGURE 18-26:
Forward a
message.

Delete a message and recover deleted messages

Most of the email you receive will eventually be deleted, just as most of the postal mail you receive ultimately ends up in your wastebasket.

To delete a message, select the message and then do any of the following:

» On the Home tab, click Delete.

» Press the Delete key on the keyboard.

» Right-click the message and choose Delete.

If you make a mistake and delete the wrong thing, you can recover it from the Deleted Items folder, as shown in Figure 18-27:

1. In the navigation bar, click Deleted Items. (Or, depending on your mail account, it may be named Trash.)

2. Drag the message from the message list to the desired folder in the navigation pane, such as to the Inbox.

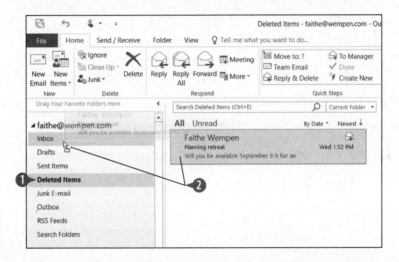

FIGURE 18-27: Retrieve a deleted message.

Creating Folders for Managing Email

As you receive more and more messages, messaging handling becomes increasingly important. You don't want to have to wade through thousands of messages in your Inbox just to find the one you need in a hurry.

To create a mail folder, follow these steps:

TIP

1. **On the Folder tab, click New Folder, as shown in Figure 18-28.**

   Or right-click the Inbox folder and choose New Folder from the shortcut menu.

2. **Type the folder name in the Name box, as shown in Figure 18-29.**

3. **Click Inbox to make the folder a subfolder of your inbox.**

TIP

   It's not required, but it's a good idea to make all of the folders that will hold received mail subfolders of Inbox. That way, when you act on the Inbox folder (for example, archive it), all subfolders will be included in that operation.

4. **Click OK.**

   The new folder appears in the navigation pane.

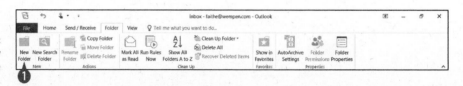

FIGURE 18-28: Choose New Folder from the Folder tab.

FIGURE 18-29: Name the new folder.

Moving Messages Between Folders

The main point of creating new folders (covered in the earlier section "Creating Folders for Managing Email") is so that you can move messages into them for storage.

To move a message, select the message in the message list, and then drag-and-drop it on a different folder in the navigation pane (see Figure 18-30).

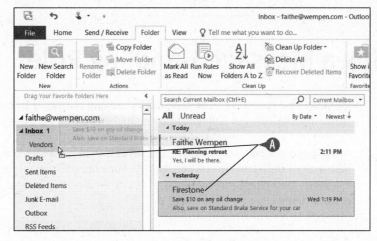

FIGURE 18-30:
Drag a message from its current location to a different folder in the navigation bar.

If drag-and-drop isn't your thing, here's another way to move a message:

1. **Select the message.**
2. **On the Home tab, click Move.**
3. **Click the desired folder.**

   If the folder you want doesn't appear, click Other Folder to browse a more complete list (See A in Figure 18-31).

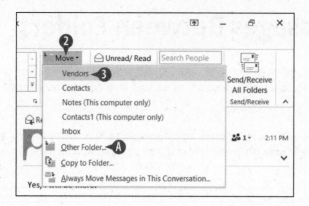

FIGURE 18-31:
Move a folder
using the Ribbon.

Creating a Message Handling Rule

You may find it tedious to be continually moving messages into different folders
manually. Outlook can help with that chore by running message handling rules.

A *message handling rule* evaluates the mail and then processes it according to your
instructions based on criteria you specify. For example, you might have a rule that
evaluates mail when it arrives and, if it's from a certain sender, moves it into a
certain subfolder.

Move messages from a specific sender

Here's a quick way to set up a rule based on a specific sender. To use this method,
you must have a message from that sender available to select:

1. **In the message list, select a message that is from the sender for which
    you want to create a rule, as shown in Figure 18-32.**

FIGURE 18-32:
Select a message
from that sender.

2. **On the Home tab, click Rules.**

3. **Click Always Move Messages from *Sender*, where *Sender* is the person's name.**

4. **Select the folder into which you want to move the messages.**

If the folder doesn't exist yet, you can click New to create it on the fly (see A in Figure 18-33).

5. **Click OK.**

The rule is created and the message moves to the new folder. All other messages from that same sender also move.

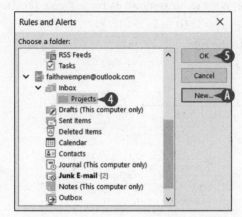

FIGURE 18-33:
Choose a folder
to which to move
the messages.

Create a message handling rule

The following steps show a method that works for multiple types of criteria, not just the sender's name. You can use this procedure to filter by subject line, sender, and/or recipient account (if you have more than one email account set up in Outlook).

1. **Select a received message that matches the criteria you want to specify.**

2. **On the Home tab, click Rules.**

3. **Click Create Rule (see Figure 18-34).**

4. **Mark the check boxes for the conditions that must apply for the message.**

The message must match *all* the criteria you choose.

TIP

If you want to set up a rule that applies if one condition *or* the other is met, create two separate rules.

5. **Specify what you want to happen when a message matches the criteria.**

   You can make Outlook play a sound, display an alert, and/or move the message.

6. **If you want the item to be moved to a certain folder, make sure the Move check box is marked, and make sure the correct folder appears in its text box.**

   Click Select Folder and choose a different folder, if needed. The dialog box for selecting the folder is the same as shown earlier, in Figure 18-33 (see A in Figure 18-35).

7. **Click OK to create the rule.**

   The rule runs.

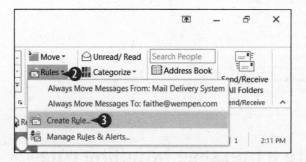

FIGURE 18-34:
Choose to create
a new rule.

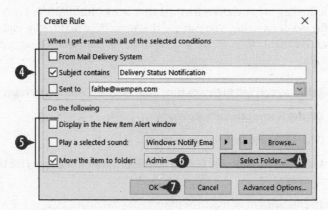

FIGURE 18-35:
Define the rule.

Modify or delete a message handling rule

Over time, your rule needs may change. Some rules may no longer be applicable, and others may need modification. If you later need to make changes to a rule, here's how:

1. On the Home tab, click **Rules** and then click **Manage Rules & Alerts.**

2. Select a rule.

The rule's description appears in the lower part of the dialog box
(see Figure 18-36).

You can delete the selected rule by clicking Delete (see A in Figure 18-36).

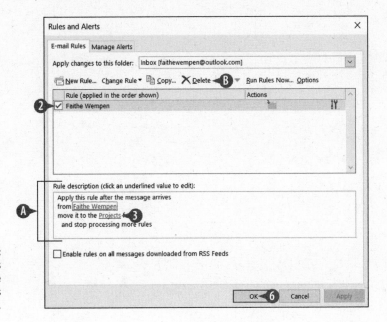

FIGURE 18-36:
Manage rules
from the
Rules and Alerts
dialog box.

3. Click an underlined portion of the rule description to modify that section of the rule.

For example, to change where to move the message, click the underlined folder name.

4. Make a change in the dialog box that appears.

The dialog box that appears depends on what portion of the rule you're modifying.

5. Then click OK to return to the Rules and Alerts dialog box.

6. When you're done modifying the rule, click OK.

Chapter **19**

Using Outlook Contacts and Tasks

O utlook is much more than just an email program. It excels at storing information that you need for your daily business and personal dealings, such as contact information and to-do lists. If you can't keep yourself organized with all these tools available to you, don't blame Outlook!

In this chapter, we show you how to enter and use contact information in the People area of Outlook. We also show how to create and manage tasks and to-do items in the Tasks area.

Adding and Editing Contacts

The People area of Outlook stores a *contact* (also called a *record*) for each person or business that you want to save for later use.

You can access the People area by clicking the People icon in the lower-left corner of the Outlook window (see Figure 19-1).

FIGURE 19-1:
Click People to
open the People
area of Outlook,
where contacts
are stored.

If you have more than one email account set up in Outlook, you might have multiple separate Contacts listings. If so, you see them listed in the navigation pane. Click the one you want to see (refer to Figure 19-1).

Create a new contact

Outlook stores complete contact information about the people you want to keep in touch with. You can store not only mailing addresses but also phone numbers, email addresses, pager numbers, and personal information such as birthdays, spouses' names, departments, and professions.

To create a new contact, follow these steps:

1. **From the People area of Outlook, on the Home tab, click New Contact (see Figure 19-2).**

FIGURE 19-2:
Start a new
contact.

2. **Fill in the fields with all the information you want to record about that contact.**

   A summary of the person's contact information appears in the upper-right corner (see Figure 19-3).

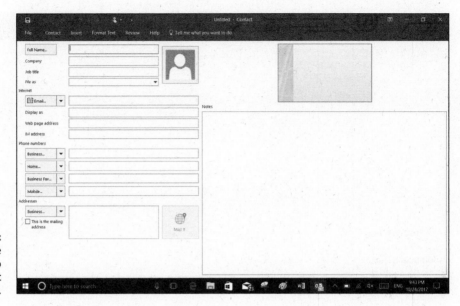

FIGURE 19-3:
Enter the
information to
store about that
contact.

TIP

You can store as much or as little information as you like about each contact, and it need not be consistent between contacts. For some people, all you need is an email address. For others, you might need multiple ways to contact the person, as well as personal details such as spouse's name and birthday.

WARNING

When creating a contact, the window in which it appears may truncate the available fields at the bottom if the window is not tall enough. You can increase the window size, but if you're using a very small screen size or low resolution, you might not be able to make the window large enough to see all the fields, and you can't scroll down to see them, because there's no scroll bar in this window. The bottommost field is the Addresses area, so if you can see that, you're good.

3. **(Optional) If you need to enter additional information about the contact, click Details and fill in any of the additional fields (see Figure 19-4).**

4. **Click Save & Close.**

If you need to make changes to a contact, you can double-click it to reopen it.

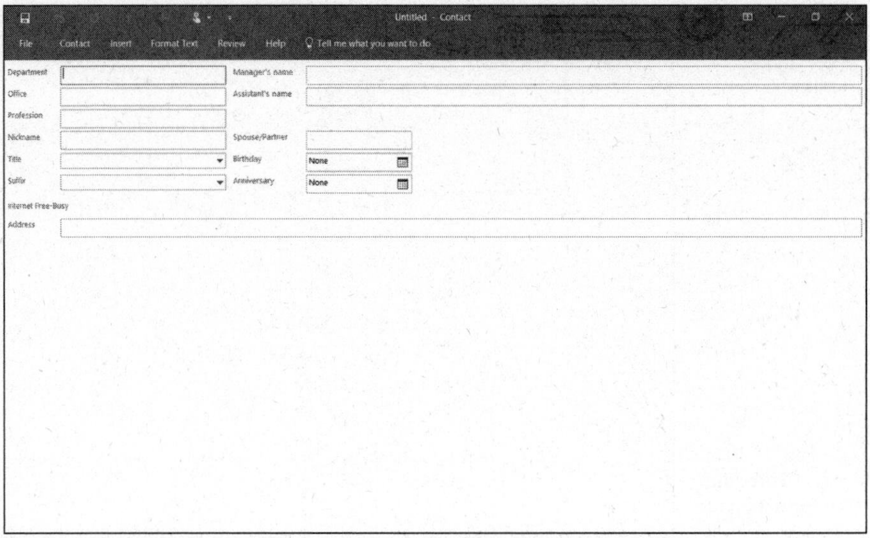

FIGURE 19-4:
Record any
additional details
as needed.

Change how a contact is filed

If someone asked you how contacts were alphabetized in Outlook, you would probably say that they're done by last name, right? And you'd be absolutely . . . *wrong.*

The File As setting determines the sort order in the People list. By default, when you create a new contact, the File As setting for it is set to *Last Name, First Name.* But you can change it to another setting if you prefer, such as the company name or the first name. Here's how:

1. **Double-click the contact to reopen it for editing.**

2. **Open the File As drop-down list and choose a different filing method for the contact (see Figure 19-5).**

    If you want both the company name and the person's name to show, choose one of the File As options that includes both. The one that appears first will be how it's alphabetized. For example, Strong, Terry (ACME Corporation) alphabetizes by Strong but also includes ACME Corporation in the title.

3. **Click Save & Close.**

Delete and restore a contact

With Outlook, you don't have to tear pages out of a paper address book to get rid of a person's information; just delete the contact:

TIP

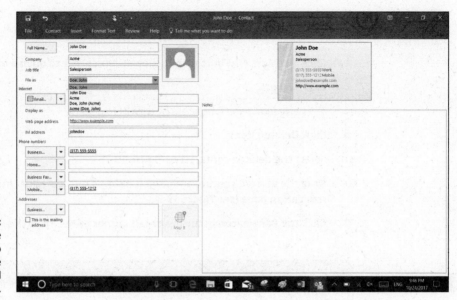

FIGURE 19-5:
Change the File
As setting to
control how the
contact is filed
alphabetically.

>> To delete a contact, select the contact and then click Delete on the Home tab (see Figure 19-6).

>> Alternatively, you can right-click the contact and click Delete.

>> You can also select the contact and then press the Delete key on the keyboard.

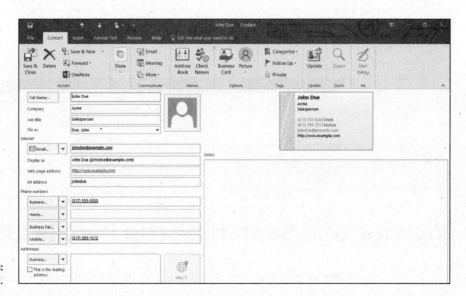

FIGURE 19-6:
Delete a contact.

To restore an accidentally deleted contact, follow these steps:

1. **Click the More (. . .) button in the lower-left corner to open a menu.**

2. **Click Folders.**

   The navigation pane is replaced by a list of folders.

3. **Click Deleted Items.**

4. **Select the deleted contact (see Figure 19-7).**

5. **Drag the deleted contact and drop it on the Contacts folder in the navigation pane (see Figure 19-8).**

6. **Click the People icon in the lower-left corner to return to the People area.**

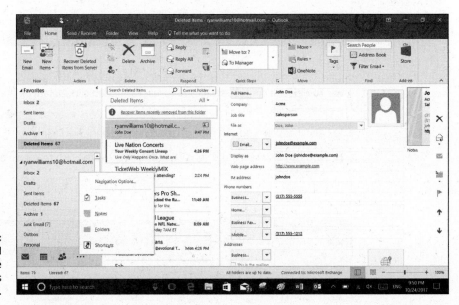

FIGURE 19-7:
Find a deleted contact in the Deleted Items folder.

FIGURE 19-8:
Drag the deleted contact onto the Contacts folder.

Viewing and Searching the People List

Depending on the view you're using at the moment, each contact may be displayed as a card, a business card, or an item in a list. Consider Figure 19-9:

>> To change the view, make a selection from the Home tab's Current View group.

>> You might need to click the More button to see all the choices, depending on the window size.

As your list of contacts grows, you might need some help finding a particular contact.

>> You can click a letter to jump to the corresponding section in the listing. This is a good way to look up a contact if you know what it was filed under (for example, the company name or the person's last name).

>> If you aren't sure how the contact was filed, you can search by entering any piece of information you know in the Search Contacts box and pressing Enter. For example, you might search by entering the person's first name or the city in their mailing address.

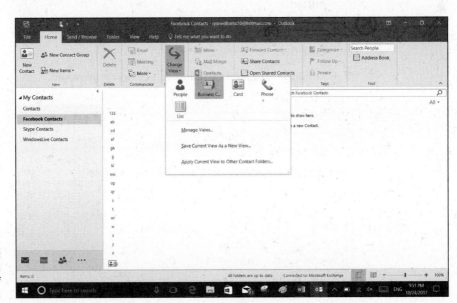

FIGURE 19-9:
Choose between different views of the People list.

Sending a Message to a Contact

You can easily address an email message to a contact in your People list. You can initiate this process from either the Contacts area of the program or the Mail area.

To send from the People area, do the following:

1. **Select the contact.**

2. **On the Home tab, click Email.**

   Outlook starts a new message with the recipient's email address pre-entered.

3. **Compose and send the email as you would normally.**

To send from the Mail area, do this:

1. **Click New Email.**

2. **In the new message window, click Address Book or click the To button.**

3. **In the Select Names window, click the contact's name (see Figure 19-10).**

4. **If the name doesn't immediately appear in the To box, click the To button.**

5. **Add other names to the To, Cc, and/or Bcc lines as desired.**

6. **Click OK.**

7. **Compose and send the email as you normally would.**

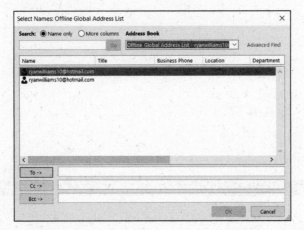

FIGURE 19-10: Choosing a contact.

Forwarding Contact Data via Email

You can share a contact by attaching the contact record to an email in one of these formats:

» **Outlook contact:** The attachment is an Outlook contact, which only Outlook can accept. The recipient must have Outlook to make use of the attachment.

» **Business card:** The attachment is in vCard format (.vcf), a standard format for personal data that many programs can accept.

Sharing contact data can be a quick way of transferring information about vendors and customers between employees; you can also use this feature to share your own contact information with people so that they can import your contact info into their address books without having to manually type it.

To attach contact information to a message, follow these steps:

1. **In the People area, select the contact to send.**

2. **On the Home tab, click Forward Contact (see Figure 19-11).**

3. **Click either As a Business Card or As an Outlook Contact.**

4. **In the New Message window that appears, enter or select the recipient(s).**

   The contact's name appears on the Subject line, but you can change this (see Figure 19-12).

   The contact information is already attached.

5. **Click Send to send the email.**

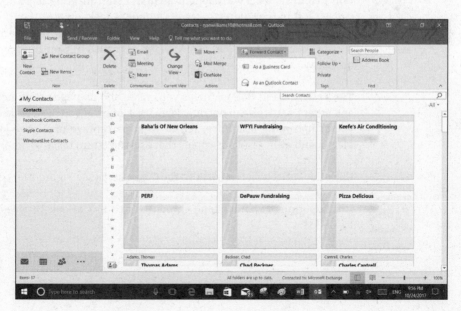

FIGURE 19-11:
Forward a contact to an email recipient.

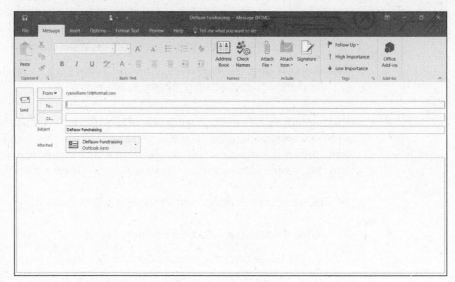

FIGURE 19-12:
Compose and
send the
message.

Creating and Managing Tasks

A *task* is a database record that contains information about something that you need to accomplish. For example, when we were writing this book, we used a task in Outlook to keep track of deadlines and our progress.

WARNING

Don't confuse tasks with appointments. A staff meeting is an appointment, and you enter it in the Calendar area of Outlook. A task, on the other hand, is an action you need to complete *by* a certain date or time, but not necessarily *at* that exact date or time. For example, a task might be to turn in your time card before 5 p.m. on Friday.

The Tasks area in Outlook helps you create and manage action items for yourself and others. Outlook can not only keep track of what you need to do but also remind you of upcoming deadlines, record what percentage of a large job you've completed, and even send out emails that assign certain tasks to other people.

Click the Tasks icon to switch to the Tasks area (see Figure 19-13).

REMEMBER

It's important to understand the difference in Outlook between tasks and the to-do list:

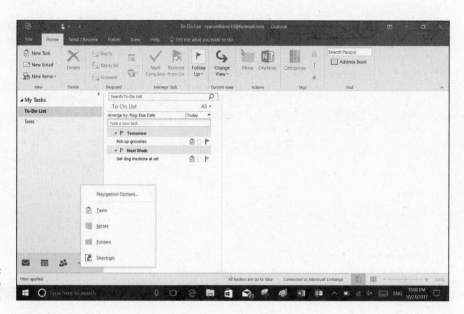

FIGURE 19-13:
Work with the
Tasks list.

» *Tasks* are specific items you create in the Tasks area of Outlook. An action isn't technically a *task* unless it was created in the Tasks section. If you click Tasks, you see only tasks created in the Tasks section.

» If you have more than one email account, each one may have its own Tasks entry, which opens a separate Tasks list.

» *The to-do list* contains everything from the Tasks list as well as other items you have marked for action, such as email messages you flag for follow-up. If you click To-Do List, you see all your tasks plus any other flagged items from other areas.

Enter a new task

Here's a simple way to enter tasks. If you have a lot of tasks to enter and you don't need to record much information about them, this method is your best bet:

1. **Enter a new task by typing it in the Type a New Task box at the top of the Tasks list (see Figure 19-14).**

- You can enter a due date in the Due Date column or leave it blank for no due date.

- The fields that are available depend on the view you have chosen. See "Change the Tasks view," later in this chapter. Simple List view is shown here.

- After entering a task this way, you can double-click the task to open it in its own window and enter additional details.

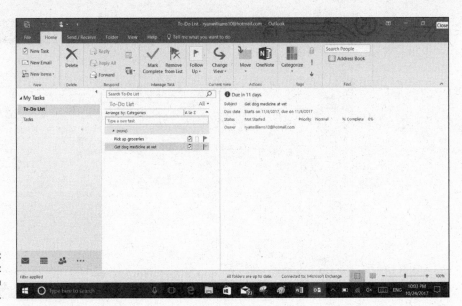

FIGURE 19-14:
Click in the box
and begin
entering the task.

To enter more information about a task as you create it, use the following method instead:

1. **From the Tasks area, on the Home tab, click New Task.**

2. **Enter data in the fields in the New Task window (see Figure 19-15).**

   You can enter as much or as little information as you like:

   - Enter a start date and/or a due date.

   - Choose a status.

   - Choose a priority.

   - Estimate the project's completion percentage.

   - Set a reminder.

   - Type any notes about the task.

3. **Click Save & Close.**

To reopen a task for editing, double-click it.

Change the Tasks view

Many different views are available for the Tasks list. Here are some tips for working with different views of your tasks:

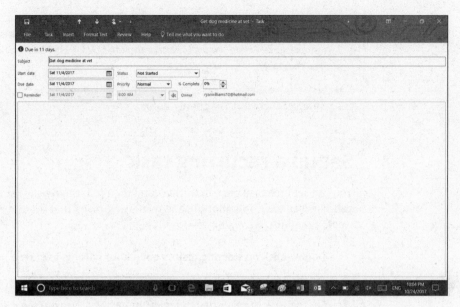

FIGURE 19-15:
Enter information
about the task.

» To choose among the available views, on the Home tab, click Change View and then click the desired view (see Figure 19-16).

» Some views show different fields. For example, Detailed view has several more columns than Simple List view.

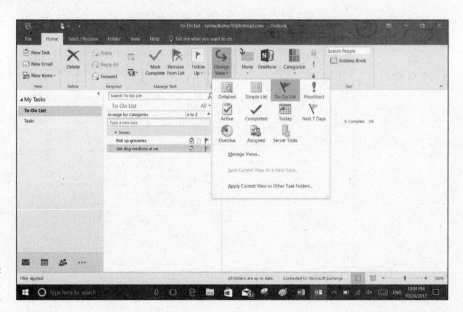

FIGURE 19-16:
Change the view,
if desired.

>> Some views also filter the Tasks list to show only items with certain statuses. For example, Active shows only uncompleted tasks, and Overdue shows only overdue tasks.

>> Some views place the tasks in a certain order. For example, Prioritized arranges them by their priority status.

Set up a recurring task

You can set up a task once in Outlook and then tell it to reoccur at a defined interval. This can save you a lot of time reentering tasks that are the same every day, week, or month. Here's how:

1. **Double-click an existing task to open it for editing, or start a new task.**

2. **On the Task tab, click Recurrence.**

3. **Set the task to recur daily, weekly, monthly, or yearly (see Figure 19-17).**

4. **Set up the details of the recurrence.**

   The options change depending on your choice in Step 3.

5. **If the recurrence should end on a certain date or after a certain number of times, set that up.**

6. **Click OK.**

7. **In the Task window, click Save & Close.**

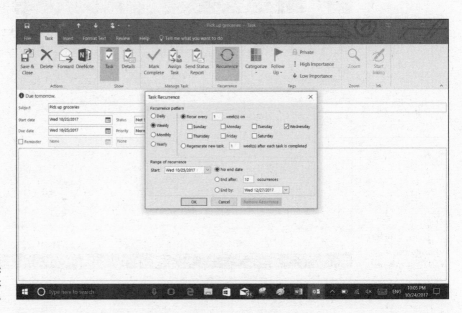

FIGURE 19-17:
Set up task recurrence.

374   PART 4 Communicating in Office 2016

If you want to remove the recurrence on a task, repeat Steps 1 and 2 and then click Remove Recurrence.

Send a status report

Your manager or supervisor will want to know how you're progressing on any work-related tasks. You can quickly send someone a status report on a task by doing the following:

1. **From the Tasks area, double-click the task to open it.**

2. **On the Task tab, click Send Status Report.**

A new email window opens.

The Subject line shows *Task Status Report* plus the name of the task (see Figure 19-18).

The status report appears in the message body.

3. **Compose and send the email as you would any other message.**

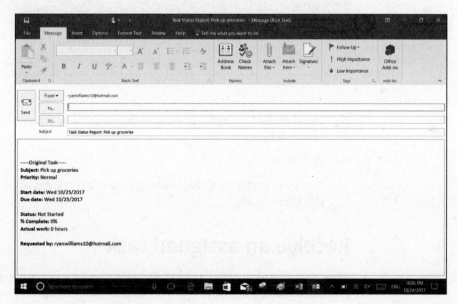

FIGURE 19-18:
Email a status
report for a task.

Assign the task to someone else

Assigning a task to someone else in Outlook accomplishes several things at once:

>> It sends an email containing the task details to the person to whom you assign it.

>> It gives them the choice of accepting or declining the task and sends their reply back to you.

>> If they accept the task, it places it on their Tasks list in Outlook (if they use Outlook).

To assign a task, follow these steps:

1. **Double-click the task to open it.**

2. **In the Manage Task section of the Task tab, click Assign Task (see Figure 19-19).**

   An email composition screen appears within the task window.

FIGURE 19-19:
Click the Assign
Task button in
the open task
window.

3. **Type or select the email address of the person who is being assigned the task (see Figure 19-20).**

4. **Click Send.**

   After you have sent the assignment, the task's icon changes in the Tasks list (see Figure 19-21).

Receive an assigned task

When you receive an email-based task assignment from another user, it comes to your inbox along with the rest of your email. When you open the assignment, you see the task information. Follow these steps:

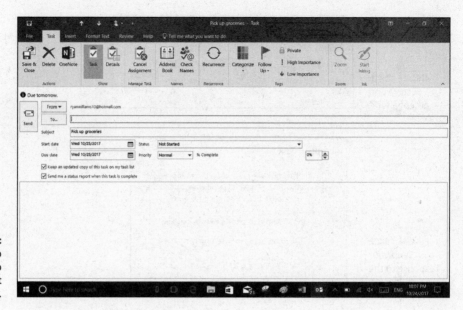

FIGURE 19-20:
Email the task to
the person to
whom you want
to assign it.

1. **Accept or decline the task:**

   (A) To accept the task, click Accept (see Figure 19-22).

   OR

   (B) To decline the task, click Decline.

2. **The sender will receive an email with your response (see Figure 19-23). If you want to edit that email, click Edit the Response before sending. If you don't want to, leave Send the Response Now selected.**

3. **Click OK.**

4. **If you chose to edit the response in Step 2, make any changes or comments on the email, and then click Send.**

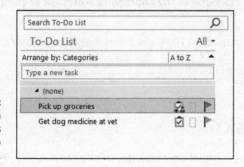

FIGURE 19-21:
The task's icon
indicates it has
been assigned to
someone.

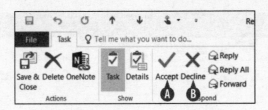

FIGURE 19-22:
Receive and
accept a task.

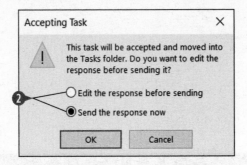

FIGURE 19-23:
Send your
response to the
requester.

Change a task status

As you make progress on a task, you will want to update its status in Outlook. Here's how:

1. **Double-click the task to open its window.**

2. **Open the Status drop-down list and choose a different status, if needed (see Figure 19-24).**

TIP

> Completing the task doesn't delete it, although a completed task may vanish from your list. When you set a task to a status of Completed, it changes which view it appears in. For example, if you're using Active view, a completed task will appear to vanish. Switch to a view that includes completed tasks, like Simple List, and you'll see it again.

3. **Set the % Complete value to the approximate percent of completion for the task.**

TIP

> If you set the % Complete to 100%, the Status field automatically changes to Completed.

4. **Click Save & Close.**

Delete a task

As we mention earlier, completing a task doesn't delete it. You might want to keep completed tasks around for later reference. If you don't want to see them, switch to a view that doesn't include completed tasks, such as Active view. If you're sure you want to delete a task, though, it's easy enough to delete it.

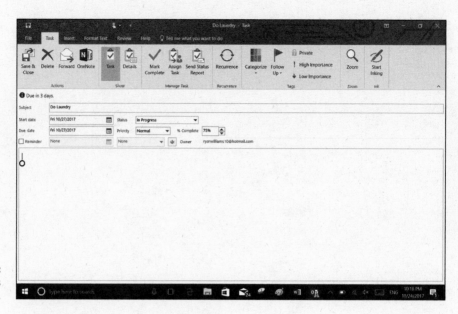

FIGURE 19-24:
Update a task's
status.

To delete a task, do any of the following:

» Right-click the task and click Delete from the menu that appears
(see Figure 19-25).

» Select the task and click Delete on the Home tab.

» Select the task and press Delete on the keyboard.

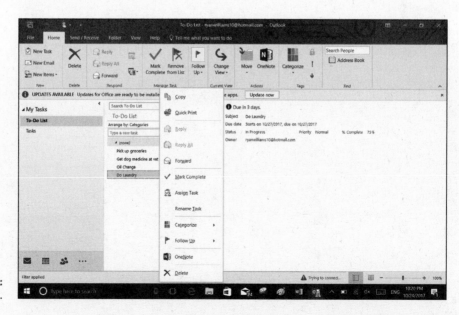

FIGURE 19-25:
Delete a task.

Chapter **20**

Getting Started with PowerPoint

PowerPoint is the most popular presentation software in the world. *Presentation software* creates support materials for people who give speeches. You can project PowerPoint slides on a big screen behind you as you speak, create handouts to distribute to the audience, and print note pages for your own reference. PowerPoint can also create self-running presentations for distribution via CD or online.

This chapter offers you some basics for working with PowerPoint. You learn how to start a new presentation, add slides and text to it, and move and resize the content on a slide. In later lessons, you learn how to add other types of content and special effects to a show.

Starting a New Presentation

When you start PowerPoint, as with the other Office applications, a Start screen appears, as shown in Figure 20-1. From there, you can

(A) Click Blank Presentation, or press Esc, to start a new blank presentation.

(B) Click one of the other templates to start a new presentation based on it.

(C) Open an existing presentation.

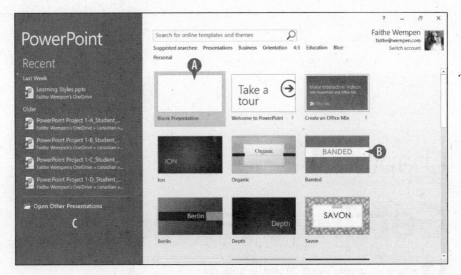

FIGURE 20-1:
The Start screen
in PowerPoint.

To start a new presentation at any other time than start-up, press Ctrl+N for a blank one or click File⇨New and choose a template.

Moving Around in a Presentation

A *slide* is an individual page of the presentation. The term *page* isn't a perfect descriptor, though, because PowerPoint slides are designed to be displayed on a computer screen or with a projector rather than printed. A *presentation* is a collection of one or more slides saved in a single data file.

At the big-picture level, the PowerPoint interface is similar to that in Word and Excel: It has a Ribbon, a File tab, and a status bar. The default view of the presentation, called *Normal view*, consists of three panes, shown in Figure 20-2.

TIP

The presentation shown in Figure 20-2 was created with the Welcome to PowerPoint template. Here are some things to note:

(A) The Slides pane is the bar along the left side. Thumbnail images of the slides appear here. It's sometimes called the *thumbnails pane* or the *slides pane*.

(B) The Slide pane (that's singular, not plural) in the middle shows the active slide in a large, editable pane. Here's where you do most of your work on each slide. It's sometimes called the *editing pane*.

(C) The Notes pane runs along the bottom of the screen. There you can type any notes to yourself about the active slide. These notes don't show onscreen when you display the presentation, and they don't print (unless you explicitly choose to print them).

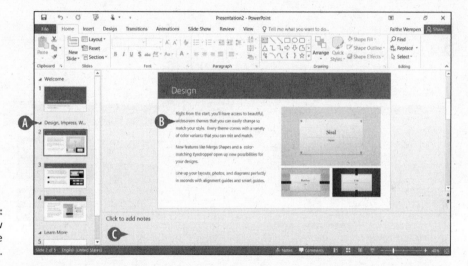

FIGURE 20-2:
Normal view consists of three panes.

(D) The Notes pane is minimized in a new, blank presentation. To see this pane, position the mouse pointer just above the (orange) status bar at the bottom of the screen and drag upward (see Figure 20-3). Drag the top border of the Notes pane down again to hide it.

(E) Another way to display or hide the Notes pane is to click the Notes indicator on the status bar.

You can navigate a presentation in many of the same ways you moved through other applications' content (see Figure 20-4).

FIGURE 20-3:
Drag upward
from the status
bar to display the
Notes pane.

(F)   Click above or below the vertical scroll bar in the Slide pane, or press Page Up or Page Down, to move one slide at a time.

(G)   You can also drag the scroll box to move more quickly as well.

(H)   You can click an up or down arrow on a scroll bar to scroll a small amount at a time.

(I)   You can also click a slide in the Slides pane to jump directly to that slide.

(J)   The Slides pane has its own scroll bar, in case you can't see all the slides there at once.

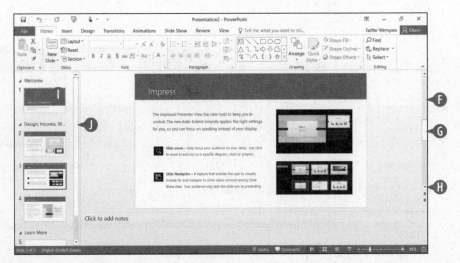

FIGURE 20-4:
Ways to move
around in
Normal view.

Choosing the Right View

PowerPoint provides several views for you to work with. Each view is useful for a different set of activities. Here are some things to remember about views:

(A)   To switch views, on the View tab, click a button for the view you want.

(B)   Master views are not regular PowerPoint views; they enable you to edit the underlying designs and layouts on which individual slides are based.

(C) Slide Show view is not represented on the View tab. To switch to Slide Show view, use the From Beginning or From Current Slide button on the Slide Show tab instead (see Figure 20-5).

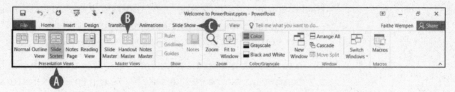

FIGURE 20-5:
View buttons on
the View tab of
the Ribbon.

You can also click one of the View buttons in the lower-right corner of the PowerPoint window (see Figure 20-6):

(D) Normal

(E) Slide Sorter

(F) Reading View

(G) Slide Show

FIGURE 20-6:
View buttons on
the status bar.

Here's a quick overview of the available views:

» **Normal:** You've already seen this one in Figure 20-4; it's the default. It consists of a Slides pane, a Slide pane in which you can edit the slide, and a Notes pane in which you can record private notes and comments.

» **Outline:** This view is identical to Normal view except that, instead of the Slides pane, an Outline pane shows a text outline for each slide.

WARNING

In Outline view, only text from the slide's text placeholders appears in the Outline pane. If you have any manually created text boxes (such as those you create with Insert ⇨ Text Box), their text doesn't appear there.

» **Slide Sorter:** This view shows thumbnail images of each slide, like the Slides pane does in Normal view, but it takes up the entire window. You can't edit slide content in this view, although you can rearrange and delete slides (see Figure 20-7):

(H) If your presentation has sections, as the Welcome to PowerPoint template's presentation does, each section appears on a separate row in Slide Sorter view. You can manage sections with the Home ⇨ Section command.

(I) To zoom in or out on the thumbnail view, drag the Zoom slider. A lower zoom means that more slides are visible at a time and they're smaller. A higher zoom means that fewer slides are visible, but you can see each one more easily.

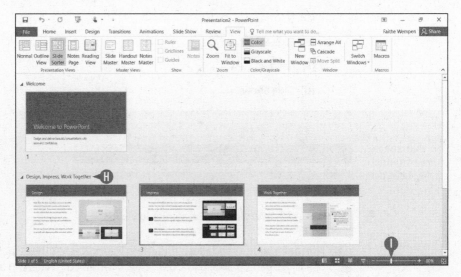

FIGURE 20-7:
Slide Sorter view is good for arranging slides.

» **Notes Page:** This view shows a vertically oriented page for each slide, as shown in Figure 20-8:

(J) The top half of the page shows the slide.

(K) The bottom half of the page provides a large text box into which you can enter and edit note text.

(L) Use the Zoom slider to zoom in to make the note text easier to see as you work with it, if desired.

» **Slide Show:** This is the view you would use to show the presentation full-screen on your monitor. Each slide fills the entire screen, one by one, and you click to advance.

>> **Reading:** Reading view is like Slide Show view except that the presentation runs in a window rather than full-screen. That's useful because you can do other things, like work with other programs or windows, while the presentation is running.

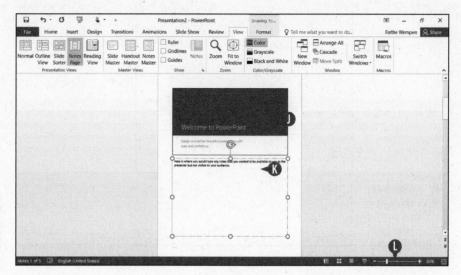

FIGURE 20-8:
Notes Page view makes it easy to compose and edit lengthy speaker notes.

REMEMBER

Most people prefer to work in Normal view most of the time when creating a presentation, so switch back to Normal view before you go any further, after experimenting with the other views.

Adding and Removing Slides

Each new blank presentation begins with one slide in it: a title slide. (Presentations based on other templates may have more.) You can easily add more slides to the presentation by using the default layout (Title and Content) or any other layout you prefer.

Several methods are available for creating new slides, and each one is best suited for a particular situation. In the following sections, you learn each of the methods.

Create a new slide in the Slides pane

In the Slides pane in Normal view, you can click to place a horizontal insertion point between two existing slides or at the bottom of the list of slides and then press Enter to create a new slide (see Figure 20-9).

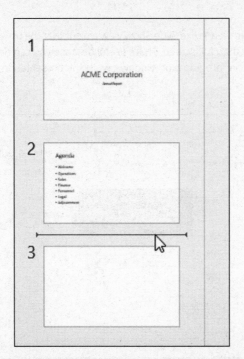

The layout of the new slide depends on the layout of the slide immediately before (above) it. If that slide uses the Slide Title layout, the new slide uses the Title and Content layout. Otherwise, the new slide uses the same layout as the preceding slide.

Create a new slide in the Outline pane

In Outline view, you can create a new slide by following these steps:

1. In the Outline pane, click at the beginning of the title of the slide that the new slide should come *before*.

2. Press Enter (see Figure 20-10).

   A new paragraph (a slide title) is created, and that causes a whole new slide to be created also.

3. Press the up-arrow key once to move the insertion point up into the new, blank slide title, and type the title text.

FIGURE 20-10:
Create a new
slide from the
Outline pane
(Outline view).

1 ☐ **ACME Corporation**

Annual Report

2 ☐ **Agenda**

• Welcome

• Operations

• Sales

• Finance

• Personnel

• Legal

• Adjournment

3 ☐ ▸◀❸

4 ☐ **Welcome** ◀❶

• Introduction of managers

• Organizational structure

Create a new slide from the Ribbon

When you create a slide using the Ribbon, you can select the layout you want for the new slide. Follow these steps:

1. In Normal view, select the slide that the new slide should come *after*.

2A. On the Home tab, click New Slide to create a slide with the same layout as the selected one (unless the selected one is a title slide, in which case the layout will be Title and Content) See Figure 20-11.

OR

3A. Click the arrow on the New Slide button, and then select the desired layout from the gallery that appears.

Duplicate a slide

If you need to create a series of similar slides, you might find it easier to copy or duplicate a slide and then make the small modifications to each copy.

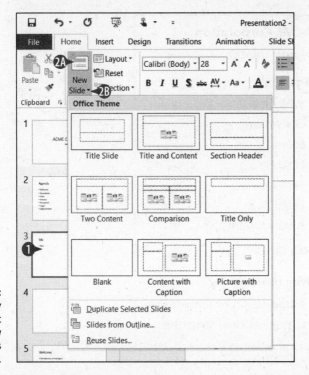

FIGURE 20-11:
Create a slide by
selecting a layout
from the New
Slide button's
gallery.

Copying and duplicating are two separate commands in PowerPoint, but they have essentially the same result.

When you *copy* a slide (or multiple slides), you place a copy of it on the Clipboard, and then you paste it from the Clipboard into the presentation. You can paste anywhere in the presentation or into a different presentation (or, for that matter, a different document altogether).

To copy a slide, follow these steps:

1. **Select the slide in the Slides pane.**

2. **Press Ctrl+C or choose Home ⇨ Copy.**

3. **Click where you want the copy to go (see Figure 20-12).**

If you want to place the copy after a certain slide, select that slide.

4. **Press Ctrl+V or choose Home ⇨ Paste.**

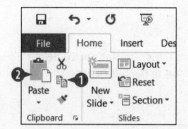

FIGURE 20-12:
Copy a slide using
the Clipboard.

When you duplicate a slide (or multiple slides), you don't have to paste, because that command accomplishes both a copy and a paste operation at the same time. However, neither do you get to choose where they're pasted; they're pasted directly below the original selection.

1. **Select the slide(s) to be duplicated.**

   To select more than one slide, hold down Ctrl as you click each one in the Slides pane.

2. **Click the arrow on the New Slide button to open its menu.**

3. **Click Duplicate Selected Slides (see Figure 20-13).**

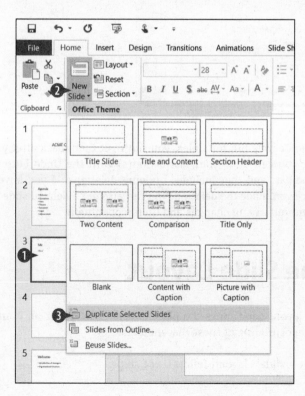

FIGURE 20-13:
Duplicate one or
more slides.

Delete a slide

Deleting a slide removes it from the presentation. To delete a slide, right-click it and choose Delete Slide, or select it in the Slides pane and press the Delete key (see A in Figure 20-14).

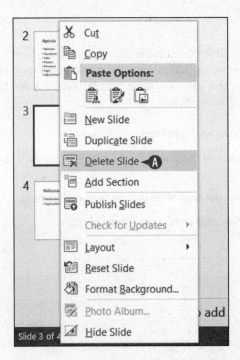

FIGURE 20-14:
Delete a slide.

TIP

There's no Recycle Bin for slides; you can't get them back after you delete them. However, you can undo your last action(s) with the Undo button on the Quick Access toolbar, and that includes undoing deletions. If you haven't saved your work since you made the deletion, you can also get a deleted slide back by closing the file without saving changes and then reopening it.

Changing the Slide Layout

A slide's layout determines the placeholders that appear on it and the arrangement and positioning of those placeholders.

To change a slide's layout, follow these steps:

1. **Select the slide to change in the Slides pane.**

2. **On the Home tab, click Layout to open a gallery.**

3. **Click the desired layout.**

TIP

The available layouts depend on several factors, including the template you started with, the theme that's applied, and any custom layouts you may have created in Slide Master view. The nine layouts shown in Figure 20-15 are the default ones that come with the Blank template.

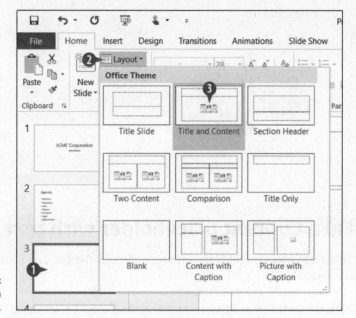

FIGURE 20-15:
Choose a
different layout.

Using Content Placeholders

The most common type of placeholder is a multipurpose Content placeholder. It gives you a choice of filling it with either text or one of six types of graphical content.

REMEMBER

You can fill each placeholder with only one type of content; if you want other content on the slide, you must use a layout with multiple content placeholders or add the extra content manually, as described in the next two sections. The available types of content are shown in Figure 20-16.

(A)   Table

(B)   Chart

(C)   SmartArt Graphic

(D)   Picture

(E)   Online Picture

(F)   Video

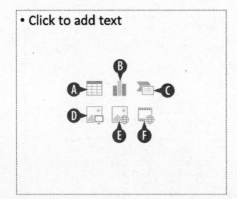

FIGURE 20-16:
The types of
graphical content
for a Content
placeholder.

Fill a Content placeholder with text

To fill a Content placeholder with text, click in the box and start typing. It's as simple as that!

Here are some things to keep in mind about Content placeholders:

(A)   Most templates and designs use bulleted lists in the Content placeholder boxes by default, which means that any text you type will automatically be formatted as a bulleted list.

(B)   You can turn off the bullet for a paragraph by clicking the Bullets button on the Home tab.

(C)   Use the Numbering button to convert a bulleted list to a numbered one.

(D)   To demote (indent) a paragraph — for example, to create a subordinated bulleted list within a list, click Increase List Level on the Home tab.

(E)   To promote a paragraph, click Decrease List Level.

REMEMBER

It might seem counterintuitive to increase something you're demoting, but think about the list level as a hierarchy, with 1 as the most superior. If you increase the level, you demote the item to a later, less important level.

TIP

Another way to demote a paragraph is to press Tab when the insertion point is at the beginning of the paragraph. Another way to promote is Shift+Tab.

You can use the commands in the Font and Paragraph groups on the Home tab to format the text in the placeholder, the same as you do in Word (see Figure 20-17). Here are a few minor differences to note:

(F) Shadow adds a shadow to the text.

(G) Character Spacing lets you adjust the spacing between letters from the Ribbon. In Word, this capability is available in the Paragraph dialog box.

(H) Clear All Formatting removes all manually applied formatting, reverting to the formatting specified by the template or the design.

(I) Columns enables you to set a text placeholder box in multiple columns.

(J) Align Text enables you to set vertical alignment within the text box of Top, Middle, or Bottom.

(K) Text Direction changes the orientation of the text to vertical, stacked, or rotated.

(L) Convert to SmartArt Graphic converts the selected paragraphs to a SmartArt graphic.

Fill a Content placeholder with a graphical element

To use one of the graphical types of content, click the corresponding icon in the Content placeholder. A dialog box appears that guides you in selecting the content to include. The process is a bit different for each of the content types. Most of these content types you have worked with in earlier chapters; the dialog boxes are the same or nearly the same as in other Office applications.

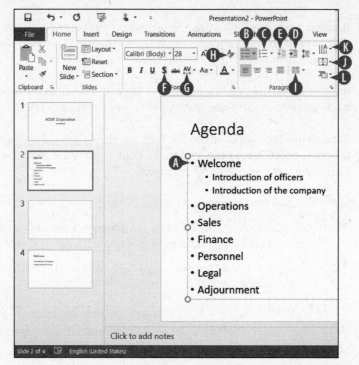

FIGURE 20-17:
Here are some text formatting buttons that are different in PowerPoint than in Word.

Just as an example, here's how to use a Content placeholder to insert a picture:

1. Click the Pictures icon in the Content placeholder (see Figure 20-18).

2. In the Insert Pictures dialog box, select the desired picture (see Figure 20-19).

3. Click Insert.

FIGURE 20-18:
Click the placeholder icon you want.

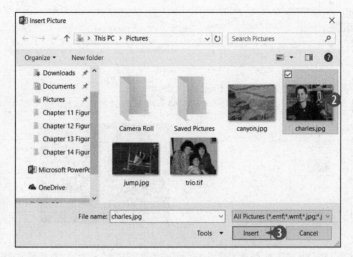

FIGURE 20-19:
In the dialog box that appears, choose the content to place in the placeholder.

Placing Text on a Slide Manually

First, a warning: Whenever possible, you should use the placeholders on the slide layouts and *not* create text boxes manually. One reason is that text in manual text boxes doesn't appear in the Outline pane in Outline view. Manually placed text boxes also aren't affected when you change layouts or designs for a slide, so with the new arrangement of placeholders, the text box might be obscured, or might obscure other content.

Nevertheless, sometimes you really do need a manual text box. For example, you might want a little informational box to appear floating next to a picture or chart to explain it.

To create a text box on a slide, follow these steps:

1. **On the Insert tab, click Text Box.**
2. **Drag to draw the desired text box on the slide (see Figure 20-20).**
3. **Release the mouse button, and then type in the text box that appears.**

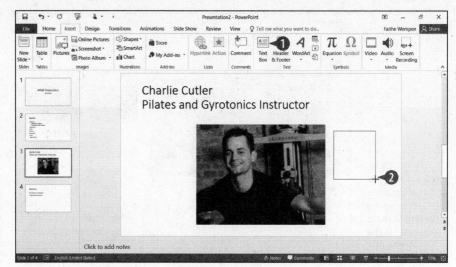

FIGURE 20-20:
In the dialog box
that appears,
choose the
content to place
in the
placeholder.

Placing a Picture on a Slide Manually

We'll issue the same warning here as in the previous section: Try not to manually place pictures if you can help it. Use placeholders whenever possible. If you make changes to the layouts or change to a different design later, you'll thank us for this advice because pictures in placeholders resize and move as needed, rolling with the changes. Manually placed pictures don't.

To manually insert a picture, do the following:

1. **On the Insert tab, click Pictures.**
2. **In the Insert Pictures dialog box, select the desired picture.**
3. **Click Insert.**

You can also insert various other types of graphics manually using the buttons on the Insert tab, such as Online Pictures, Chart, and SmartArt.

Moving and Resizing Slide Objects

Objects on a slide are all free-floating frames. You can move and resize them just like in Word and Excel:

(A) Drag an object by any part except its selection handles to move it. If it's a picture, you can drag it by any part, including the middle. If it's a text box, you have to drag it by its border (see Figure 20-21).

(B) Drag a selection handle to resize it. To maintain the aspect ratio, hold down Shift and drag only the corner selection handles.

(C) Drag the rotation handle to rotate it.

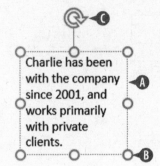

FIGURE 20-21:
Drag the object's border to move it, or drag a selection handle to resize.

You can specify an exact size for an object in the Size group:

(A) The tab on which the Size group appears depends on the object type. For example, for a picture, it's on the Picture Tools Format tab, and for a chart, it's on the Chart Tools Format tab.

(B) Set an exact height in the Height box.

(C) Set an exact width in the Width box (see Figure 20-22).

FIGURE 20-22:
Control an object's size precisely with the Height and Width settings.

Deleting Slide Objects

To delete an object on a slide, select the object and press Delete on the keyboard. You can get a deleted object back immediately after deleting it by using Undo. Click the Undo button on the Quick Access toolbar or press Ctrl+Z (see A in Figure 20-23).

5

The Parts of Ten

Find out how to troubleshoot some common problems.

Get introduced to some tools you can use in addition to everything else you've already learned.

- maintenance

- » **Preventing problems through best practices**

- » **Using Task Manager to fix all kinds of problems**

- » **Freeing up storage space with Disk Cleanup**

- » **Finding out which apps and games use the most storage space**

- » **Troubleshooting problems using the built-in troubleshooting wizards**

Chapter **21**

10 Ways to Prevent and Fix Problems with Windows 10

Prevention is one of the best ways to ensure that you'll have a long, pleasant, and safe computing experience. Windows 10 helps you do so by including prevention tools.

Also, you find some practices that can help you stay out of trouble when using any Windows computer or device. Finally, if terrible luck still manages to find you, we'll review some tips you can use to troubleshoot your way.

Perform Recommended System Maintenance

Windows 10 includes the System Maintenance tool, which is a hidden tool that you can run on demand to find out whether your system has issues. This tool checks for unused files and shortcuts, performs maintenance tasks, verifies that the system time is set correctly, and so on. If problems are found, the System Maintenance tool fixes them automatically.

To manually run the System Maintenance tool, follow these steps:

1. **In the search bar on the taskbar, type** perform recommended maintenance.

   A list with search results appears.

2. **Click the Perform Recommended Maintenance Tasks Automatically search result.**

   The System Maintenance Wizard starts.

3. **Click Next (see Figure 21-1).**

   The wizard begins the process of detecting possible issues.

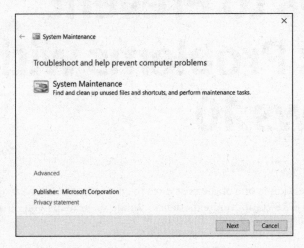

FIGURE 21-1:
Starting the
System
Maintenance
Wizard.

4. **If the wizard recommends that you do the troubleshooting as an administrator, click Try Troubleshooting as an Administrator.**

   When the wizard finishes, it shows a summary of its findings. If it finds issues, it also shows you actions that you can take.

5. **Click Close.**

Prevent Problems with Your Windows Computer or Device

Just as in medicine, when you're dealing with computers, prevention is a much better tool than medication. That's why, if you want to face as few issues as possible, the best approach is to consider these simple, effective rules:

>> Don't download apps and programs from untrusted sources. Stick to websites that have a good reputation and with well-known software.

If you need to download and install an app that you know nothing about, before you even consider downloading it, search on Google or Bing for information about it.

>> When you install apps, never use the quick-install option; always use the custom install.

Many free desktop apps bundle all kinds of junk and third-party apps that you don't need. If you always choose to install them quickly and don't go for a slower custom install where you configure in detail what gets installed, you're just asking for trouble. You may install toolbars that hijack your computer, useless desktop apps that take up space and system resources, apps that display ads you don't want, and so on.

>> Be careful what you click on while browsing the web. It doesn't matter which browser you're using, clicking random links and ads invites trouble.

Use browser add-ons like Web of Trust (WoT) that help you quickly evaluate the trustworthiness of the websites that you're visiting.

>> Shut down your Windows computer or device from time to time. Usually, you want your devices to start as fast as possible, so you might use Sleep and other low-power modes. However, a simple shutdown once a week helps Windows update files, shut down processes, and start from scratch the next time you turn it on.

>> Read error messages; don't just click through them. When you encounter an error message in Windows 10, don't just click OK automatically. First, take some time to read it completely and understand what's going on. If it's something serious, take a screenshot of that message so that you can share it with your company's IT support department or someone else who can help you solve the problem.

>> Use a security product on your Windows device. At the very least, use the built-in Windows Defender and Windows Firewall to protect your computer or device from malware and network attacks. The best idea is to purchase a commercial security product from a well-known security company such as Kaspersky, Bitdefender, Norton, or ESET.

>> Keep Windows 10 and your security software up to date at all times. Yes, updates are annoying, but they're also quite useful. Keeping your software up to date means that your system is less likely to get infected by malware and is less vulnerable to all kinds of threats, and you get new features and regular bug fixes.

>> Perform regular maintenance using the tools covered in this chapter to keep your system in good shape.

Start Task Manager

Task Manager is one of the most useful tools that you can use to troubleshoot performance problems with your Windows 10 computers and devices. With it, you can view which apps are running, which aren't responding, which apps consume too many system resources, which make your system's startup time longer, and so on.

The fastest way to start Task Manager is to press Ctrl+Shift+Esc on your keyboard. You can also use a mouse or touch gestures. Here are the steps for starting Task Manager:

1. **Right-click the Start button.**

A pop-up menu appears, showing several options.

You can also access the pop-up menu by pressing Windows+X on your keyboard. Use search by typing **task manager** in the search bar on the taskbar and clicking the appropriate search result.

2. **Click Task Manager to start it (see Figure 21-2).**

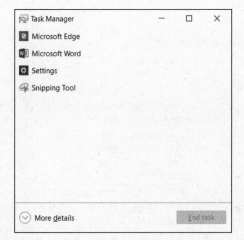

FIGURE 21-2:
Starting Task
Manager.

View All Running Apps and Processes

When you start Task Manager, you see a list of only the apps that you're running (refer to Figure 21-2). The only data shown for each app is its name. In this list, you see both apps from the Windows Store and desktop apps.

To view a more complete list with all the apps that you're running and the processes started by Windows 10, click More Details at the bottom-left corner of Task Manager. A new Task Manager window appears with many tabs that contain lots of detailed information. By default, the Processes tab is loaded, and there you see a long list of running apps and processes, split into the following categories:

>> **Apps:** The apps that you're running

>> **Background processes:** Processes that are started by either Windows 10 or the apps that you install

>> **Windows processes:** Processes that are automatically started by Windows 10 and that are required in order for the operating system to function correctly

All these tabs are shown in Figure 21-3. For each entry, you see the percentage of the CPU (processor) it's using, how much RAM memory it's using, how much data it writes on the disk, and how much of your network connection it's using.

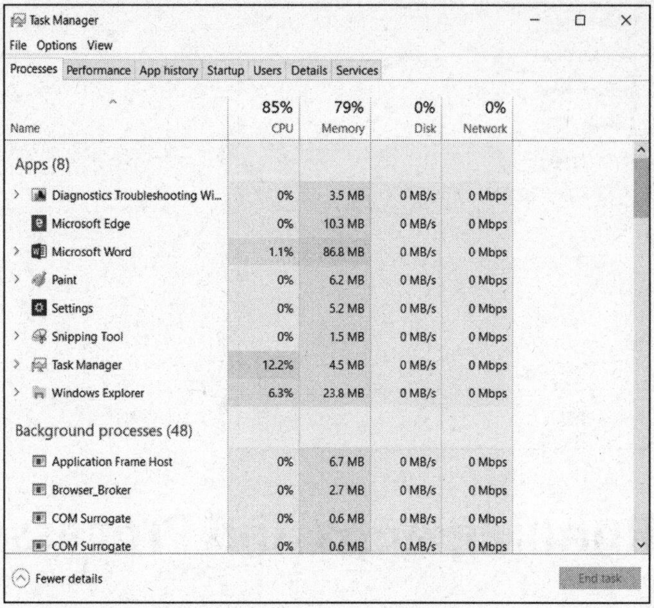

Task Manager

File Options View

Processes | Performance | App history | Startup | Users | Details | Services

Name	85% CPU	79% Memory	0% Disk	0% Network
Apps (8)				
> Diagnostics Troubleshooting Wi...	0%	3.5 MB	0 MB/s	0 Mbps
Microsoft Edge	0%	10.3 MB	0 MB/s	0 Mbps
> Microsoft Word	1.1%	86.8 MB	0 MB/s	0 Mbps
> Paint	0%	6.2 MB	0 MB/s	0 Mbps
Settings	0%	5.2 MB	0 MB/s	0 Mbps
> Snipping Tool	0%	1.5 MB	0 MB/s	0 Mbps
> Task Manager	12.2%	4.5 MB	0 MB/s	0 Mbps
> Windows Explorer	6.3%	23.8 MB	0 MB/s	0 Mbps
Background processes (48)				
Application Frame Host	0%	6.7 MB	0 MB/s	0 Mbps
Browser_Broker	0%	2.7 MB	0 MB/s	0 Mbps
COM Surrogate	0%	0.6 MB	0 MB/s	0 Mbps
COM Surrogate	0%	0.6 MB	0 MB/s	0 Mbps

Fewer details   End task

FIGURE 21-3:
The Processes tab in Task Manager.

End Apps That Aren't Responding

At times, some apps may stop responding to your commands, making it impossible to use them. When that happens, it's best to force them to close using Task Manager and then start them again. To close an app, follow this procedure:

1. **Start Task Manager.**

2. **In the list of running apps, select the app that you want to close by clicking it.**

3. **Click the End Task button in the bottom-right corner of the Task Manager window.**

Determine Which Apps Use the Most System Resources

Task Manager offers you the tools you need to find out which apps are using most of your computer's resources. This information is especially useful when apps start running too slowly or when your computer doesn't seem to understand what you want it to do. If you find an app that's using too many resources, you can use

408   PART 5 The Parts of Ten

the End Task option to close it and free up system resources so that your computer and apps will run faster.

Here's how to find the apps that use the most resources:

1. **Start Task Manager.**

2. **If the Processes tab isn't shown, click More Details.**

3. **In the Processes tab, click the CPU column to sort apps and processes by processor usage.**

4. **Identify the apps that use more of your system's processor than you want (see Figure 21-4).**

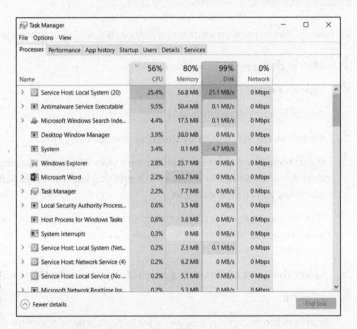

FIGURE 21-4:
The apps that use the most CPU power.

5. **Click the Memory column to sort apps and processes by memory usage.**

6. **Identify the apps that use more of your system's RAM memory than you want.**

7. **Click the Disk column to sort apps and processes by hard disk usage.**

8. **Identify the apps that write the most data on your system's hard disk.**

9. **Click the Network column to sort apps and processes by network usage.**

10. **Identify the apps that use more of your system's network connection than you want.**

11. Click the Name column to view apps and processes using the default view offered by Task Manager, which is sorted by name and type.

12. Close Task Manager.

Increase Disk Space Using Disk Cleanup

If you're running out of disk space on your Windows 10 computer or device, you can use the Disk Cleanup tool. This tool scans your system for files that can be removed and then helps you remove them. These unnecessary files can be of several types, such as temporary Internet files, log files made by the apps that you installed, thumbnails, and temporary files.

To free up some space on your computer or device, follow these steps:

1. Click in the search bar on the taskbar.

2. Type the words free up.

A list of search results appears.

3. Click Free Up Disk Space by Deleting Unnecessary Files.

4. If you have more than one partition on your Windows 10 computer or device, you're asked to select which one you want to scan. Select the partition you're interested in.

Disk Cleanup automatically starts and scans your computer for files that can be safely removed. When it finishes, you see a list of the types of files that can be removed.

5. Select the types of files that you want to remove (see Figure 21-5).

6. Click OK.

You're asked to confirm that you want to permanently delete the files.

7. Click Delete Files and wait for Disk Cleanup to do its job.

TIP

After Step 4, if you click Clean Up System Files instead of moving forward with Step 5, Disk Cleanup restarts and rescans your computer. This time, it looks also for system files that can be cleaned up like previous Windows installation files, temporary Windows installation files, and so on. Select the types of files that you want to remove and continue with steps 6 and 7.

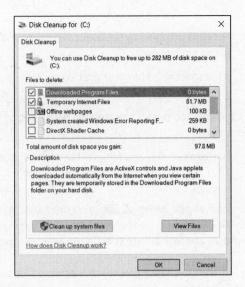

FIGURE 21-5:
The Disk
Cleanup tool.

Investigate How Your Storage Space Is Used

Windows 10 includes a new feature called Storage. You can use it to find how storage space is used on your computer or device. This information is useful because you know how the storage space is used and understand what you can delete to save some space.

When displaying how your storage space is used, Storage splits things into the following categories:

>> **System and Reserved:** This space is for files that Windows requires in order to run. Never delete system files, even if you're running out of space.

>> **Apps and Games:** These are the apps and games that are installed on your computer or device.

>> **Pictures, Music, and Videos:** This is the space occupied by the files in your Pictures, Music, and Videos user folders and libraries.

>> **Mail:** This is the space occupied by the Mail app for storing your email messages.

>> **Maps:** This is the space occupied by the maps that you have downloaded.

>> **Documents:** This is the space occupied by the files in your Documents user folder and library.

>> **OneDrive:** This is the space occupied by the OneDrive folder and the files that you're synchronizing to the cloud.

>> **Other Users:** This is the space used by other user accounts on your computer or device.

>> **Temporary Files:** Includes temporary files that are generated by Windows or the apps that you're using.

>> **Other:** These are unrecognized files and folders that can't be classified by Windows 10.

TECHNICAL
STUFF

Their order isn't the same as the order of the preceding list; Windows 10 automatically sorts all these categories by the amount of storage space they take. Therefore, these categories are in a different order on your computer or device.

When you open any of the preceding items, Windows 10 offers you different options for creating storage space in the item's category. To find how the storage space is used on your computer or device, follow these steps:

1. **Open Settings.**

2. **Click System.**

   Your system settings are shown.

3. **Click Storage.**

   Now you can see the total storage space that's used on your computer or device.

4. **Click This PC.**

   Windows 10 takes a few seconds to analyze how your storage space is used.

5. **Check each category and find how much storage space it uses (see Figure 21-6).**

6. **When you finish, close Settings.**

TIP

If you have a microSD card plugged into your Windows 10 tablet or laptop, you can use Storage to view how storage space is used on it, too.

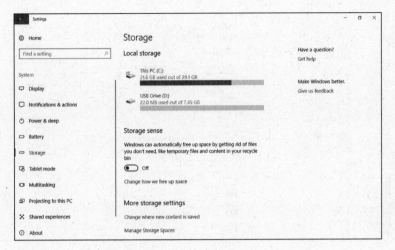

FIGURE 21-6:
Using your
storage space.

Find Which Apps and Games Use the Most Storage Space

If you're close to running out of storage space on your Windows 10 computer or device, one thing you can do is find out which apps and games from the Windows Store use the most space. If you don't use some of those apps and games, you can uninstall them and free up storage space.

If you want to find how much storage space each installed app and game uses, follow these steps:

1. **Open Settings.**

2. **Click Apps.**

   Your apps settings are shown.

3. **Click Apps & Features.**

   Windows 10 analyzes all installed apps.

4. **Look at the list of apps and games and identify those that require the most storage space (see Figure 21-7).**

5. **When you're done, close Settings.**

TIP

You can remove the apps and games you no longer need to use straight from the App Sizes section. Simply click the app that you want to remove and then click Uninstall twice to remove it.

FIGURE 21-7:
Installed apps
and games and
their size on disk.

Troubleshoot Problems Using the Windows Troubleshooting Wizards

Windows 10 includes many troubleshooting wizards that can help you solve lots of problems. For example, you can fix issues with programs that aren't compatible with Windows 10 and with problems related to Internet Explorer and to the hardware for different components, such as the network card, the sound card, printers, and Internet connections. You can find these wizards in the Troubleshoot panel, and they're easy to use (see Figure 21-8).

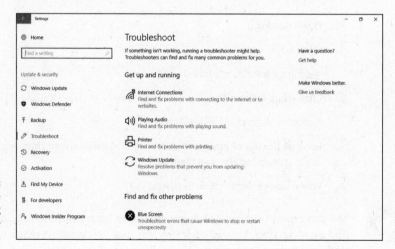

FIGURE 21-8:
The
troubleshooting
wizards available
in Windows 10.

With the help of these wizards, you can identify both what's causing the problems you're having and the solutions to fix them. In some scenarios, the troubleshooting wizards automatically fix the problem.

Here's an example of how these troubleshooting wizards work. For this example, mute the sound on your device. The Playing Audio troubleshooter can find and fix the problem.

1. Click in the search bar on the taskbar.

2. Type troubleshoot.

A list of search results appears.

3. Click the Troubleshoot search result.

The Troubleshoot window appears.

4. Click Playing Audio to start this troubleshooting wizard.

5. Click Run the troubleshooter.

Wait for the troubleshooter to identify the problems that you're having. When it finishes, you receive a message telling you that the troubleshooting is completed and that the problems were found and fixed automatically.

6. Click Close.

The sound is no longer muted on your Windows 10 computer or device.

Get Help from Your Company's IT Department

When you use Windows 10 at work, you may encounter issues that you can't fix on your own, even after reading this chapter. When that happens, contact the IT support team at your company and talk with them about your issues. Be sure to follow these guidelines:

>> **Describe your issues clearly and completely.** It's crucial that the IT staff understand what's wrong with your Windows 10 computer or device so that they can help you more effectively.

>> **Describe accurately what you were doing when the problem occurred.** Use your own words, You don't have to be technical. However, be as detailed and as accurate as possible in your description of the problem.

>> **Ask for clarification if you don't understand something.** If technical terms or questions seem foreign to you, don't hesitate to ask the IT support team to use simpler, more accessible language. Doing so increases the effectiveness of your dialogue and also the chances of getting your problem solved faster.

>> **Keep calm and be level-headed.** Don't take your computing issues personally and express your frustration in a nonconstructive manner. Explain your problems calmly and be patient. The IT support team is there to help you as fast as possible.

>> **Set some time aside for solving your problem.** If you haven't figured things out on your own, your problem probably isn't that easy to understand and fix. Don't expect it to be solved in five minutes. Allow the IT support team time to understand what's going on and find the best fix.

>> **Learn from your mistakes.** If you repeat the same mistakes, you repeat the same problems. When a problem is solved, ask the IT support team to explain what was wrong and what you can do to make sure that the problem doesn't reoccur.

Chapter **22**

Ten Additional Features Available from Microsoft Office

Windows 10 and Office 2016 offer all the functionality you need to get work done in the office, wherever that office might be. But what happens if you need to talk to people in other offices, or make somewhere else your office for a bit? And what if you need to get files from your laptop on your phone or tablet somewhere else? Luckily, you can take advantage of all sorts of other tools available to you to manage these tasks. Hit the road, keep track of all your tasks and thoughts, and launch stellar PowerPoint presentations with the features in this chapter.

Skype

Microsoft bought Skype to add a stellar communications product to its lineup. Skype's name is almost synonymous with simple video conferencing over the Internet. We've talked to coworkers, conducted job interviews, and even just chatted with friends over Skype. IT may have already installed this app on your machine, or you may need to download it from the Microsoft Store. Simply connect a good headset and camera to your computer for the best communication.

OneNote

OneNote comes bundled with Office 2016 and stands ready to help you capture all your thoughts throughout the workday. Microsoft calls this program a digital network, but it's much easier to include links to websites, images, audio, or video in OneNote than it is on paper. Plus, you can instantly share these notes with your coworkers as necessary (be careful who and what you type about) and synchronize those notes across your devices. This feature is really helpful if you enter something on your mobile device that needs to be ready for the presentation on Monday.

OneDrive

You're probably tired of hearing about the cloud by now, but Microsoft's spot in this ubiquitous cliché is especially helpful. This service connects directly to your Microsoft or work account and stores your most important files on Internet-accessible servers. You'll always have your files backed up, and you can work on your files from several different locations. You can also customize which folders back up automatically from your computer to OneDrive. Your workplace may have a preferred cloud backup solution, but if not, consider OneDrive a solid solution.

Mail Merge

We're sure you don't feel like making a single document for each one of your hundreds or thousands of customers, or filling out mailing labels for each one. Mail merge helps you combine a generic document with a data list and personalize your communication to each one of your customers.

In Word, click Start Mail Merge in your document and follow the wizard to make the merge happen. You'll need a data list, such as an Excel spreadsheet, that contains the information about your customers. Insert the merge fields and perform the merge, and you're good to go. This description skims over a lot of possibilities, but mail merge can help you personalize everything from letters to mailing labels to catalogs without issue.

Excel Databases

We talk about data lists in the previous section, and Excel databases can help you manage the information for data lists with no hassle. Well, there's a little hassle, but certainly much less than handwriting records. Use Excel databases to keep records on customers, products, or whatever you need to track. Sort, filter, and query the information to find the exact group of data you need to target (maybe you want to send advertising to people in Wisconsin about parkas), and then use that information in mail merges or many other situations.

Sound and Video in PowerPoint

PowerPoint doesn't just have to include text and pictures of cats, although we don't mind that. If you want to jazz up your presentations a little, click the Insert tab in your PowerPoint presentation and click Audio or Video. The audio can be a file on your computer, a recording you make just for the slide, or background music for the slide. The video can be from either your computer or an online source. Just make sure you can access the Internet from where you present or else you'll leave a lot of cat video enthusiasts disappointed.

PowerPoint Presentations

You don't want to show everybody all the slides in your presentation at one time, so be sure to display your next PowerPoint presentation properly. Choose the Slide Show tab in your presentation and choose whether to start the presentation from the beginning or a specific slide, or other options. Use the arrow keys to move between slides, and press the Esc key to exit the display.

Presenter View

You want to show your audience a great presentation, but you don't want them to see what's going on behind the scenes. PowerPoint makes Presenter View available to you for just that reason. Presenter View lets you see what slides are coming up and reorganize your presentation on the fly, all while the audience sees only the slide you want them to see. Click the Slide Show tab in PowerPoint and make sure you select the Use Presenter View check box. When you start the presentation, you'll be in total control on your laptop while your audience sees only the projector.

Did I mention you'll need two monitors or a monitor and a projector to make this happen? You'll need to choose which monitor is yours in Presenter View to make sure you have the control.

Slide Annotations

If you're presenting your PowerPoint file from a laptop to a larger screen, you can include notes for each slide. Maybe you want to remind yourself what to talk about or you just want to entertain yourself with a short joke during an extremely long presentation on actuarial tables. No matter how you choose to use them, annotations can help you move your presentation along. Look for the field for each slide that says Tap to Add Notes, and then do just that. When you use Presenter View, you'll see the notes!

Online Office Features

Office 2016 already gives you great local functionality, but Office Online features let you take your Office functionality . . . online. It's a very descriptive name. When you want to work with documents online, such as on a corporate website, features like Word Online and Excel Online let you use Office tools to work on those documents. Open documents directly in your browser and do your work without switching over to another program. You might not get all the functionality of the full program, but more than likely you'll get the job done.

Chapter **23**

Ten (or So) Ways of Doing Your Job in Windows 10

This chapter focuses on practical tasks that you may encounter in your work environment. For example, you find out how to connect your computer to a second display and project the image on it. You also find out how to use this second display with the Windows Mobility Center so that you can deliver presentations like a pro.

At work, you probably print and scan all kinds of documents, so we cover these tasks in this chapter, too.

Perhaps you work with multinational teams or use multiple languages at work. If so, you'll be glad to know that you can find some important details on those topics in this chapter. First, you see how to set and view the time in multiple locations across the world. Then you see how to switch between multiple keyboard input languages when you type, as well as how to switch between multiple display languages.

Lastly, we cover a tool that is surprisingly useful: the new Calculator app from Windows 10. You never know when you might need to do some quick calculations, and in such cases, this app will come in handy.

Project to a Second Display

In the business world, it's customary to project your work on a second display so that others can see it. For example, you might connect a projector to your laptop, you might connect a large TV in a meeting room, or you might connect some other kind of display. To project your work to another display, you first must connect that display to your Windows 10 computer or device, which you do though a port such as VGA, DVI, HDMI, or Mini DisplayPort, depending on how current your computer and the second display are. After you connect the second display, the simplest way to project an image to the display is to press Windows+P on your keyboard and then select how you want to project the image (see Figure 23-1).

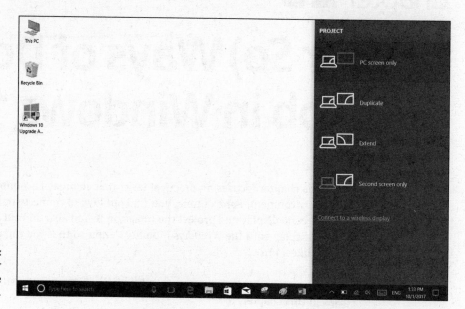

FIGURE 23-1:
Options for projecting the image.

As you can see in Figure 23-1, here are your options:

>> **PC Screen Only:** Displays the image on your main display; it ignores the second display.

>> **Duplicate:** Shows the same image on both displays.

>> **Extend:** Extends the image on the second display; you can use both displays like one single desktop. You can move windows from one display to the other.

>> **Second Screen Only:** Displays the image only on the second display.

   To bring the image back to the main display, either disconnect the second display or press Windows+P again and select PC Screen Only.

Another way to project to a second display is to use search. Here's how it works:

1. **Click in the search box on the taskbar.**

2. **Type** Project.

   A list with search results appears.

3. **Click the Project to a Second Screen search result.**

4. **Click the option you want for projecting the screen.**

Deliver Presentations with the Windows Mobility Center

The Windows Mobility Center centralizes information and settings most relevant to mobile computers and devices such as laptops, netbooks, Ultrabooks, and 2-in-1s.

TECHNICAL STUFF

The Windows Mobility Center isn't available on desktop computers.

Windows Mobility Center's role is to help you be mobile and to enable you to take quick actions, such as

>> Change the brightness of the screen.

>> Change the sound volume.

>> Change the active power plan.

>> Connect or disconnect external displays.

>> Set synchronized partnerships with such devices as portable music players and USB removable drives.

>> Set the Presentation mode to either On or Off.

If you're a typical business user, you're likely to find that the most useful features of the Windows Mobility Center are the ability it gives you to connect external displays and to turn on Presentation mode. These settings are especially useful when you must switch your presentation from room to room and connect your device to different kinds of external displays. However, before you start using the Windows Mobility Center for presentations, make sure that you connect a second display, as shown in the previous section.

Here's how to start the Windows Mobility Center and use it to turn on Presentation mode:

1. **Click in the search box on the taskbar.**

2. **Type** mobility.

    A list with search results appears.

3. **Click the Windows Mobility Center search result.**

    The Windows Mobility Center window appears (see Figure 23-2).

4. **Review all the settings that you're interested in.**

5. **Minimize Windows Mobility Center.**

6. **Deliver your presentation.**

7. **When you finish the presentation, click Turn Off in the Presentation Settings section.**

8. **Close the Windows Mobility Center.**

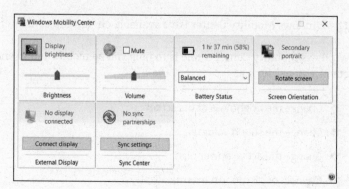

FIGURE 23-2:
The Windows
Mobility Center.

Print Your Documents and Presentations

To print the documents and presentations you create, you, of course, need to install a printer. Once you install a printer, you need to access the Print menu. Here, you select the printer you want to use, set up how items are printed, and then click the Print button. The universal keyboard shortcut for printing in Windows 10 is Ctrl+P, and this command accesses the Print window in most apps. However, you can also use clicks and taps to print.

As an example, here's how to print a document from the Word app:

1. **Start the Word app.**

2. **Open a document that you want to print.**

3. **Click File.**

   The File menu appears.

4. **Click Print.**

   The Print dialog box appears (see Figure 23-3).

5. **Select the printer that you want to use.**

6. **Configure how you want to print the document.**

7. **Click Print.**

8. **After the document prints, close the Word app.**

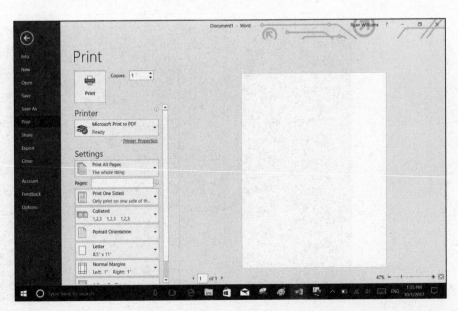

FIGURE 23-3:
Printing a document from the Word app.

TIP

The process for printing documents is similar in all Microsoft Office apps.

Scan Documents

Windows 10 offers an improved Scan app that you can use to quickly scan and save documents to your computer. To use this app, you must first install a scanner on your computer. Many modern printers are multifunctional and include both printing and scanning features so that you can use one device for both tasks.

Before scanning a document, insert it in the scanner and then follow these steps:

1. **Click in the search box on the taskbar.**

2. **Type** scan.

   A list with search results appears.

3. **Click the shortcut for the Scan app.**

   The Scan app window appears. You may need to download the app from the Store.

4. **In the Scan app, select the scanner that you want to use.**

5. **Select the available scanning parameters, such as the document source and the scan's file type (see Figure 23-4).**

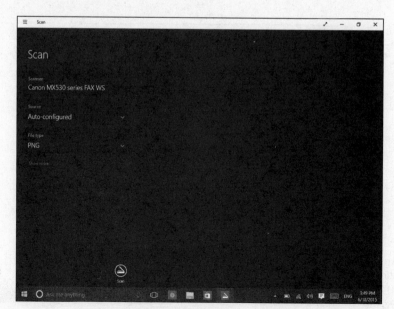

FIGURE 23-4:
Scanning a document.

6. **Click Scan.**

   After the Scan app does its job, you're informed that the scan was saved to the Scans folder on your computer.

7. **Click View to view your scan.**

8. **If you're satisfied with the result, close the document you just scanned.**

9. **Close the Scan app.**

The Scans folder is in your Pictures library or your User folder.

TIP

View Time Around the World

These days it's becoming common to be part of a multinational project team that spans continents and multiple time zones. If that's your case, you surely want to use the Windows 10 Alarms & Clock app. With this app, you can set alarms and timers and use the stopwatch. Most importantly, you can set and view the time in multiple locations across the world, and here's how to do so:

1. **Click Start.**

2. **Click All Apps.**

   The list of installed apps appears.

3. **Click Alarms & Clock.**

4. **Click World Clock (see Figure 23-5).**

5. **Click the + button at the bottom of the app window.**

6. **In the search field that appears, type the name of the city whose time you want to find.**

7. **Click the search suggestion that fits that city.**

8. **View the time in the newly added location.**

9. **Close the Alarms & Clock app.**

Add all the cities where your teammates work so that you can easily keep track of the time in their location and schedule meetings and conference calls at times that work best for all of you.

TIP

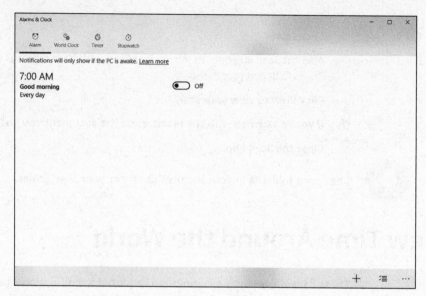

FIGURE 23-5:
The Alarms &
Clock app.

Add Multiple Time Zones to the Start Menu

To check the time quickly in multiple locations across the world, you can pin to the Start Menu the locations that you add in the Alarms & Clock app. Here's how:

1. **Start the Alarms & Clock app.**

2. **Click World Clock.**

   The time appears in the cities that you have added to this app.

3. **Right-click the city that you want to pin.**

4. **Click Pin to Start (see Figure 23-6).**

5. **Close the Alarms & Clock app.**

6. **Click Start to see the time shown for the location that you just pinned to the Start Menu.**

TIP

You can pin as many locations as you want.

FIGURE 23-6:
Pinning the time
for a location to
the Start Menu.

Switch Between Keyboard Input Languages

If you type in multiple languages, you've installed more than one keyboard input language, and you need to quickly switch between languages as you type. The quickest way is to press the Windows+Space keys on the keyboard. This keyboard shortcut switches to the next available keyboard input language. Press these keys again, and you switch to the next language. However, you can also change the keyboard input language by using the mouse, like this:

1. **On the right side of the taskbar, click the Input Indicator that displays the current keyboard input language.**

   For example, this button says ENG when the English keyboard language is active.

   A list appears, showing all the available languages (see Figure 23-7).

2. **Click the language that you want to use.**

   The language Input Indicator changes, now showing the language you just selected.

3. **Start typing, using the newly selected language.**

Before you can switch to a new keyboard input language, you need to install it. Refer to Chapter 7 to find out how to add a keyboard input language.

REMEMBER

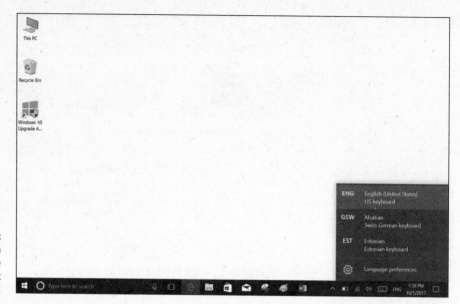

FIGURE 23-7:
The list with
available
keyboard input
languages.

Switch Between Display Languages

In addition to keyboard input languages, Windows 10 allows you to install and use multiple display languages. Here's how to set up your operating system to translate in a different language:

1. **Open Settings.**

2. **Click Time & Language.**

3. **Click Region & Language.**

4. **In the Languages section on the right, select the language that you want to use for Windows 10.**

5. **Click the Set as Default button for that language (see Figure 23-8).**

   The selected language is placed ahead of the previous display language, and you're told that the selected language will be used the next time you sign in.

6. **Sign out of Windows 10.**

7. **Sign in to Windows 10 using your user account.**

   The operating system now uses the language that you selected.

REMEMBER

Before you can switch to a new display language, you need to install it (refer to Chapter 7 for more on this topic). To revert to the previous display language, follow the same procedure and select the previous display language at Step 4.

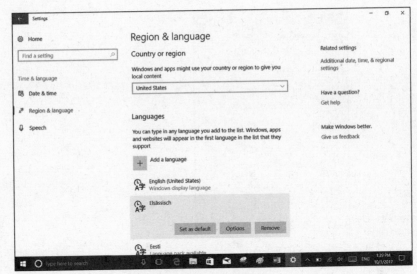

FIGURE 23-8:
Setting a new display language as the default.

Make Complex Calculations

Windows 10 includes a new, improved, touch-friendly Calculator app. With this app, you can do these types of calculations:

>> **Standard mathematical:** You can do simple calculations, such as addition, subtraction, and multiplication.

>> **Scientific:** You can work with advanced scientific values, such as degrees, radians, and grads.

>> **Programmer:** You can use functions that are useful to software developers.

>> **Conversion:** You can make all kinds of conversions: volume, length, weight and mass, temperature, energy, area, and speed.

Figure 23-9 shows the Calculator app in Windows 10 and the options you have for making standard mathematical calculations.

Here's how to start the Calculator app and switch between different types of calculations and conversions:

1. Click Start to open the Start Menu.

2. Click All Apps.

The list with available apps appears.

3. Click Calculator to open the app.

The Calculator app appears.

FIGURE 23-9:
The Calculator
app in
Windows 10.

4. **Click the burger button (three stacked lines, like a burger on a bun), at the top-right corner of the Calculator app (see Figure 23-10).**

   A menu appears, with several options.

5. **Click Scientific to switch to scientific calculations.**

6. **Click the burger button again.**

7. **Click Temperature to switch to temperature-related conversions.**

8. **Close the Calculator.**

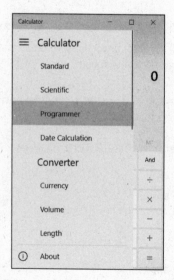

FIGURE 23-10:
Changing the
type of
calculations you
make in the
Calculator app.

Index

formatting. *See also* paragraph formatting

   character, 203

   chart element text in Excel, 323–324

   chart elements in Excel, 321–328

   copying with Format Painter, 215–216

   removing in Word, 207

formatting shortcuts (Quick Analysis), 303

formula bar, 258

formulas

   controlling order of precedence in, 281–282

   copying in Excel, 284–286

   moving in Excel, 284–286

   referencing cells in, 282

   writing in Excel, 280–284

Formulas tab, 292

forwarding

   contact data via email with Outlook, 368–370

   messages in Outlook, 351–352

Free Lossless Audio Codec files, 78

Function Library, choosing from, 292–293

functions

   ABS function, 297

   AVERAGE function, 289–290

   COS, 297

   COUNT, 289–290

   finding in Excel, 290–292

   IF, 297–298

   inserting in Excel, 286–293, 290–292

   MAX, 289–290

   MIN, 289–290

   NOW, 293–294

   NPER, 295–296

   PMT, 295–296

   PV, 295–296

   RATE, 295–296

   ROUNDUP, 297

   showing current date/time with Excel, 293–294

   SIN, 297

   SQRT, 297

   SUM, 288–289

   TAN, 297

   TODAY, 293–294

G

games

   checking storage space for, 413–414

   removing, 413

generating

   bulleted lists in Word, 240–242

   charts in Excel, 307–328, 309–310

   contacts in Outlook, 362–364

   desktops, 20–21

   documents in Office, 188–190

   files in File Explorer, 82–83

   folders for managing email in Outlook, 353–354

   folders in File Explorer, 82

   footers, 249–250

   formulas in Excel, 279–305

   functions in Excel, 279–305

   headers, 249–250

   message handling rules in Outlook, 356–359

   numbered lists in Word, 240–242

   page breaks in Word, 252–253

   PDF versions of Word documents, 225–226

   picture passwords, 166–167

   range names by selection, 300–301

   range names using Define Name, 302–303

   range names using Name box, 301–302

   shortcuts to files/folders in File Explorer, 85–86

   slides from Ribbon in PowerPoint, 389

   slides in Outline pane in PowerPoint, 388–389

   slides in Slides pane in PowerPoint, 387–388

   tasks in Outlook, 370–379

   text boxes on slides in PowerPoint, 397–398

   VPN connections, 146–147

   Word documents. *See* Word (Microsoft)

   worksheets in Excel, 274–277

   XPS versions of Word documents, 225–226

getting started (Windows 10)

   about, 7–8

   accessing Control Panel, 14–15

   accessing desktop, 13

   accessing settings, 14

   Action Center, 16–17

L

landscape, 244

language packs, downloading, 136–137

Large Icons view, 107

legend, 308, 319

libraries, 70

Libraries section (Navigation pane), 104–105

LibreOffice documents, 78

line chart, 309

line numbers, adding in Word, 254–255

line spacing, adjusting in Word, 237

List view, 107

lists, 240–241

live tiles, 11

loan terms, calculating in Excel, 295–296

Lock Screen (Windows 10)
  about, 8–9
  changing app status on, 128–129
  changing picture, 127–128

locking devices, 23–24

M

macro-enabled file type, 196

Mail (storage category), 411

Mail Merge, 418–419

Mail section (Outlook), 332, 334

Make This PC Discoverable switch, 44

malware, protecting yourself from, 175

managing
  downloads in Internet Explorer, 55–56
  email. *See* Outlook (Microsoft)
  files. *See* File Explorer
  folders. *See* File Explorer
  order of precedence, 281–282
  tasks in Outlook, 370–379
  Wi-Fi settings, 44–45
  worksheets in Excel, 274–277

Maps (storage category), 411

margins, setting in Word, 242–244

Matroska multimedia files, 78

MAX function, 289–290

maximizing Ribbon in File Explorer, 75–76

Medium Icons view, 108

message handling rules
  creating in Outlook, 356–359
  deleting in Outlook, 358–359
  modifying in Outlook, 358–359

messages, email
  addressing in Outlook, 343–344
  attaching files to in Outlook, 344–346
  composing in Outlook, 342–346
  deleting in Outlook, 352–353
  forwarding contact data via, 368–370
  forwarding in Outlook, 351–352
  managing. *See* Outlook (Microsoft)
  moving between folders in Outlook, 355–356
  moving from specific senders in Outlook, 356–357
  reading in Outlook, 346–353
  receiving in Outlook, 346–353
  replying to in Outlook, 350–351
  sending in Outlook, 342–346
  sending to contacts in Outlook, 367–368
  Word documents, 221–223

Microsoft account, 162

Microsoft Edge, 51–52. *See also* Internet Explorer (IE)

Microsoft Excel. *See* Excel (Microsoft)

Microsoft Office. *See* Office (Microsoft)

Microsoft Office files, 77

Microsoft Outlook. *See* Outlook (Microsoft)

Microsoft PowerPoint. *See* PowerPoint (Microsoft)

Microsoft Word. *See* Word (Microsoft)

MIN function, 289–290

minimizing Ribbon in File Explorer, 75–76

mixed reference, 286

mobile USB modems, connecting to Internet using, 41–42

modifying
  account settings in Outlook, 339–341
  app status on Lock Screen, 128–129
  axis scale of charts in Excel, 314–315
  bullet character in Word, 242

About the Authors

Ciprian Rusen is a recognized Windows Consumer Expert and a Microsoft Most Valuable Professional (MVP). He has published several books about Windows and Microsoft Office, and he's a very active tech blogger at www.7tutorials.com. On this website, you can find many tutorials about Windows, Android, Windows Phone, and Xbox One. If you want to keep up to date on the latest Microsoft consumer products, be sure to subscribe to his blog, too.

Faithe Wempen, MA, is a Microsoft Office Master Instructor and the author of more than 150 books on computer hardware and software, including PowerPoint 2013 Bible and Office 2013 eLearning Kit for Dummies. She is an adjunct instructor of Computer Information Technology at Purdue University, and her corporate training courses online have reached more than one-quarter of a million students for clients such as Hewlett-Packard, Sony, and CNET.

Ryan Williams is an author, technical editor, and musician living in New Orleans, LA. His previous publications for Wiley include books on digital music, bass guitar, and social media. When not sitting in front the computer writing, he is sitting in front of the computer playing or recording music, then asking his daughter not to spend so much time sitting in front of computers.

Publisher's Acknowledgments

Acquisitions Editor: Steve Hayes

Senior Project Editor: Paul Levesque

Copy Editor: Rebecca Whitney

Editorial Assistant: Matthew Lowe

Sr. Editorial Assistant: Cherie Case

Production Editor: Vasanth Koilraj

Cover Image: © Gang Zhou / iStockphoto

Take dummies with you everywhere you go!

Whether you are excited about e-books, want more from the web, must have your mobile apps, or are swept up in social media, dummies makes everything easier.

Find us online!

dummies.com

Leverage the power

Dummies is the global leader in the reference category and one of the most trusted and highly regarded brands in the world. No longer just focused on books, customers now have access to the dummies content they need in the format they want. Together we'll craft a solution that engages your customers, stands out from the competition, and helps you meet your goals.

Advertising & Sponsorships

Connect with an engaged audience on a powerful multimedia site, and position your message alongside expert how-to content. Dummies.com is a one-stop shop for free, online information and know-how curated by a team of experts.

- Targeted ads
- Video
- Email Marketing
- Microsites
- Sweepstakes sponsorship

20 **MILLION** PAGE VIEWS EVERY SINGLE MONTH

15 MILLION UNIQUE VISITORS PER MONTH

43% OF ALL VISITORS ACCESS THE SITE VIA THEIR MOBILE DEVICES

700,000 NEWSLETTER SUBSCRIPTIONS TO THE INBOXES OF

300,000 UNIQUE INDIVIDUALS EVERY WEEK

# of dummies

Custom Publishing

Reach a global audience in any language by creating a solution that will differentiate you from competitors, amplify your message, and encourage customers to make a buying decision.

- Apps
- Books
- eBooks
- Video
- Audio
- Webinars

Brand Licensing & Content

Leverage the strength of the world's most popular reference brand to reach new audiences and channels of distribution.

For more information, visit dummies.com/biz

PERSONAL ENRICHMENT

Staying Sharp dummies

9781119187790
USA $26.00
CAN $31.99
UK £19.99

Facebook dummies
Carolyn Abram

9781119179030
USA $21.99
CAN $25.99
UK £16.99

Guitar dummies
Mark Phillips, Jon Chappell

9781119293354
USA $24.99
CAN $29.99
UK £17.99

Investing dummies
Eric Tyson, MBA

9781119293347
USA $22.99
CAN $27.99
UK £16.99

Beekeeping dummies
Howland Blackiston

9781119310068
USA $22.99
CAN $27.99
UK £16.99

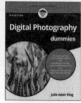
Digital Photography dummies
Julie Adair King

9781119235606
USA $24.99
CAN $29.99
UK £17.99

Meditation dummies
Stephan Bodian

9781119251163
USA $24.99
CAN $29.99
UK £17.99

Pregnancy ALL-IN-ONE dummies
6 Books

9781119235491
USA $26.99
CAN $31.99
UK £19.99

Samsung Galaxy S7 dummies
Bill Hughes

9781119279952
USA $24.99
CAN $29.99
UK £17.99

iPhone dummies
Edward C. Baig, Bob "Dr. Mac" LeVitus

9781119283133
USA $24.99
CAN $29.99
UK £17.99

Crocheting dummies
Karen Manthey, Susan Brittain

9781119287117
USA $24.99
CAN $29.99
UK £16.99

Nutrition dummies
Carol Ann Rinzler

9781119130246
USA $22.99
CAN $27.99
UK £16.99

PROFESSIONAL DEVELOPMENT

Windows 10 dummies
Andy Rathbone

9781119311041
USA $24.99
CAN $29.99
UK £17.99

AutoCAD dummies
Bill Fane

9781119255796
USA $39.99
CAN $47.99
UK £27.99

Excel 2016 dummies
Greg Harvey, PhD

9781119293439
USA $26.99
CAN $31.99
UK £19.99

QuickBooks 2017 dummies
Stephen L. Nelson, MBA, CPA, MS in Taxation

9781119281467
USA $26.99
CAN $31.99
UK £19.99

macOS Sierra dummies
Bob "Dr. Mac" LeVitus

9781119280651
USA $29.99
CAN $35.99
UK £21.99

LinkedIn dummies
Joel Elad, MBA

9781119251132
USA $24.99
CAN $29.99
UK £17.99

Windows 10 ALL-IN-ONE dummies
10 Books
Woody Leonhard

9781119310563
USA $34.00
CAN $41.99
UK £24.99

SharePoint 2016 dummies
Rosemarie Withee, Ken Withee

9781119181705
USA $29.99
CAN $35.99
UK £21.99

Fundamental Analysis dummies
Matt Krantz

9781119263593
USA $26.99
CAN $31.99
UK £19.99

Networking dummies
Doug Lowe

9781119257769
USA $29.99
CAN $35.99
UK £21.99

Office 2016 dummies
Wallace Wang

9781119293477
USA $26.99
CAN $31.99
UK £19.99

Office 365 dummies
Rosemarie Withee, Ken Withee, Jennifer Reed

9781119265313
USA $24.99
CAN $29.99
UK £17.99

Salesforce.com dummies
Liz Kao, Jon Paz

9781119239314
USA $29.99
CAN $35.99
UK £21.99

Coding dummies
Nikhil Abraham

9781119293323
USA $29.99
CAN $35.99
UK £21.99

Learning Made Easy

ACADEMIC

9781119293576
USA $19.99
CAN $23.99
UK £15.99

9781119293637
USA $19.99
CAN $23.99
UK £15.99

9781119293491
USA $19.99
CAN $23.99
UK £15.99

9781119293460
USA $19.99
CAN $23.99
UK £15.99

9781119293590
USA $19.99
CAN $23.99
UK £15.99

9781119215844
USA $26.99
CAN $31.99
UK £19.99

9781119293378
USA $22.99
CAN $27.99
UK £16.99

9781119293521
USA $19.99
CAN $23.99
UK £15.99

9781119239178
USA $18.99
CAN $22.99
UK £14.99

9781119263883
USA $26.99
CAN $31.99
UK £19.99

Available Everywhere Books Are Sold

dummies.com

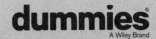
dummies
A Wiley Brand

Small books for big imaginations

9781119177173
USA $9.99
CAN $9.99
UK £8.99

9781119177272
USA $9.99
CAN $9.99
UK £8.99

9781119177241
USA $9.99
CAN $9.99
UK £8.99

9781119177210
USA $9.99
CAN $9.99
UK £8.99

9781119262657
USA $9.99
CAN $9.99
UK £6.99

9781119291336
USA $9.99
CAN $9.99
UK £6.99

9781119233527
USA $9.99
CAN $9.99
UK £6.99

9781119291220
USA $9.99
CAN $9.99
UK £6.99

9781119177302
USA $9.99
CAN $9.99
UK £8.99

Unleash Their Creativity

dummies.com

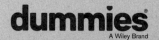